FOLLOWING HO CHI MINH

BUI TIN

Following Ho Chi Minh

The Memoirs of a
North Vietnamese Colonel

<small>TRANSLATED FROM THE VIETNAMESE
AND ADAPTED BY</small>
<small>JUDY STOWE AND DO VAN</small>

<small>WITH AN INTRODUCTION BY</small>
<small>CARLYLE A. THAYER</small>

<small>UNIVERSITY OF HAWAII PRESS
HONOLULU</small>

Published in North America by
University of Hawaii Press
2840 Kolowalu Street
Honolulu, Hawaii 96822

Library of Congress Cataloging-in-Publication Data
Bùi Tín, 1928 –
    [Hoa xuyên tuyêt. English]
    Following Ho Chi Minh: the memoirs of a North Vietnamese colonel
    by Bui Tin: translated by Judy Stowe and Do Van: introduction by
    Carlyle Thayer.
        p.   cm.
    Translation of: Hoa xuyên tuyêt.
    Includes index.
    ISBN 0-8248-1673-0
    1. Bùi, Tín, 1928 –   . 2. Vietnam—Politics and
government —1945 – 1975. 3. Vietnam—Politics and government —1975-.
4. Communists —Vietnam—Biography.   5. Vietnam. Quân dôi nhân dân
—Officers —Biography.   I. Title.
DS560.72.B85A3   1995
959.704 —dc20   94-10878
                                                                    CIP

CONTENTS

ILLUSTRATIONS

INTRODUCTION

by Carlyle A. Thayer

Bui Tin grew to manhood in one of the most tumultuous periods of Vietnamese history. At the age of eighteen, he was swept up in the 1945 August Revolution when nationalist forces led by Ho Chi Minh seized power in Vietnam. Bui Tin stood among the crowd in Hanoi's Ba Dinh Square on 2 September 1945 and witnessed Ho's historic proclamation of independence.

In what he now describes as a romantic and impetuous decision, but nonetheless a major step in his life, Bui Tin left home for the first time and enlisted in the Vietnam People's Army. He was immediately assigned to the first military class to be trained in Hanoi. His instructors included such legendary revolutionary figures as Truong Chinh, Pham Van Dong and Vo Nguyen Giap. Throughout his entire career, including the epic eight year resistance war against the French (1946–54), Bui Tin never lost his loyalty to General Giap and respect for him.

At the end of the war, Vietnam was partitioned and Bui Tin continued his military career in the north. He notes that in the early 1950s the influence of Chinese Communism began to be felt in Vietnam after Mao Tse-tung's forces triumphed in the Chinese civil war, and it was Chinese advisers and their advice which Bui Tin blames in part for the conduct of the land reform campaign in North Vietnam. The campaign went badly off course and resulted in the deaths of over 10,000 people. The experiences of land reform, political victimisation and arbitrary rule during this period must have planted the seeds of Bui Tin's later disaffection.

In the 1960s Vietnam was still divided and many Vietnamese, including Bui Tin, felt that national unification was a vital task. When the Vietnam Communist Party made the historic decision to resume armed conflict in the south, Bui Tin once again returned to the front. In 1961 he made the first of two gruelling trips down the Ho Chi Minh Trail to report on conditions below the seventeenth parallel. He made his second trip in early 1964 and on returning to the north in October was assigned to the army newspaper, *Quan Doi Nhan Dan*, where he began a second career as a journalist.

He was on hand on 30 April 1975 shortly after Communist tanks crashed through the gates of the Independence Palace in Saigon. As a full colonel and the most senior Communist official present, he played an historic role in the transfer of power and the surrender of the Republic of Vietnam. In the words of one westerner, Bui Tin was always 'in the most important place at the right time.'

After reunification Bui Tin continued his career in journalism as a member of the editorial board of *Quan Doi Nhan Dan*, with special responsibility for reporting on foreign affairs, defence and security matters. He personally reported on the border war which erupted between Vietnam and Pol Pot's Cambodia in 1977. Late the following year, he accompanied the armoured spearhead of Vietnamese forces which invaded Cambodia, and was one of the first ranking Vietnamese military officials to enter Phnom Penh. Once again he was at the most important place at the right time.

In 1990, at the age of sixty-three and with a distinguished career spanning nearly forty-five years, Bui Tin could have looked forward to honourable retirement. He had also become a doting grandparent—he was immensely proud of his two granddaughters. Yet, acting on his own volition, he made the momentous decision—perhaps the last major step of his life—to leave Vietnam and live abroad. He did so in order to make public a growing list of personal misgivings about Vietnam and its political system which had been haunting him at least since 1975. As a result Bui Tin was fired from his job and expelled from the Communist Party. His career record was vilified, his family placed under police surveillance, and his son-in-law denied the opportunity to take up a scholarship at Harvard University.

Bui Tin's memoirs, written as an exile abroad, have retained a sense of balance about developments in Vietnam and about the historical period through which he lived. This has not pleased the extremists among the anti-Communist Vietnamese community living in France and the United States, who would prefer to see a more wholehearted condemnation of the Vietnam Communist Party and its historical legacy. Bui Tin, however, would prefer to build bridges between the present regime in Hanoi and Vietnamese living abroad. He advocates political pluralism and gradual change but skirts around the question of how Vietnam can develop a multi-party system. He argues that his ideas are not the sole solution but simply a stimulus for discussion.

This book is not an autobiography. This is important in itself, since it indicates that Bui Tin is not motivated primarily to highlight his personal achievements. As its title states, the book is a memoir. But it is a memoir the likes of which has not been written previously by a Vietnamese Communist official.[1] Bui Tin is an insider with intimate knowledge of Vietnam's political system and its secretive leaders, and as a senior journalist he had access to the most powerful of the latter. He observed them at meetings in Hanoi and on various battlefields, accompanied them on overseas trips and he participated in preparing their official biographies. He reveals facts and details which cannot be found elsewhere and which are still regarded as state secrets in Vietnam.

But *Following Ho Chi Minh* is much more than this. It is a memoir which makes ethical, moral and political judgments about contemporary Vietnam, its political system and its leaders, and none of these is more startling and more calculated to produce an outburst by party conservatives in Hanoi than that Ho Chi Minh was 'a human being not a saint'. Two hagiographies of Ho Chi Minh's life are now revealed to have been written by Ho himself using a pseudonym. Bui Tin points to evidence that Ho was not a celibate, as his offical biographies state, but may have been twice married.

Because Bui Tin's memoir is written by a son of the revolution who reflects values that are deeply held in Vietnamese political culture, it will provoke heated discussion among Vietnamese intellectuals at home and abroad. Vietnamese culture dictates that the 'family' keep such matters to itself; and Vietnamese Communist political culture dictates that such sensitive matters be kept from foreigners. Bui Tin has violated both of these norms. In doing so he has opened the closed world of one of the few remaining Communist systems to scrutiny and judgment by outsiders—including the Vietnamese people.

Traditional Vietnamese society accorded a special role and great prestige to scholars and intellectuals. As early as the fifteenth century, the country borrowed and adapted Confucianism and the mandarin system of governance from China. But it was not till 1802, with the founding of the Nguyen dynasty, that there was a thoroughgoing attempt to adapt the Chinese Confucian model to Vietnam. A key component of this system was the selection of government officials through impartial examinations based on knowledge of Confucian texts and commentaries. This was the or mandarin, governed by applying ethical precepts, and conscious of a duty to be loyal to the king and to serve the nation.

These twin loyalties were put to the test as a result of the imposition of colonial rule and the collaboration of the Vietnamese monarchy with the French. For example, in the late nineteenth century the Vietnamese court was split on the question of collaboration. In 1885, one group kidnapped the newly-enthroned child King, Ham Nghi, and attempted to rally support for the anti-French cause under his banner. The French reacted by installing the king's brother on the throne. This action caused some mandarins to transfer their loyalities to the new leader on strictly legalistic grounds. In the end, not only was the 'Loyalty to the King' movement crushed, but the Vietnamese monarchy itself, as the source of moral authority, was mortally wounded. Those mandarins who collaborated with the French 'were tools of foreign rulers, and they knew it'.[2]

Early in the twentieth century a variety of factors resulted in the first stirrings of modern Vietnamese nationalism among the mandarin élite. They were broadly divided into reformist and activist camps, as exemplified by the two major historical figures, Phan Chu Trinh (1872-1926) and Phan Boi Chau (1867-1940). In the mid-1920s this first generation of Vietnamese nationalists passed from the scene, having been unsuccessful in their quest, and they were replaced by a more radical and revolutionary second generation.

No figure stands out more prominently in modern Vietnamese history than Ho Chi Minh. Born in 1890 (or 1892) the son of a mandarin official, he was an 'inter-generational' figure and derived his authority in part from this fact. He received both classical and Western education and, like the first generation of modern nationalists elsewhere in Asia, he travelled extensively abroad. Ho founded the Revolutionary Youth Association, the precursor of the Vietnam Communist Party, and among his early recruits were the offspring of mandarin officials, such as Pham

Van Dong. These individuals combined the traditional value system inculcated by Confucianism—loyalty and service to the national community based on moral and ethical values—with the new revolutionary and scientific values of Marxism-Leninism. The relationship between these systems has been described by Marxist scholar Nguyen Khac Vien in an influential essay 'Confucianism and Marxism':

> Marxism was not baffling to Confucians in that it concentrated man's thoughts on political and social problems. By defining man as the total of his social relationships, Marxism hardly came as a shock to the Confucian scholar who had always considered the highest aim of man to be the fulfilment of his social obligations. Although there was certainly a wide gap between the purely moral definition of social obligations in Confucianism and the scientific definitions of social relationships in Marxism, both doctrines shared the same frame of reference and concerns. Bourgeois individualism, which puts personal interests ahead of those of society and petty bourgeois anarchism, which allows no social discipline whatsoever, are alien to both Confucianism and Marxism. The Confucian can make the transition from a traditional society to a socialist one. He is never actually hostile to the principle of collective discipline (as is the bourgeois intellectual) since he always sees social discipline as an indispensable part of the development of his own personality.
>
> Marxist cadres also drew freely from the political morality of Confucians. The notion that leaders should exemplify high moral standards was deeply ingrained in Confucian countries.[3]

Bui Tin was born into a family of mandarins. His paternal great-grandfather held the highest examination rank, and after serving as a provincial governor rose to the rank of deputy Minister of War; his grandfather was also appointed provincial governor. Bui Tin's father earned degrees in classical literature and French before starting a public career as a provincial judge. He too served as province governor before rising to the rank of Minister of Justice. In this capacity he was charged with drawing up new criminal and civil codes for central Vietnam. In October 1945, he joined Ho Chi Minh's government as Inspector-General and was elected to the National Assembly in 1946. His son thus inherited much intellectual baggage from his family, and from his father in particular.

Bui Tin was schooled at home by his father in Confucian morality and ethics, and his mother imparted humanistic values. At the age of thirteen he studied French literature at Khai Dinh high school in Hue, the imperial capital, and remembers reading Montesquieu, Voltaire, Rousseau, Victor Hugo and Daudet, which remained deeply ingrained in him. Bui Tin grew to political manhood embodying the ideals of these two traditions. In an echo of a famous essay by Ho Chi Minh, 'The Path Which Led Me to Leninism',[4] he also proclaimed that it was nationalism—not Marxism—which led him to join the Viet Minh.

Bui Tin left home with his character deeply influenced by his parents' values. These remained with him for life and formed the basis on which he came to judge both his peers and high-ranking Party and military officials. Bui Tin places a high premium on education as the basis for enlightened moral behaviour. He is an admirer of General Vo Nguyen Giap, not only for his military genius, but for his deep knowledge of traditional Vietnamese laws and values.

Bui Tin joined the Vietnam People's Army and the Vietnam Communist Party for patriotic reasons. During the ensuing thirty years of warfare which he experienced, he never lost faith in the ultimate goal of the struggle: to expel the foreign invader and to reunify the country. In his view, the Party, the army and the people were one.

But after the euphoria of victory and reunification in 1975, according to Bui Tin, a turning-point was reached. Vietnam's leaders became drunk with victory and defiled the act of liberation, turning it instead into annexation. The wartime policy of national reconciliation was replaced by subjugation. Former enemies who should have been treated as prisoners-of-war were now turned into political criminals and placed in re-education camps. Property and equipment were looted and shipped north. Bui Tin writes that a 'primitive and childish conception of class struggle' was imposed on the South which stigmatised not only the vanquished but their families as well, and condemned them to a life of institutional discrimination. By way of example, he recounts the 1978 campaign to end bourgeois trade which resulted in the mass exodus of ethnic Chinese and Vietnamese entrepreneurs by boat. The campaign was orchestrated by the Ministry of the Interior and the Cong An, who put themselves above the law. Hapless victims were charged in gold for the 'privilege' of leaving Vietnam. After making payment and travelling to the point of embarkation, they were subject to further indignity when they were stripped of their remaining valuables and possessions before being allowed to depart.

According to Bui Tin, the main rift in the Communists' ranks was between the intellectuals and the 'professional revolutionaries'. The latter, led by party Secretary General Le Duan in alliance with his fellow Politburo member Le Duc Tho, formed an un-scrupulous group of 'red capitalists'.

One of the most shocking examples of how the system became degraded occurred in Cambodia. Bui Tin initially supported the decision to intervene, having personally witnessed the atrocities committed by Pol Pot's forces against Vietnamese villagers along the border. But, according to him, Vietnam's leaders became stricken with the 'disease of subjective arrogance'. They treated their Cambodian allies much like colonial subjects. Even worse, Vietnam's privileged élite kept their sons out of combat and harm's way. It was the children of Vietnam's urban dispossessed and poor peasantry who bore the brunt of battle, malaria and the maiming caused by mines: 52,000 died and 200,000 were wounded. This revelation 'astounded' Bui Tin and caused him to be 'harassed by doubts'. His feelings were not assuaged when on returning to Hanoi he found how bleak was the plight of wounded war veterans. His sense of social justice was further affronted.

As Vietnam's domestic socio-economic crisis mounted in the late 1970s and early 1980s, calls for reform were made from within the Vietnam Communist Party. In July 1986 Party Secretary General Le Duan died in office and was replaced by Truong Chinh, who in the lead-up to the sixth national party congress in December, endorsed the calls for reform. Bui Tin was moved to write a personal petition and pass it on to him. He never received an official response. The sixth congress, however, adopted a reform program known as *Doi Moi* and elected Nguyen Van Linh the next party chief. Linh initially moved in a determined manner to end central planning and to develop a market economy. He also sponsored limited political reforms. Intellectuals, writers, artists and editors were encouraged to criticise social ills such as corruption. Efforts were made to end the rubber-stamp role of the National Assembly by giving it enhanced law-making powers.

The brief flowering of political reform was cut short by the massacre of pro-democracy demonstrators in Tien An Men and by the collapse of Communism in Eastern Europe in 1989. A crackdown took place in Vietnam, and newspaper and journal editors who had been outspoken were punished or dismissed from their posts. A leading advocate of increased political reform, Tran Xuan Bach, was expelled from the Politburo, and a secret party directive banned all public discussion of pluralism and multi-party democracy. Bui Tin was subjected to censorship and to such close scrutiny that by mid-1990 he felt that he had become a 'major target' because of his increasingly outspoken views. In these circumstances he resolved to leave Vietnam and make public the causes of its poverty, misery, despair and isolation.

NOTES

1. The one possible exception is Hoang Van Hoan's memoir, *Giot Nuoc Trong Bien Ca* (A Drop in the Ocean) (Beijing: Nha Xuat Ban Tin Viet Nam, 1986). Hoan was dropped from the Politburo in 1976 and later defected to China. He refrained from commenting on the contemporary period and, according to Vietnamese officials interview by me, did not reveal material which was considered a state secret. Hoan is unabashedly pro-China and his memoir is in part a polemical attack on the now deceased party Secretary General Le Duan (in office September 1960-July 1986), who leaned towards the Soviet Union.

2. David G. Marr, *Vietnamese Anticolonialism, 1885-1925* (Los Angeles: University of California Press, 1971), 48.

3. See; David Marr and Jayne Werner (eds), *Tradition and Revolution in Vietnam* (Berkeley: Indochina Resource Center, 1974), 47.

4. In Bernard B.Fall (ed.), *Ho Chi Minh on Revolution: Selected Writings, 1920-66* (New York: Praeger, 1967), 5-7.

AUTHOR'S PREFACE

In Vietnam, we celebrate Tet, the festival of the Lunar New Year, as the beginning of spring as well. But in February 1991 at the start of the Year of the Goat, Tet Tan Mui, I was in Paris where winter was still very much in evidence. A deep layer of snow covered the garden of the house where I was living in the outskirts of the city. How, I wondered, could natural life survive under such a freezing blanket!

Then almost overnight it seemed as if a miracle occurred. The snow melted and within a few days a little white flower burst into bloom. The English call it a snowdrop. In French it is *perce-neige*, the flower that pierces through the snow. But there is no name for it in Vietnamese since in our tropical climate there are no snowdrops. Nonetheless the sight and symbolism of the flower fired me with enthusiasm to look back over my life and to think.

All Vietnamese who love their country hope that, no matter what difficulties and hardship they have had to encounter, a new spring will finally dawn in a spirit of unity, construction and progress. But the situation in Vietnam now is a matter of great concern to all its citizens both inside and outside the country. There is a crisis there which affects every level of society, and everybody dreams day and night of a change that will help Vietnam escape from its poverty and the stagnation of its political and economic life. They want to escape too from anarchy and social injustice.

Walking around the streets of Hanoi in recent years, I have felt continuous mental torture. The children look thin and frequently speak in obscenities. The women are gaunt and anxious. Sewage spills here and there. Sometimes arguments explode, abuse is hurled and knives are brandished. The city teems with gamblers, thieves, pickpockets, prostitutes and opium smokers.

So what was all the sacrifice of the Revolution about? Was it so that our people would suffer more hardship after our victory

than during the war? If Nguyen Du, who wrote our national
epic poem at the beginning of the nineteenth century, were still
alive, he would weep even more on seeing what the people
of Hanoi and Saigon have been reduced to. Nguyen Du recounted
in verse the story of Kim Van Kieu, a high-born and well-educated
lady, who because of social corruption was prevented from marrying
the man she loved and instead was sold off as a prostitute. Hence
for ten years she went from one man to another, often being
tricked despite her noble spirit. This epitomises the fate of Vietnam.

My home in Hanoi is 221C Kham Thien Street. In the old
days, it used to be quite quiet. Now there are over 200 tailors'
shops. There I have many old and dear friends through whom
I have been able to feel the pulse of society as a journalist should.
There is a worker over forty years old with four children, three
boys and a girl. He has been laid off from a state-run factory,
his wife is a street-sweeper and he survives as best he can. He
does a bit of building work, carpentry, repairing bicycles or tailoring.
In winter he even makes Western-style 'NATO' jackets according
to a pattern which emanates from Thailand. In the evenings too,
he takes his young son along to set up a stall selling tea and
cigarettes outside the district finance office where they collect
lottery tickets. Then there is the woman who sells congee. She
is fat and good-natured, although her husband died recently of
throat cancer. Meanwhile an old lady of over eighty hawks titbits
to the children.

Also down the street, a retired colonel who specialised in anti-
aircraft warfare now sells yoghurt. A more junior officer who
made a name for himself in 1954 at the time of the battle for
Dien Bien Phu by sabotaging French aircraft before they took
off from the airfield near Hanoi, now makes a living by pumping
up bicycle tyres. His problem is that even his pump is old and
requires frequent repairs. As for a doctor who graduated from
Paris and works at the Central Eye Hospital, he lives alone in
a room 12 metres square. He does nothing but read, cook on
an oil stove or collect dirty water in a leaking bucket. He does
not even have time for breakfast before going to work. Yet such
people are intent on surviving all these hardships on their own.
They are accustomed to electricity and water cuts as well as the
stinking environment. They even cheer when the light comes
back on. But what do they really feel inside about human fate?

One story which circulated widely in Hanoi was about a retired official who was so hard up that the only thing he wanted to do was to go to prison where at least he would get something to eat, no matter what the quality and quantity of the food. So he went out into a crowded street and shouted 'This regime is composed of stupid and irresponsible people.' He received some strange looks but nobody arrested him. Instead he was advised that the regime was a collective entity and nobody in particular. He would therefore do better to make his complaint more personal. At that he went around shouting 'The Party General Secretary is an idiot.' Naturally he was arrested and taken to court where he was sentenced to six years' imprisonment, comprising six months on a count of disturbing public order plus five and a half years for 'revealing state secrets'!

I myself have felt growing dismay about what has been happening in Vietnam ever since April 1975 and what we called our Great Spring Victory when the whole of the country was finally liberated. But it was not until I arrived in France that my views could be expressed fully in public.

Compared with most other Vietnamese and particularly those from the North, I am lucky. I have travelled widely and not only to communist countries like China, the Soviet Union and the German Democratic Republic. I have also visited neighbouring South East Asian countries, as well as Australia and various cities in Africa and Latin America. All these travels opened my eyes but it had long been one of my dreams to visit France.

From the age of thirteen to seventeen, I studied French literature at Khai Dinh High School in Hue and still remember my teachers there, what they looked like, the sound of their voices and their gestures. Indeed it would be hard to forget that rich experience during my youth. The works of Alphonse Daudet, Victor Hugo, Anatole France as well as the political ideas of Voltaire, Montesquieu and Jean-Jacques Rousseau have been part of my intellectual baggage ever since I left home and school to go and join the Resistance against the French in 1945.

Perhaps that was why I had to wait so long to visit France. Then at the beginning of 1990 I received an invitation through the Vietnamese Embassy in Paris to attend the annual fair organised every September by *L'Humanité*, the French Communist newspaper. It was sent to me in my capacity as Deputy Editor of its Vietnamese counterpart, *Nhan Dan*. After a great deal of thought, I accepted the invitation.

Throughout my life I have taken many major steps. The first was to leave home in 1945 and join the Resistance and a few months later the Communist Party. I then played a role in the battle of Dien Bien Phu in 1954. A few years later I travelled to the South several times along the Ho Chi Minh Trail to report on the situation there and then became a journalist. As a result in 1973, I was appointed a member of the delegation which oversaw the departure of American troops from South Vietnam. After that I went south again to report on the war there just before our forces finally reached Saigon in April 1975. On that occasion, I was proud to be present at the surrender of the South Vietnamese Government. In 1979 as well, I was one of the first Vietnamese to enter Phnom Penh following the defeat of Pol Pot. Going to Paris in 1990 was equally important for me.

During the course of this career, I have written many articles as well as eight books on the subject of the war and its aftermath. They were factual but looking back I can see that their aim was more or less propagandist. This one is different. I am writing it as the result of the pain felt by somebody who has been a member of the Vietnamese Communist Party for forty-five years before being expelled in March 1991. I am not bitter or resentful. I have tried to write conscientiously and clearly without exaggerating, embroidering or distorting the facts. I have written principally for the youth of Vietnam. They are the future of the country, and will lead it into the twenty-first century. If they understand its past and present, they will be able to construct its future more successfully. As for all my other friends, both Vietnamese and foreign, I hope they will find here the confessions of a man who realises the mistakes of his own generation and does not wish to see them repeated.

Like the snowdrop, I have survived the winter and now I am breaking through the ice. This book, which was published in Vietnamese in the United States in December 1991, has been well received by our overseas community there as well as those in Canada, Europe and Australia. Despite the tight controls imposed by the Vietnamese authorities, it has also managed to reach my friends and other people at home who have warmly welcomed

At the Vietnam War Memorial, Washington, October 1991.

it. Indeed its clandestine circulation in Vietnam has provoked anxiety and even anger among diehard circles there, as is evident in the continuing attacks in the Party press against me personally.

The translation and adaptation of this book into English has been carried out by two friends for whose help I would like to take this occasion to express my gratitude.

I wish however to dedicate it to my friend Stanley Karnow who, through his erudition and his heart, knows the history of our country so well. His book *Vietnam, A History*, as well as the television series of the same name which he masterminded, has been very well received and is considered by many American universities as a scholarly basis for the study of the history of Vietnam. It is precisely because he has adopted the position of a scientifically objective researcher that he has been criticised by both right-wing fanatics and leftist extremists. That simply exemplifies their true colours.

I would also like to dedicate this book to Stanley's wife Anne, an artist who paints with a great deal of sensitivity, and their daughter Catherine, a talented photographer. Catherine too has captured the heroic and pitiful character of our people in a journey she made on her own by train from Saigon to Hanoi and then through the remote northern mountains. In her relentless search for memorable photos in a country as under-developed as Vietnam, she overcame many difficulties to which such a sensitive American girl is unaccustomed.

Finally I dedicate the book to my American friends, the journalists and veterans, the politicians and the aid workers in whose hearts there is always a place for my country, and those who wish to see it change into a democracy.

Last but not least, I offer this book to all those who fought with valour and sacrifice in a country so far from home for values to which they were dedicated. As a Vietnamese soldier, I can only hope for reconciliation.

Paris, 1994

1

REVOLUTION

On the afternoon of August 17, 1945, a couple of days after the Emperor of Japan ordered his forces to lay down their arms so putting an end to the Second World War, I went to the ornate French-style Opera House in the centre of Hanoi to attend a meeting of city officials. Their aim was to express support for Tran Trong Kim, the prime minister installed in Hue by Emperor Bao Dai following the coup in March earlier that year when the Japanese ousted the French administration throughout Indo-China.

Suddenly, in the midst of this meeting, the microphone was seized by a group of men toting pistols. They took turns making speeches announcing the end of the reign of Emperor Bao Dai and the establishment of a new regime. They were in fact cadres of the Viet Minh, the movement founded by Ho Chi Minh in 1941 to struggle for the independence of Vietnam from both the Japanese and the French. Now that the Japanese had ac-knowledged their defeat, this meeting at the Opera House turned out to be the start of what we call the August Revolution.

I also vividly remember how on that occasion an extremely large red flag with a gold star at its centre was draped from the roof. At the same time young men from the Viet Minh carrying each other on their shoulders ran around the square in front of the Opera House waving red flags with the gold star and distributing them to the crowds gathering there. The slogan 'Support the Viet Minh' spread wider and wider that evening as it turned into night. Hanoi began to seethe with excitement.

I too was fired with enthusiasm. Like the rest of my generation and indeed most Vietnamese people, we were bursting with op-timism and excitement. At last the era of French colonialism

1

seemed to be over. Just to make sure, I joined a group of people who climbed over the iron gates of Bac Bo Phu, the seat of the former French senior administrator of Tonkin and took over the building. We then went to what had been the residence of the French Governor-General less than four kilometres away, which was now occupied by the Japanese who had not yet been disarmed. Still they did not take any action against us.

Then a couple of weeks later on September 2, 1945 when President Ho Chi Minh declared the independence of Vietnam in Ba Dinh Square, I was also present. So too were many families from Hanoi dressed in their best clothes, including officials in Western-style suits complete with jacket and tie, all of them waving little red flags with gold stars. Beside them were girls from the outskirts of the city wearing traditional dress in brown or black mingled with various other colours. Many of them were carrying bunches of flowers. I myself was among the ranks of the Viet Minh youth although I broke away from them to move closer to the black limousine being used by Ho Chi Minh. I even managed to touch its door as he departed after making his historic speech.

The next day was equally memorable because of the arrival of Chinese troops. Knowing so little about the world outside Indo-China and what it had decided about the future of our country, few of us were aware that the great powers – in other words the leaders of the United States, the Soviet Union and Britain – meeting in Potsdam in July 1945 had agreed to partition Indo-China along the 16th parallel for the purpose of disarming the Japanese army. South of this parallel was the responsibility of South East Asia Command led by the British and to the north the Chinese army loyal to Chiang Kai-shek.

Some of these Kuomintang troops reached Hanoi on September 3. To greet them, the Chinese community in the city organised a large band of musicians dressed in white uniforms to march north over the Paul Doumer bridge across the Red River. Together with my younger brother and many other people, I waited at the bridge for their return. But when the brass band and the reception committee re-appeared, there was obvious dismay because behind them what was supposed to be a victorious army turned out to be a rabble in total disarray. Many of the Chinese troops were so small that they were perhaps only thirteen or fourteen years old. Their uniforms were too big for them. They were smelly, tired, hungry and suffering from skin disease. Unable to march in step, a lot of them also had shoulder poles carrying their belongings. They were just peasants who had been hastily drafted into the army in order to move into Vietnam. People in Hanoi nicknamed them the Swollen Legs Brigade because a lot of them had oedema.

Those days and weeks at the beginning of September 1945 were full of surprises. At the age of eighteen, I became fully engrossed in the active political life of the country. Following on the heels of the Chinese Army came several exiled political organisations like the Quoc Dan Dang, the Vietnamese equivalent of the Chinese Nationalist Party, the Kuomintang. It set up an office in Quan Thanh Street with loudspeakers blaring out and published a couple of daily newspapers. As for the Viet Minh, it publicised its views in *Cuu Quoc* (National Salvation) and *Co Giai Phong* (Liberation Flag) which made compulsive reading early every morning. As a result many of us young people enlisted in the Liberation Army singing patriotic songs as we went. Regardless of hardship and the sacrifices we might encounter, we had the blood of warriors stirring in our veins. We were romantic and impetuous.

Initially, my friends in the Viet Minh took me to a house next to Bac Bo Phu, which we had occupied on August 19. It had since then become the headquarters of the Quang Trung Brigade which had just come down from the northern mountains where it had been formed during the war to fight the Japanese in the first instance.

It was the first time I had ever spent a night away from home. Previously I had always lived under the same roof with my parents as well as eight elder sisters and a younger brother. We had always enjoyed the warmth of a close-knit family. My father was a mandarin, a high government official who enjoyed a good standard of living. Our family employed a chauffeur, two rickshaw-drivers, a person who went to market, a cook and four general servants.

Now all I had with me was an old and thin pair of trousers, a brown woollen short-sleeved sweater with a hole in the front, and a small shoulder bag with a towel in it. Yet there I was, sitting on a long bench all day learning, sleeping soundly at night without tossing around, and eating rice scooped out of a bamboo basket together with my comrades in a squad of the Liberation Army. Although I had been a Boy Scout since the age of fourteen, this was very different. My life had completely changed.

Within a couple of weeks, I was selected to join the first military class to be trained in Hanoi. Its syllabus derived from the courses previously developed to fight the Japanese. Later I was credited with being one of the first cadets of Vietnam's main military training establishment, whose honorary chairman was Ho Chi Minh. He gave the opening lecture. Then came Anh Than,* who was introduced as a member of the Viet Minh Central Executive Committee. In reality he was Truong Chinh, the General Secretary of the Communist Party of Indo-China. He instructed us about the international situation at the end of the war as well as the current role of the Vietnamese Revolution. Another lecturer was Anh To, in other words Pham Van Dong, then Minister of Finance in the revolutionary government; he talked to us about the ethics of the revolution. But practical training was provided by Anh Van—that was the code-name always used by General Vo Nguyen Giap. At that time he was Minister of the Interior and he taught us about the principles of guerrilla warfare. In the afternoons there would be military drill followed by rifle and bayonet practice, as well as grenade-throwing, followed by lessons in section and platoon tactics.

Our training lasted all of two weeks. Then, because the situation in southern Vietnam was becoming very tense and fighting broke out in Saigon on September 23, seventy-two of us from my class were chosen to form the 'Advance to the South' mission. We set off by train from Hanoi, and in each province dropped off two or three comrades to form the nucleus of a resistance force. I myself left the train at Quang Tri, north of Hue, with two friends, Dai and Kinh.

Quang Tri was regarded as a very important location because of its position at the junctions of the main north-south road, Highway One, and Highway Nine which traverses the mountains into Laos and reaches as far as Savannakhet on the east bank of the Mekong river opposite Thailand. Part of this highway

---

* *Anh* = elder brother; *Than* = cautious.

had been constructed between 1942 and 1944 under the supervision of Prince Souphanouvong of Laos, a French-trained engineer who later became a resistance leader.

My task in 1945 was to act as a military instructor trying to teach the local people about guerrilla warfare – conducting ambushes, laying mines and sabotaging the railway. Then we moved up to a big French-owned rubber plantation near Khe Sanh and on into Laos. Our aim was to search for and eliminate about 100 soldiers, remnants of the French army who had fled in March 1945 when the Japanese staged their complete military take-over of Indo-China. These French soldiers, being unable to reach China or cross into Thailand, were believed to be operating in the area of Tchepone and Muong Phine in southern Laos. So before I was nineteen, to my great surprise, I was a company commander engaged in operations against the enemy in which I had to worry about getting arms and basic necessities such as rice and salt.

A year later in early 1947, when the French landed fresh troops at Quang Tri, I also had to worry about patrolling enemy positions and leading my unit to conduct ambushes before melting back into the population living close to the long beaches of central Vietnam. There were even times when having eaten all our rice, although it had rotted after being stored under the sand, we were happy to chew boiled sweet potatoes flavoured with pickles provided by the old people living nearby. Sometimes the entire unit suddenly became afflicted with scabies and other skin diseases. Yet we still continued to sing lustily around the camp fire. Often, too, I had to send away my deputy commander, Nguyen Dung, before closing the eyes of our dead comrades. Dung was my closest friend. We were as alike as two peas in a pod. But in 1947 when our 4th company was operating as part of the 14th battalion in Quang Tri province, he was killed in battle by the French and so I had to close his eyes as well.

Nonetheless, despite the hundreds of friends who died, all of us, including schoolchildren, gladly plunged into battle after battle. Towards the end of 1947, I returned to Laos to help set up a joint Vietnamese-Lao battalion with Thao Ke and Thao Ma, who later became chief of the province of Sam Nua. I happened to meet Thao Ke again in 1987 when I went to Vientiane to give a lecture to the Lao Journalists' Association. By then he had retired, but he told me that Thao Ma was still active as head of a geological company prospecting for gold.

With Thao Ke I was able to reminisce about the old times in Tchepone when we held a ceremony at the local Buddhist temple to mark our cooperation and then went to a Chinese coffee shop to celebrate. In those early days of the Revolution, there was a sense of being a young man at a time of great turmoil. One could apply the strength of youth to bolster a new nation. Patriotism, comradeship, a feeling of national pride, a firm belief in justice...these were the sources of happiness for a whole generation of young people.

When I joined the Communist Party at the age of nineteen, I swore an oath under the light of an oil lamp always to be loyal to the idea of liberating the people and the whole of mankind. Oh, what joy and happiness to take part in the struggle for such beliefs! Lacking education, I knew little about political theory. I had read a few Communist manifestos but did not really understand them. I equated joining the Party with patriotism and gaining independence. A life full of activity, yet simple, beckoned; it would be bright and glorious without a ripple of concern discernible in the future.

Perhaps my desire to serve my country stemmed from my family background. My paternal great-grandfather was Bui Tuan who studied assiduously to become a mandarin of the highest rank. He then held several important positions before becoming governor of a northern province encompassing modern-day Thai Nguyen and Bac Ninh; he was also appointed Deputy Minister of War. In 1869 when the Chinese Black Flag rebels started to attack across the border, my great-grandfather together with Ong Ich Kiem suppressed the trouble with a show of strength which is recorded as illustrious in the history of our country.

Bui Tap, my grandfather, also belonged to a generation of outstanding mandarins and scholars who administered the country and acted as provincial governors during the early period of French rule. But alas he died at the early age of forty-seven, leaving my father and his two elder brothers orphans before they had reached their teens. They therefore went to live in the small district of Van Dinh just south of Hanoi with an uncle who taught them classical Chinese and Vietnamese literature. They were very bright and studied hard. There is even a story that they often went to sweep up the leaves in the grounds of a nearby Buddhist temple so that they could burn them at night to provide enough light to continue studying.

In 1906, these three brothers moved to a prominent school in Hue, the imperial capital, where they all graduated from the same class; this is very rare. In fact my father, Bui Bang Doan, obtained a degree in classical literature when he was only seventeen. He then continued studying for a further three years to get another degree in French. After that he was successively appointed a judge in Ninh Binh and governor first of Cao Bang province on the border with China and afterwards of Bac Ninh. Then in 1933 at the age of forty-three he was recalled to Hue to become Minister of Justice in the imperial administration. This appointment made by Emperor Bao Dai was seen by the French as a wise move. My father was at that time by far the youngest minister in Bao Dai's administration apart from Ngo Dinh Diem who, after a very varied career, was ultimately to become the first President of (what is often referred to as) the Saigon regime.

During the next twelve years, which he spent in Hue, my father supervised the legal system throughout the provinces in what was then called Annam in the centre of present-day Vietnam. He also maintained a standard of complete honesty and did not take advantage of his position. At the same time he was directly involved in drafting new Criminal and Civil codes of law for Annam. These codes were written in French and Vietnamese as well as being translated into Chinese.

I still remember my father's political views at that period. He was anxious to regain the political independence of Vietnam but through non-violent means. He wanted to expand the educational system in order to improve the people's knowledge and create a legal basis for a fair society to catch up with modern ideas. A Confucian by upbringing, he was loyal to the Emperor and wished to see a constitutional monarchy established. On the other hand, he highly valued French culture and civilization, insisting that everybody should make the most of it to raise cultural standards. For instance, along with all my sisters and my brother, I had to learn French at high school in Hue. Every Sunday too was very special. The house was decorated with flowers. My father liked chrysanthemums best. All day we would eat only French food with knives and forks on a table properly set with napkins.

Bowls and chopsticks were forbidden. So too were Vietnamese clothes. My brother and I had to wear European-style shirts and shorts. My father would also read French poems and literature to us, although I remember, when we were very young, that he would sometimes relax a little, carrying us around the room on his back. As for my sisters, on Sundays they used to show off their talents by making ice-cream and a great variety of other desserts. They also specialised in knitting and sewing.

Naturally my father's career and his attitude towards life had a great influence on me. He taught me from a very young age to be honest and straightforward without kowtowing or licking the boots of anybody. I will never forget how my father always sat up straight. Whenever he slept, either at night or during a siesta, he always assumed the same position with his two hands clasped over his stomach. In fact, throughout his life he was never undignified. Descending from his room to the living quarters or the courtyard, he always walked straight and turned corners at a right angle, never taking any short cuts. Maybe some people found this attitude fussy. But this is the character of a gentleman, and has to be so. He cannot compromise. He has to be strict with himself.

Other people have similar memories of him. For instance, in July 1990 when I visited a village in the province of Ha Nam Ninh just south of Hanoi, I met by chance an old man aged ninety who recalled that in 1927 when my father came to take up the post of district chief, the first notice he issued stated: 'Anybody who has a request to make, should not bring along any sort of offering.' In all the hundreds of cases he judged throughout his career, he never accepted a penny and declined every bribe. And when he travelled for his work, he would not eat or drink in the homes of the people because mandarins were strictly forbidden from importuning those under their charge. His integrity and uprightness were really absolute.

Presumably it was because of this reputation that in September 1945, a few days after proclaiming our independence, Ho Chi Minh wrote to my father asking him to join the new revolutionary administration then being set up in Hanoi. Our family still has the letter. It is short and states: 'I have been informed that you have many talents and a reputation for honesty. Therefore you are invited to help shoulder the work of the state.'

At that time, Ho Chi Minh held very broad views. He wanted to use talented people from the old regime with knowledge and a sense of justice in order to unite the people. But initially my father turned down the invitation on the grounds of old age and poor health. By then he was fifty-six, though actually only a year older than Ho himself. Instead the real reason was the Confucian adage which states: 'A loyal servant does not serve two masters.'

Still Ho Chi Minh was so insistent that in October 1945 my father agreed but only after consulting the family. Since lineal seniority matters so much in a traditional Vietnamese family, that meant first and foremost his two elder brothers Bui Bang Phan and Bui Bang Thuan, both of whom had by then retired from their provincial governorships.

At first Ho appointed my father as Government Inspector-General, his deputy being Cu Huy Can, one of the Viet Minh representatives who had just been to Hue to accept the abdication of Emperor Bao Dai. This prompted my father to inquire what power he had. The new Head of State said he had full power and my father proceeded to apply it decisively and impartially in a number of cases, some of which involved corruption and the abuse of power by high-ranking communist cadres in the provinces of Vinh Phu and Ha Nam.

Nonetheless in the elections held under the aegis of the Viet Minh on January 6, 1946, my father stood as candidate in Ha Son Binh and gained a large majority. He subsequently acted as head of the standing committee of the National Assembly from the end of 1946 onwards. As such he spent a lot of time with Ho Chi Minh when the revolutionary administration fled Hanoi to the comparative security of the Viet Bac military zone close to the border with China. There they became close friends because they respected one another despite their ideological differences. In fact they sometimes exchanged poems. One of them, written in 1948, is in my opinion one of the best poems Ho Chi Minh ever wrote.

Such was the esteem in which my father was held that when he died of a brain haemorrhage in April 1955, he was accorded a state funeral and there were plans to bury him in Mai Dich cemetery in Hanoi along with other prominent revolutionaries. But before he breathed his last, he had asked to be interred in his native village of Ung Hoa in Ha Dong province among his loved ones.

Apart from a small house in this village, my father had no property either in Hanoi or anywhere else where he had worked. When he died, he left nothing of any substance to his ten children, eight girls and two boys. We did not even own a bicycle between us. But we told each other that human values were what mattered most and we had inherited a standard of honesty through the career of a prominent mandarin who, throughout his life, had lived simply and unassumingly and was respected by every class in society for his honesty and humanity. In fact his sense of social justice was probably the main reason why I have always sought to achieve it by involving myself in the future of my compatriots and my country.

Father was laid to rest beside my mother on whose grave I burnt some joss-sticks. She was his second wife. The first, who bore him five daughters, died at an early age before he went to Hue to become a minister. My mother came from a poor family in the district of Binh Luc, south of Hanoi. I will always recall her seductive voice as she sang old traditional melodies to lull my father to sleep. She also loved to work. She was always sewing, making cakes, cooking, pickling vegetables and concocting sauces. She was indeed regarded as a great woman. The best thing I remember about her was her loving heart. She really liked to get to know people and become good friends with everybody, no matter how simple they might be.

After the Revolution, when I went away to join the army, I did not tell my family where I had gone. In vain my mother visited several camps trying to find me. After that she always looked after young soldiers as if they were her own children when they dropped by at the house where she was living in a village outside Hanoi. The tenderness and unselfishness of my mother, whose life was devoted to others on the basis of humanity, had a decisive influence on my own feelings and continues to act as a driving force to this day.

Following two relentless years in the Resistance against the French, I managed to find time to visit my mother briefly. She prepared some delicacies with leaves culled from the garden, made some cakes and encouraged me to eat. Several days later during the mid-autumn festival in 1948, when some French troops were parachuted into the district and made a sweep through the village, an informant pointed out our house as that of the wife of a high-ranking Viet Minh official, meaning my father. Immediately a legionnaire rushed in and shot my mother in the chest with a round of fire from his sub-machine gun. She died on the kitchen floor. After that it was impossible not to feel vindictive. Whenever I went into battle, behind every opposing gun was the enemy who had killed my mother.

When we embarked on the struggle for our independence of course nobody realised it would result in more than thirty years of war which would have widespread effects on every Viet-namese family without exception. But people endured and held firm in the belief that independence and freedom were more precious than anything else and that once they were achieved, everything else would follow. In other words every sacrifice was worthwhile in the longer term. But was it all inevitable?

This question has long been debated among politicians and academics alike, though rarely within Vietnam itself, at least not in public. I was eager therefore in October 1990, soon after I arrived in Paris, to accept an invitation to attend a seminar on this issue, organised by the foundation set up in honour of the late General Leclerc, the commander of the French troops who returned to Indo-China in 1945. I was accompanied to this seminar by two officials from the Vietnamese embassy. Also present were several French generals and prominent historians of the period* as well as Roland Dumas, Minister of Foreign Affairs. The seminar focussed on who was directly responsible for the outbreak of full-scale war between the French and the Viet Minh on December 19, 1946.

On both sides it is a matter of controversy. There are those who think the French provoked the war with their bombardment of the port of Haiphong on November 24 while reinforcing Hanoi with tanks to make a show of strength on the streets. Suddenly these tanks attacked the Financial Directorate (which was housed in what is now the Ministry of Foreign Affairs) on the pretext that the Viet Minh could not maintain law and order – the French

---

* They also included Pierre Messmer who had been parachuted into Vietnam in 1945 and was for a time held captive by the Viet Minh, before being appointed to a key position relating to Indo-China. Much later he became prime minister of France during the early 1970s.

were therefore taking over. But after that they ordered all their troops back to barracks. So did the French have a gradual plan of escalation leading to the outbreak of full-scale war? Or did the Viet Minh draw up their own plan weeks beforehand with the intention of triggering off the outbreak of war by blowing up the Yen Phu electrical power plant in Hanoi on the night of December 19?

Some French historians affirm that Vo Nguyen Giap, the Vietnamese commander, ordered the explosive for the attack without informing Ho Chi Minh. That is a purely subjective conjecture lacking any foundation because in such a momentous affair Giap would never have taken the lead. In other words it is a conjecture which completely ignores the mechanism and spirit of the Viet Minh method of operating.

After studying many documents, I believe that back in 1946 both sides had very similar aims but misunderstood one another. There was a common feeling that peace talks had broken down irretrievably and the outbreak of war was inevitable. Both sides had a plan to cope with a worst-case situation. Each side also had the intention of taking the opportunity to reduce its level of activity immediately if its opponent gained the upper hand, in order to avoid losing power completely. And both sides were conscious that they did not want to embark on total war because in December 1946 Léon Blum, the leader of the French Socialist Party, had just taken over the premiership in Paris, while Marius Moutet, the Minister responsible for the Colonies, was even then on his way out to Indo-China.

However, once the two armies got their teeth into one another, there were many eager young extremists for whom any small scuffle, any minor outbreak of fighting could become a major fire. Neither side wanted to engage in full-scale war but they were both well prepared and ready for the worst in order to avoid being caught on the hop. The resultant skirmishes were the spark which set off the conflagration, and that was how our country became involved in a tragic war.

In my opinion, the fault really lay with the outmoded colonial mentality of French politicians, including those belonging to the Socialist and Communist Parties. As far as the French were concerned, patriotism consisted of recovering their colonies and maintaining the original glory of the French empire. According to General Leclerc, before he left to take up his duties in Indo-China, Maurice Thorez, the General Secretary of the French Communist Party, took him by the shoulder and said '*Cognez, cognez fort*' (Hit them, hit them hard).

In fact, during his talks in Paris in 1946 Ho Chi Minh accepted the formula of a free Vietnam within the French Union but the French would not agree. But what if the French government had dealt with its colonies like the British did with India? What would have happened then? Perhaps Vietnam within a French Union would have calmed down and developed, so avoiding all the suffering and destruction of later years.

The initial years of the Resistance were really rather elating and heroic, with the spirit of the nation developing to a high level. In October 1945 there was the 'gold week' in Hanoi when the whole population were encouraged to donate their wealth to further the cause of independence, and millions of piastres in banknotes, gold and property were contributed. Shortly afterwards the Communist Party formally dissolved itself and became the Marxist Study Association. It was still led by Party General Secretary Truong Chinh, although it was rarely mentioned on the radio or in the press particularly when compared with the Resistance Government set up by Ho Chi Minh in March 1946. This body comprised many well-known non-Party figures who would these days be described as technocrats. But Truong Chinh was not dismayed. He wrote books like *The Revolution Will Win*, and he had a network of professional revolutionaries, men who had little education but were dedicated to the cause, having learnt their politics in imperialist prisons. They remained the Party's regional representatives whose duty was solely political.[*]

From 1947 onwards, the Resistance built up the Viet Bac war zone in the northern highlands followed by liberated zones 4 and 5 at points down the coast stretching from Nghe An to

---

[*]   These were: Le Thanh Nghi in charge of Zone 3, the coastal region north of the Red River, Hoang Van Hoan in Zone 4 to the south of Haiphong, Do Muoi along Route 5 from Hanoi to Haiphong, Tran Quoc Hoan in the area immediately surrounding the capital, Nguyen Duy Trinh in Zone 5 covering central Vietnam including Hue and Da Nang, Le Duc Tho in the south overall, and Pham Hung in the southern Mekong Delta region. All these men were to become prominent Politburo members from 1961 onwards, lasting until the 1980s and in the case of Do Muoi the 1990s.

Phan Thiet in the South. The sense of struggle truly ran deep
and strong. Close bonds of brotherhood linked cadres, combatants
and compatriots. Our national tradition of opposing foreign aggression is a heritage which imbues everybody, whether rich or
poor, secular or religious.

By 1950, my unit was part of the 304th Division which was
deployed in the Ha Nam Ninh/Hoa Binh battlefield south of
Hanoi before extending its activities to Dien Bien Phu. There
we held politico-military seminars and indoctrination sessions. We
conducted night-time exercises in the cold and mud with everybody
very sleepy. At the same time some battlefield studies were carried
out on maps and models, and others on the ground itself. Still
there were many attacks on enemy positions while they counter-
attacked with bombing raids and long-range artillery. We were
not deterred. We interrogated the French soldiers and legionnaires
we had captured and carried on our daily life. That consisted
of drills and exercise, pitching camp and maintaining hygiene,
all of which we carried out with a light heart. Despite everything
we could still laugh, sing and play jokes on one another, because
we continued to love life and be optimistic.

The situation started to change towards the end of 1950 after
we forced the French to abandon their garrisons along the northern
border, and the Resistance of the Vietnamese people was able
to link up with the People's Republic of China which was founded
in October 1949. The ever-increasing amount of military and
civilian aid from China enabled the Viet Minh to strengthen
its position. But it became more complex and tension grew. Many
people left the Resistance and returned to the French-occupied
zone as large numbers of Chinese advisers arrived and were attached
to every unit at all levels. The friendly, even cosy atmosphere
which had previously existed disappeared with talk of orthodox
class warfare. Marxism had come to Vietnam via Maoism.

When two Chinese advisers joined the 304th Division where
I was director of the political school in 1952, everything they
said seemed different, new and somehow wonderful. As a result
everyone from top-ranking generals to the rawest of recruits hurried
along with their books to learn from the advisers. What is the
Communist Party? It plays the leading role in every aspect of
society. It is constant, correct and absolute. Class struggle is objective, decisive and obligatory. The collective masses are opposed
to individualism and its role in history. The individual is as worthless

as a grain of sand, and to be crushed underfoot. The meaning of democratic centralism is collective leadership. What is the Lin Piao strategy? The guiding strategy is four fast, one slow. What is assault strategy? The political commissar makes the final decision. We learned also about the role of the cell and the Party member but above all about Mao Tse-tung Thought, with the peasants and workers forming the backbone of the Revolution.

The wind from the north first engulfed the Viet Bac region and then all the other liberated zones. Chinese books, films and songs were everywhere and all of us in the Resistance regarded them as first-class works. For instance Mao Tse-tung's song 'The East is Red' assumed the status of an official anthem alongside our own national anthem 'Advance the Army' (*Tien Quan Ca*). Only after that came a song in honour of Ho Chi Minh and the '*Internationale*'.

At the same time, a campaign got underway to encourage the reading and speaking of Chinese while a constant stream of cadres was sent north to study in Peking, Shanghai, Nanking, Nanning and Canton. For instance, Peking University threw open its doors to hundreds of Vietnamese students. China was the immense rear area for the Vietnamese Revolution. It was a tremendous advantage but we had to pay very dearly for it. Having just escaped from the long night of being slaves to the French, we were dazzled by the new light of the Chinese Revolution which was acclaimed as our role-model. We accepted everything impetuously and haphazardly without any thought, let alone criticism.

Looking back it was a time of happiness but also of shame and childishness. From the beginning of 1952, every unit had to set up three-man cells. Each evening after they had eaten, these cells had to examine together their actions and thoughts during the day. Every member of the cell had to reveal his fears of hunger, hardship and death as well as his thoughts of envy, lust or enjoyment. This system was said to be necessary to maintain discipline, but it weighed heavily on human dignity and the personality of the individual who was always forced into repentance.

To generalise, the uniformity imposed on us at that time was painful. In fact we were all in uniform: men in Mao jackets, women in black trousers and Mao jackets. Still, women were allowed to wear their hair long if it was tied firmly into a pony-tail.

Curly hair was regarded as bourgeois and an imitation of the imperialists. Thinking, writing, working, all forms of behaviour including eating, all had to be uniform to conform with the masses. Life just became a barracks, a spiritual prison, and many aspects of this attitude still persist, so negating our traditional values, our individualism.

All these developments reached a climax at the 2nd Party Congress held in the Viet Bac region in February 1951, when it re-emerged as the Lao Dong or Workers' Party. It was stated in Party regulations that 'the basic theory of the Party is Marxism-Leninism, Stalinism and Mao Tse-tung thought'. Nobody had any doubts and naturally nobody reacted. At that time those tenets were as natural as the morning light and the breath of life, and essential for human existence.

In truth it has to be said that the thinking of Ho Chi Minh and the rest of the leadership in those days was to regard Mao Tse-tung thought as the only way to follow. But to lose the identity of a nation, of oneself and one's own power of thought is a colossal mistake. It was as if we took a white sheet of paper, poured black Chinese ink on it and proclaimed that the light had dawned.

I recall that not long after the Second Party Congress, a French journalist asked Ho Chi Minh why he had written so little about politics. The reply came back 'What is there for me to write? All the theory that is needed has been worked out and written by Mao Tse-tung.' That was the overall trend of thought at the time.

Personally I respected Ho Chi Minh because in 1945, when I enlisted in the Quang Trung Brigade, my duty for more than a month was to stand guard with an American carbine at Bac Bo Phu, the mansion where Ho worked. At that time, he did not know who my father was, but it was Ho's idea that I join the first military class formed in Hanoi.

Much later when I became a newspaperman, I had the opportunity on many occasions to observe Ho Chi Minh when he gave interviews to journalists from the Soviet Union, China and several other countries. He was always relaxed and natural, without any affectation. It is true he lived very simply and honestly. He loved children and sympathised with women as well as the poor. He hated vanity, ostentation and formality. He was also very discerning and subtle with everybody, no matter what their experience and standing. But I entirely reject any suggestion that he was a clever actor. It has to be recognised that he was a cultured and well-travelled man as well as somebody who was very human.

In fact he was very much a human being and certainly not a saint. I was therefore extremely interested to learn from the French scholar Daniel Hemery that Ho Chi Minh probably had two wives. One was Marie Briere, a French Socialist Party member whom he met in Paris during the early 1920s. The other was Tang Tuyet Minh, a midwife whom he married in Canton on October 18, 1926. Yet when a report about this latter marriage was printed in the Saigon youth newspaper *Tuoi Tre* in May 1991, its editor Kim Hanh was disciplined and dismissed from her post.

What is wrong with saying that when he was young Ho Chi Minh fell in love like any other ordinary mortal? Somebody who is subtle and hides his feelings is very human and certainly capable of love. It is stupid to extol Ho as a saint who led an exemplary life without a thought for love, marriage or the joys of having a family.

On the other hand, in my opinion Ho Chi Minh was not very smart in writing two books under different pseudonyms about his own life. They contain many passages of self-praise. Naturally the people love and admire 'Uncle Ho' very deeply. He saw that as self-evident and simply reflecting the truth. But to write praising oneself is not right and could be said to be tasteless, especially since one of these books was published as early as 1948 when we were all deeply involved in fighting the French.*

Then there were the many occasions when he referred to himself as 'Uncle'. That was all right with young people and children. Indeed it is part of our Vietnamese tradition. However, we do not refer to our many national and historical heroes such as Le Loi and Tran Hung Dao as 'Uncle'. Therefore to call oneself 'Uncle' of the people as a whole while still alive was to abuse that tradition. In any case there were many people far older than Ho who were more deserving of this form of address.

---

* These books were *Stories about the Activities of Chairman Ho*, first published in Shanghai in 1949 under the name Tran Dan Tien, and *Tales told during a Journey* by T. Lan, published in 1963.

In fact in 1945, when he was only fifty-five, Ho Chi Minh styled himself 'the Father of the Nation'. Perhaps he was simply emulating Stalin.

During the 1950s in Vietnam, Stalin – just like Mao Tse-tung –was excessively praised. The mass media created an extraordinary picture of a hero who had saved mankind from the disaster of fascism and paved the way for more than a dozen countries in Europe and Asia, including Vietnam, to stand up and gain their independence. How can one forget the verses penned by To Huu, our Party poet, on the death of Stalin in 1953:

> *Stalin, oh Stalin, alas He is gone!*
> *Do heaven and earth still exist?*
> *Devotion to father, to mother, to husband,*
> *Devotion to Him ten times more than to oneself.*
> *Love for the children, for the country, for the race*
> *But so much more love for Him.*
> *In the old days, we were so withered and desolate*
> *With Him there is joy*
> *In the old days, there was hunger and torment*
> *With Him there is more than enough rice to fill the pot.*

At that time teachers were specially trained to explain to their pupils that it was Stalin who brought rice and clothes, and smiles to the faces of the children. I have to admit that I too was absolutely shattered and heartbroken when I heard of his death. Later I was to learn better but To Huu, who had been a respected poet, continued to politicise his work, including verses eulogising Mao Tse-tung.

The main disciples of Mao in Vietnam were Truong Chinh, the Party General Secretary, and his close associate Hoang Quoc Viet, who was also a member of the Politburo. Other early members of this body were Vo Nguyen Giap and Le Duc Tho. In 1947 they were joined by Nguyen Luong Bang (known as Sao Do, the Red Star) and Pham Van Dong, while Le Duan, who was to dominate the Party in the 1960s and 1970s, came later.

Of all these men the best known was Vo Nguyen Giap, who joined the Party early and so ranked high, although he first es-tablished his reputation elsewhere. Having graduated in law from Hanoi University in 1936, he became a teacher of history at Thang Long High School in Hanoi where he enjoyed the con-fidence of his students. Many of them still recall how passionately he taught the history of the French Revolution with warm praise for its leaders like Danton, Marat and Robespierre. Giap was intelligent and had a good memory. He was always engrossed in the latest books and newspapers. In later years his office was simply strewn with books lying everywhere, unlike other generals who arranged them neatly for show but never read them. As a result, he continued to be respected and trusted by numerous cadres and officers.

Vo Nguyen Giap was responsible for training a whole generation of young officers to study hard and follow his example of living simply and honestly. For example, in September 1945 he just appeared suddenly in my military class in Hanoi to teach basic guerrilla warfare and the role of armed struggle in the Revolution. I subsequently met him at various other military training establishments.

General Giap was helped by his scientific thinking and good knowledge of Marxist dialectics from an early age. That enabled him to command and lead the army. Very penetratingly and quickly he summed up and grasped every new situation to raise the perceptions of others. Hence he was personally responsible for developing military science in Vietnam and inspiring two generations of cadres. It could be said that our military victories stemmed from the correct political and military policies pursued by a Minister of Defence and Commander in Chief who made a deep impact.

At first, our training was very rudimentary and we only gained experience gradually. Although I became a regimental commander at the age of the twenty-two, I was still like a child. I did have some training in using guns and throwing grenades, but my knowledge of strategy and tactics was very limited. So was that of most of my comrades in arms. A few of them had previously received military training from the French, but they were mostly NCOs. As a result General Giap expended a lot of energy on reviewing the performance of every unit at six-monthly intervals, as well as analysing the tactics of the French.

Initially, the French did not put a lot of effort into Indo-China. They sent only small units comprising mainly legionnaires plus Senegalese and Moroccan troops. There were very few French men among them because they hoped to recruit locally. In fact they increased their war effort only gradually since they expected to gain a quick victory over us, whereas we tried to prolong the war in order to defeat them. What is more, they were fighting far from home with little international support, but we had the advantage of relying on the people and rallying patriotism on our own home ground. So gradually we were able to change the character of the war and by 1954 engage the enemy in division strength and choose our own battleground.

This evolution marked a major transformation in our tactics. At first we had only attacked French positions for a few minutes before withdrawing. Then we gradually prolonged the battles as we grew in strength. But Dien Bien Phu was altogether a different proposition. The French began to build up their position there in late 1953, so General Hoang Van Thai and certain Chinese advisers headed by General Wei Kuo-ching were sent to observe the situation. Their advice was that we should attack as soon as possible before the French had time to dig themselves in and construct an airfield in this remote valley. The attack was planned for the end of January 1954, but about six hours before it was due to be launched, General Giap ordered a halt to all operations.

This decision almost led to a mutiny. Everybody from the highest-ranking generals right down to the ordinary soldiers protested because they were all prepared to accept hardship and had already written letters in their own blood about their readiness to sacrifice everything, even their lives, for complete victory. Even the three other members of the Party Committee in charge of the battlefront, Generals Hoang Van Thai, Le Liem and Dang Kim Giang, were opposed to Giap. He however insisted that he was Supreme Commander, with full powers issued by Ho Chi Minh. As such he said it was his right to stop the attack. There was to be no discussion. Everybody had to obey him and he would explain later. At the same time, Giap sent a message to all units. It contained only one sentence. 'Stop attack tonight, regroup to former position, obey strictly, explanation follows.'

There were several reasons why General Giap called off this attack at the last moment. Up till then the largest battle we had carried out involved one division only. How then could we command and co-ordinate five divisions at Dien Bien Phu? He was also worried that we had never before carried out prolonged attacks lasting more than twenty-four hours. In any case he pointed out that the assessment of the situation at Dien Bien Phu had been carried out two months earlier. Since then the French had considerably reinforced their position there. So, like a gambler, we were staking everything on a single throw and risked losing the entire war.

Instead Giap's solution was to mobilise porters from every province to provide support for the battle to come. They brought supplies of ammunition, rice and salt. Each porter was required to work for a month or more, depending on where he came from. They were organised in units with a bicycle allocated to every two men. They had to take it in turns uphill and downhill carrying up to 250 kilos of supplies. They travelled through jungles and mountains at night and rested during the day to avoid detection by the enemy. The French, however, did not have much air cover and we created mock targets for them to attack by lighting fires in places of no tactical value – the rising smoke was simply a decoy.

One characteristic of this war was that while we could remain hidden, the enemy was totally exposed. During what turned out to be a fifty-five-day battle for Dien Bien Phu, we always had the French within our sights. We could look down on them in the valley below but they could not see us. We could pick out our targets one by one and so eliminate them while digging in closer and closer and minimising our losses. When we closed the airfield at Dien Bien Phu and the French had to bring in supplies by parachute, they sometimes missed the target and we benefited. As a result, their morale decreased, they could not evacuate casualties, and with the onset of the rainy season their trenches filled with water. In other words, the French were living in hell and lost the war.

I myself was involved in training troops for the battle of Dien Bien Phu and was wounded there, fortunately not too seriously, in a French air attack which killed many of my friends. So I was very interested to attend an exhibition arranged by the Ministry of Defence at the Army Museum on Dien Bien Phu Avenue in Hanoi to mark the thirtieth anniversary of the battle. Also present on that occasion in May 1984 were General Giap and his close friend General Hoang Van Thai, who was Chief of Staff throughout the war against the French. Therefore they were together in the Muong Phang command post at Dien Bien Phu.

At the exhibition which included models of the battlefield, General Giap reminisced about the events which had taken place

thirty years earlier, and talked about each of the divisional commanders then present. Then, walking towards the symbolic flagpole
on the citadel, he signalled to General Thai and me to come
close as if he wanted to confide something. 'Look journalist,
this is Brother Thai. Ask him whether it is true that when I
decided to change the plan of attack, he did not understand and
even opposed me!' General Thai smiled amiably and said 'Yes,
it was exactly like that. We had prepared everything and our
soldiers were highly motivated. All they were waiting for was
the order to fire, so it was very difficult to hold them back.
But if we had not done so, it would have been far more difficult.
We might not have won the battle and then the future of the
Resistance would have been endangered. So all the effort to build
up our five divisions was well worthwhile.'

That account was further borne out on the thirty-fifth anniversary
of our victory in 1989 when I asked General Vo Nguyen Giap
to write an article telling the whole true story about events for
the Sunday magazine edition of *Nhan Dan* of which I was then
editor. He agreed to do so and entitled his account 'The Most
Difficult Decision'. It attracted a lot of public attention because
it differs markedly from that in standard Vietnamese history books.
General Giap referred to several generals whose names have not
been publicly mentioned for a long time like Dang Kim Giang
and Le Liem* as well as high-ranking officers such as Do Duc
Kien and Nguyen Minh Nghia, who were all deeply involved
in the battle. He also praised the Chinese advisers present at
Dien Bien Phu under the leadership of General Wei Kuo-ching.

General Giap was very careful in drafting this article. He amended
it frequently and often phoned me about it. Above all he was
concerned about the illustrations which accompanied it. He was
insistent that there should be a photo of Uncle Ho plus the
text of his order stating 'General in the battlefield, you have
full authority to make decisions. But once you have engaged
the enemy, victory must be achieved!'

---

* General Dang Kim Giang, who was head of support services at the battle of
Dien Bien Phu, was later arrested as a 'revisionist' and died in prison, without
ever being brought to trial or any mention being made of his death. Le Liem
likewise died in obscurity; he had left the army in 1954 and for a time served
as Deputy Minister of Education.

2

REFORM

The French finally surrendered at Dien Bien Phu on May 7, 1954, the eve of the opening of a major international conference in Geneva to discuss peace in Indo-China. In the resulting agreements signed on July 27 that year, there were provisions for the departure of the French, but we did not consider it a great victory. Due to pressure at the conference form Chou En-lai, the Chinese Foreign Minister, and his Soviet counterpart Molotov, we were forced to accept the partition of Vietnam along the 17th parallel, whereas we wanted it further south at Deo Ca. We believed that we could easily have gained all that territory if fighting had continued. Still we could look forward to nationwide elections as provided for in the Geneva Agreements, although that hope too soon became an illusion because the regime set up in the South, afraid that it would not win, sabotaged the whole idea with the help of the Americans.

At least, however, the north of the country was liberated and we could now go ahead freely with the process of creating a new society. Land reform had already started in the area of Thai Nguyen, where Hoang Quoc Viet was in charge, and was proving very popular with the army because many soldiers were poor peasants. So too were the thousands of porters who played such an important role at Dien Bien Phu. Thanks to an intensive propaganda campaign, they all believed they would be given land. At first we did not realise what a mistake it was going to be.

Land reform occurred after we had heard hundreds of Chinese advisers introduce the process on the basis of experience in their own country. I still recall eight lectures on the subject given to all middle-level cadres. Not a single one of us could escape them. They were a hurdle we had to jump in order to 'grow

23

up and become a genuine revolutionary'. The eight stages of growing up involved numerous sessions of team discussions and debate to help one another criticise mistakes. Then there were sessions to air the grievances of the peasants and tell stories illustrating the cruelty of landlords and imperialists. We were also taught that cases which seemed correct could be a divergence from the truth. So we watched films and plays about landlords and peasants. Everything was cut and dried. He is a landlord even though he owns only 10 square metres. Therefore he is bad, greedy, cruel and the evil hand of imperialism. All peasants are good. They have a revolutionary spirit and are disciplined.

Such thinking was widespread. It could be said that the spread of Maoism after 1951 began to stultify our consciences and has caused lasting harm right up till now. We forgot our basic national values and lost our sense of pride and self-confidence. We put an end to the exciting and innocent period of respect uniting those who joined the Resistance. Instead we imposed a yoke on the special nature of our peasantry. Repression was mistaken for enlightenment and progress.

For instance there were landlords who joined the Resistance and were subsequently branded as fake on the pretext that they had enlisted simply in order to destroy the Revolution from within. I remember in 1955 such an accusation being made against a cadre in Nghe An province who came from a middle-level peasant family. He was paraded before a group of 'grassroots' peasants who competed with one another to insult and humiliate him. First one shouted at him to stop staring at the crowd and bow his head in shame as a landlord. Then another yelled at him to hold his head up and show his cruel face. After that he was accused of being stubborn and provocative by looking the peasants in the eye. And so it went on and on.

To find only two cruel landlords in any one village was not enough. One had to try again, even though the system of land tenure in northern Vietnam was different from that in China and few people owned more than a few hectares. Nor, for that matter, did we have cities like Shanghai and Wuhan full of capitalist businessmen. Yet a campaign modelled on the Chinese experience was also launched to eliminate national capitalists on the basis of class warfare, while placing all industrial production and trade under state control. Articles in the press talked about labour and exploitation as well as social inequality along orthodox Marxist lines. As a result, the atmosphere grew as tense in urban areas as it was in the countryside with numerous people being accused of capitalist exploitation of their workers, profiteering, trafficking, speculation, profligacy, decadence etc.

During this struggle, there were some truly nonsensical stories. Business owners who lived simply and worked alongside their employees were assumed to be dishonest tricksters putting on an act to carry out even greater exploitation. Trading invoices with foreign companies were seized upon as evidence of links with capitalist imperialism. Family photos of weddings and other parties as well as outings to the popular beach resort of Do Son were criticised as proof of debauchery. Those people who possessed copies of the poems of Lamartine and Baudelaire or even the works of Victor Hugo and French dictionaries were branded as worshipping imperialist culture. Students, too, from the petty bourgeoisie were told they were not solid and trustworthy. They were simply looking forward to getting enjoyable and secure jobs in the future. The well-known writer Nguyen Tuan was also labelled as bourgeois because he wrote an interesting article about *pho*, the noodle soup which is one of the traditional dishes of northern Vietnam, rather than concentrating on class warfare which was then in full swing. He was said to be a parasite indulging in the spirit of enjoyment and cultural sensuality. Hence he was ostracised by his friends who were afraid of having contact with somebody with 'political problems'.

The categorisation of the bourgeoisie was strictly applied. There were three types. Type A were people who had a full grasp of state and Party policy. Those who merely accepted these policies were Type B. Everybody else was classified as a class reactionary belonging to Type C. In those days one had to stay close to the poor peasants to study and make progress. I have friends who were regimental commissars and battalion commanders and were inspired by the mood of the times. They felt moved from the bottom of their hearts to admire the 'marvellous and purified spirit' of the poor peasants and sow deep roots by finding an 'ideal' wife among them. After the mistakes of land reform were corrected, these gentlemen were stuck. No rectification was possible, and for the rest of their lives they have had to swallow the bitter pill with happy faces because there was no way they could harmonise their feelings and intelligence with those they had chosen as lifetime companions.

Every period has its fashionable figures. In 1954 and 1955 those who were supreme were the leaders of the land reform brigades. In their hands the power of life and death was absolute. They applied the rules and used the people's courts to make a judgement with a simple show of hands. There were no lawyers, and in fact there was no law. Sentences were carried out by a rifle section selected from local guerrillas who were landless peasants with no relatives among the middle peasantry or landlords. As for the leaders of the land reform brigades, they always went around with solemn faces, wearing blue Mao jackets in summer and felt ones in winter. They did not wear Ho Chi Minh sandals but rather leather shoes which creaked authoritatively. They also carried shiny briefcases and travelled in Chinese jeeps. I once met one of them in Nghe An who scarcely knew how to write. All he could do was scrawl his signature in large letters to approve dozens of death sentences. To him the people concerned were class enemies or enemies of the people.

The promotion of such individuals had serious long-term consequences. Many of them became cadres in the Cong An, the Public Security Force, which, together with the army, has always been considered the most important branch of the regime, providing it with stability. In other words, workers and peasants are the grassroots from which come the cadres to man these important branches. But there were not many workers in Vietnam and most of them were independent artisans. Therefore landless peasants were often selected to become the most important cadres. I do not mean to imply that all of them are sub-standard, stupid and bad-mannered because there are some who are willing to learn how to become capable cadres. However, some are extremely degenerate and have become more so since the end of the war.

Take the case of Muoi Van, for example. He had had only four years of schooling and his understanding of society was very arbitrary when he was appointed head of a land reform brigade in Hoa Binh in 1955. I discovered this in 1982 when, as chief of the Cong An in Bien Hoa province just north of Saigon, he was sentenced to death after being exposed for corruption and the embezzlement of public funds. With power in his hands, he had apparently acted without restraint, acquiring large houses, gold and diamonds for his relatives and friends as well as drinking heavily and running after girls. There was nothing to stop him. Only those who have a modicum of education appreciate the necessity of abiding by moral values in life and avoiding excesses. Muoi Van symbolised the worst sort of cadre who ignored his duty and pleased himself.

During the period of land reform and re-education for middle-level cadres in 1956, I too was subject to review. Some stalwart cadres who had been landless peasants criticised me as an exemplary case of decadence because from an early age I had studied at a school reserved for the children of the French and the Vietnamese élite. Therefore I must have become imbued with poisonous colonial culture. I also came from a family of great feudalists. These two words colonialism and feudalism were the worst, and represented the ultimate in decadence. I was accused of being the shameless bastard of these two 'isms' with my knowledge worth less than a clod of dung which, as Mao said, was useful for manuring the fields. They told me that the only thing which saved me was my being a Party member.

I did not in the least resent such people calling me bad names. They were the victims of a blind, almost religious faith. But later somebody did come to apologise to me when the mistakes of the land reform programme were being corrected.

Ho Chi Minh was also criticised for the policies pursued after the North was liberated in 1954. For instance former government employees – *les fonctionnaires* – were retained in office with their original salaries for a couple of years. In my view, this was a good idea, although it caused a stir of envy among those who had been in the Resistance. Then there were reform classes for prostitutes to learn another vocation which would be more economically productive. I know too that Ho Chi Minh was very concerned about the treatment of prisoners of war, both Vietnamese and French, as well as other nationalities in the Foreign Legion. He laid down that they were not to be abused or beaten and had to be fed the same rations as our soldiers.

But the real problem was posed by the mistakes of land reform which caused the deaths of more than ten thousand people. Most of them were Party members or patriots who had supported the Revolution but nonetheless were reasonably well off. They were shot having been condemned by what amounted to kangaroo courts, although they were called people's tribunals. This was the result of the mechanistic application of Chinese experience imposed by their advisers. Admiration of China was widespread at this period because of blind attitudes and a lack of self-confidence. In my opinion, Ho Chi Minh was to blame. Initially he was very hesitant about land reform, then at the beginning of 1952 he was criticised by Stalin for pursuing a policy based on nationalism rather than class warfare. But it was Mao Tse-tung who really forced his hand.

A very interesting illustration of this attitude occurred in the early stages of land reform near Thai Nguyen, when an action brigade arrived to work with the peasants on a plantation owned by Mrs Nguyen Thi Nam. She had helped communist revolu- tionaries as far back as 1937 and had on occasion even sheltered Truong Chinh and Hoang Quoc Viet. What is more, her two sons had joined the Revolution and by 1954 were high-ranking officers. But the Chinese adviser quickly concluded that she was a cruel landowner who had to be eliminated. Some simple peasants naively related that Mrs Nam was good and kind; she went to the pagoda, handed out charity and looked after many revolutionary fighters, so she should be considered a landowner belonging to the Resistance. For their pains, these peasants were adjudged to be lackeys seeking to protect a landowner, by a Chinese adviser as well as a brigade leader who came from Nghe An. The atmosphere became even more tense as grassroots hired labourers arrived to begin the political struggle leading to the holding of a people's court.

Hoang Quoc Viet who was in the area and realised what was going on, rushed to Hanoi to inform Ho Chi Minh. He listened attentively and then said, 'It's not right. The campaign should not start off by shooting a woman and certainly not one who has looked after Communist cadres and is the mother of a regimental political commissar in the People's Army.' Ho Chi Minh then promised to intervene by talking to Truong Chinh, the head of the Land Reform Programme, about this urgent matter. But it did not happen. Mrs Nam was quickly condemned to death on the advice of Mao Tse-tung's representative who accused her of deceitfully entering the ranks of the revolution to destroy it from within.

Years later, I asked Hoang Quoc Viet what he thought about

this case and he told me, 'When I spoke to Uncle Ho, he knew it was not right, but he dared not tell them.' By 'them' he meant the sons of heaven, the representatives of Mao Tse-tung. Here Ho Chi Minh made a big mistake. Did he not realise he was head of state and Chairman of the Party? By remaining silent and failing to intervene in the case of Mrs Nam, he showed a lack of responsibility not only towards her and her family but also towards all the other people who were victimised and killed during the land reform programme. He allowed his country and his Party to be usurped by foreigners.

Reaction in the countryside became very strong during the transition from Stage 2 to Stage 3 of the land reform programme when mistakes were made and became increasingly evident. Clearly a decision had to be made to analyse the situation and rectify it. Ho Chi Minh himself was determined in this matter, despite the unwillingness of the Chinese advisers who were very stubborn and conservative. If the decision had not been taken, the disaster would have been much worse. Therefore, although Ho Chi Minh was not directly involved in guiding the land reform programme, he carried out self-criticism while several other people were demoted. They included Truong Chinh who bore the main responsibility for land reform together with Hoang Quoc Viet. Then there were Le Van Luong, who was supposed to check that everything was proceeding correctly, plus Ho Viet Thang, the day-to-day administrator of the programme. According to one of my friends who worked with these leaders from 1954 to 1956, they all toadied to the Chinese advisers who sat around with their feet on the table, drinking *mao tai* and spitting on the floor while issuing orders on what the Vietnamese people should do.

In my opinion, the mistakes of land reform have still not been summed up in a serious and constructive way. And its leaders were never really disciplined. They were simply moved to other positions, although for Truong Chinh in particular, that was a hard blow. He lost his position as Party General Secretary which he had held since 1941. That was also about the time he adopted the name Truong Chinh, meaning Long March, a name which the Chinese considered deeply gratifying.

All Truong Chinh's work up till 1956, whether in writing or in practice, was obviously copied from the Chinese and specifically Maoist experience, irrespective of Vietnamese reality. Dang

Xuan Khu, as he was originally called, was the son of a scholar who taught Chinese. Hence, in his youth Truong Chinh read a lot, and was familiar with both Chinese and French literature. He was also assiduous and careful by nature, which caused him to be nicknamed Anh Than or 'Cautious Elder Brother'. He really paid attention to every sentence, every word, even down to the last dot and comma. It was the same when he spoke. He was courteous and spoke with flawless grammar, choosing his words precisely. Truong Chinh also wrote poetry under the pseudonym Song Hong (Red Wave). But these poems were prone to triteness and lacked a sense of harmony. They were more like exhortations. But his political comments were clear, concise and reasoned.

I met Truong Chinh on numerous occasions, most frequently after 1985 when I and Nguyen Van Phung, the deputy head of the Party History Institute, interviewed him for biographical purposes. It was very evident that he was extremely proud of all he had done for the Party. For example, Truong Chinh talked to us about his methods of operating secretly during the Second World War, which he said were rather special. He claimed to have been very clever and resourceful in avoiding the periodic security sweeps carried out by the French secret police. Sometimes he would disguise himself as a teacher or alternatively a trader, a ferryman or a petty official. He also recounted how, before the August Revolution, there were people who wanted to set up a safety zone for the Party Central Committee in the mountains close to the border with China, but he had insisted that it be situated no more than a day's bicycle ride from Hanoi in order to keep in touch with developments both at home and abroad.

Truong Chinh then went on to explain how he had established an organisation among the workers of the Taupin printing plant, where on most afternoons a French official would bring documents from the Indo-China ruling council for copies to be made. These documents were internal reports for distribution to about sixty high-ranking officials within the administration. They concerned the international situation during the war as well as what was happening in the country itself. So the printing took place under strict security and the French took measures to ensure the plates were destroyed afterwards. But, according to Truong Chinh, a copy of these documents was conveyed that same evening, thanks to his organisation, to the Party in its safety zone either at Dong Anh or Bac Ninh. There was also an official in Hanoi who set up a radio monitoring organisation which drew up daily reports about official broadcasts for collection by a man on a bicycle who would deliver them to the Party Central Committee in its safety zone. Clearly Truong Chinh was very proud of these past exploits of his.

However, after the mistakes of the land reform programme, for which he was directly responsible, it was as if Truong Chinh did not wish to say anything more on the subject. He was very strict and disciplined, asking those around him always to be punctual, to write and speak according to Party resolutions and to follow the Party line. He was in a state of shock, having attended the 20th Congress of the Soviet Communist Party in February 1956, when he heard Khrushchev deliver his secret speech denouncing Stalin's excesses. In fact although Truong Chinh – like the heads of all other foreign Party delegations – had been given a copy of this speech before returning home from Moscow, he kept it firmly locked in his briefcase and did not discuss it.

Yet once Truong Chinh lost his position towards the end of 1956, there was a need to explain the details of the rectification of the land reform campaign to cadres and families of those affected by injustice and the death sentences carried out. In this climate of unrest and indignation, when the people had to be calmed down, who was there who could represent the Party leadership in carrying out this difficult task?

The atmosphere became increasingly tense. A number of families who had been victimised and received no redress made their way to Hanoi where they gathered outside the office of the Party Central Committee and what was in effect the Presidential Palace. Wearing traditional mourning clothes, the children among them included, they submitted petitions and waited for an answer in angry mood. In the end, the authorities had to acknowledge their presence and promise that their complaints would be considered at district level. Gradually, this was accepted, especially after meetings were arranged with families who had suffered great losses during our military campaigns. Then everybody was invited to the major sports ground in Hanoi on October 29, 1956 and addressed there by General Vo Nguyen Giap. Speaking on behalf of Chairman Ho and the Politburo, he acknowledged that mistakes had been made and expressed regret, while putting forward proposals to make immediate amends. But he also reminded those present that during the war and especially at the battle of Dien Bien Phu, our soldiers had had to keep the guns in position with their own physical strength, and thousands of them had died. Therefore although the loss of life during the land reform campaign was equally regrettable, everything should be seen in the context of contributing to the progress of the Revolution.

Ho Chi Minh also chose Vo Nguyen Giap to go out and campaign throughout the country. He was thus at the receiving end of all the anger of those local representatives who had passed through the destruction of land reform, as well as the repentance and apologies of the people. The commander of the victory at Dien Bien Phu was of course able to pacify the widespread indignation through his sincerity and aura of heroism resulting from such a historic victory.

Still the question remained who would replace Truong Chinh as Party General Secretary. Several cadres close to Ho Chi Minh at the time said that he had two people in mind. They were Vo Nguyen Giap and Le Duan, but Ho was inclined to favour the former with whom he had worked closely for many years. However Le Duan was appointed because of the criteria then prevailing. He had spent two long periods in prison amounting to almost ten years in all. This was a significant qualification for rising to the top of the Party, since it was considered that the more one had been put to the test, the more trustworthy one was. In fact, imprisonment was regarded as the university of politics and here General Giap did not qualify because his degree in law resulted from a conventional education.

In this matter the ideas of Le Duc Tho became decisive since at that time he took over the task of Party Organisational Secretary, after previously working in the south together with Le Duan and Pham Hung. These three men progressively tried to neutralise Ho Chi Minh as well as the Prime Minister, Pham Van Dong. With the latter it was not difficult, since he had no wish to become involved in an internal power struggle both as a matter of principle and because of weakness of character. But the main aim of this struggle was to downgrade the role and the reputation of General Giap.

Unlike the rest of the top Communist Party leadership in 1956,

Le Duan was considered to be a southerner. Born in a village near Quang Tri just north of Hue, he had spent all his life in the South, where he had taken advantage of his position as a railway official to travel around and assess the situation. But he derived his concepts of philosophy, politics and economics from what he had learned in French when he was imprisoned on the island of Poulo Condore, which we call Con Dao, out in the South China Sea. He often referred to ideas in French like *'quantité et qualité'* or *'valeur marchande'* without the ability to explain what they meant. He was very self-confident and thought a lot of himself. For example there is a story that Tran Van Giau and Pham Van Bach, two of the leaders of the Provisional Revolutionary Committee set up in Saigon in August 1945, were subsequently 'excluded from office' for committing a 'crime' at the time of the Revolution. They forgot their comrades, including Le Duan, still imprisoned on Con Dao island, and only sent a boat to pick them up a week later.

However, that was probably only a pretext. In fact a major struggle took place in the South for control of the Viet Minh. In contrast to the North of the country where the 'professional' revolutionaries came to dominate the Party to the detriment of intellectuals, most of the original leaders of the Revolution in the South were educated men. Many had been abroad to study in Europe including Tran Van Giau who ended up in Moscow in the early 1930s learning Marxism in the same class as Maurice Thorez, the French Communist Party leader, and Josip Broz Tito, the future President of Yugoslavia. But that did not deter Le Duan.

On his release from Con Dao, Le Duan thought he was assigned too low a position, incommensurate with all he had suffered in prison: he was appointed head of civilian defense forces whereas he thought he should play a military role. Looking northwards, he attributed his plight to Vo Nguyen Giap, a man he knew only by reputation as a French-educated graduate who had taught at one of the foremost high schools in Hanoi but had never suffered imprisonment. What is more, Giap occupied a leading military position in 1954 and had appointed Nguyen Binh, a former member of the Kuomintang-backed faction, as leader of the Viet Minh forces in the South. This view was shared by other long-term Party members including Le Duc Tho who was

sent south in early 1946 as a 'professional' revolutionary to take
control of the Party there. He succeeded not only in ousting
Tran Van Giau and other leading Southern intellectuals, but also
in eliminating General Nguyen Binh who was betrayed to the
French. At the same time, Le Duc Tho promoted the cause
of Le Duan who came to occupy an increasingly important political
role; this accounts for the subsequent collusion between the two
men.

Soon after the Geneva Agreements, when Le Duan decided
not to 'regroup to the North' like so many other Viet Minh
combatants and Party members, he proposed the use of revolutionary violence to oppose the repression in the South. But did
Ho Chi Minh also concentrate too much on guiding the revolutionary struggle in the South and make light of other problems
such as education and culture, leaving those responsible for them
to make mistakes without bothering to interfere? Or was he directly
implicated in these matters? These are very difficult questions
to answer.

In 1956 there occurred what became known as the *Nhan Van,
Giai Pham* affair. These were the names of two literary magazines
published in Hanoi by a group of writers, poets and musicians
who had joined the Revolution, some of them had also joined
the Party but later become disillusioned – not just with land reform
but also with the Party's strict control over intellectuals.

For instance, the writer Tran Dan, who had been present at
the battle of Dien Bien Phu, penned a novel not just about
the triumph but also about the suffering and human feelings of
those involved. Still he was sent to China to write the script
for a film on the battle, only to find it was virtually dictated
to him in terms of 'heroic socialist realism' by the political cadre
who had accompanied him. Then on his return to Vietnam,
he was victimised by the Party for falling in love with a girl
who was classified as a class enemy because her parents had been
property-owners and fled to the South in 1954. Yet while his
poems reflected bitterness over the way the situation had developed
in the North, Tran Dan still criticised the regime in the South
as increasingly subject to decadent American influence.

The writers in the *Nhan Van, Giai Pham* group like Tran
Dan were apparently emboldened to express their views openly
by the Hundred Flowers campaign launched in China in May

1956. But just as in China, the resulting upsurge in artistic creativity and literary criticism was soon suppressed. In November 1956, *Nhan Van* and *Giai Pham*, after only a few issues, were forced to close down largely at the instigation of To Huu, the poet on the Central Committee who had a major influence over the Party's cultural policies.

At the time, the affair aroused little public interest because awareness of democracy was low, as were the cultural standards of the people. The North was also isolated from the outside world with the exception of the Soviet Union and China, the two so-called great paradises. There was even the saying, 'What the Soviet Union and China are today, Vietnam will be tomorrow.' The people in the countryside went to see Chinese films like *The White Haired Girl* or Soviet films about agricultural collectives to praise them and discuss the next Five Year Plan in a revolutionary spirit. The heroes in these Soviet and Chinese films were far more familiar to Vietnamese youth than the writers of the *Nhan Van, Giai Pham* group.

In fact the whole of society ganged up to follow the ideas of the leadership because it was truly stirred up rather than afraid. What is more, the question of reform through labour was used as a stimulus and given prominence. For instance, cadres were eager to go and dig dykes in Gia Lam, construct an irrigation system in Hung Hai or work in the collectives. So the fact that a group of writers had been sent to the countryside for labour reform did not arouse public opinion. It was called an '*affaire*' but nothing appeared in the official press about it at the time. Later there were some articles using quotations from the works of the banned writers to criticise them and pass judgement in an arbitrary fashion. But in those days nobody could get hold of copies of *Nhan Van* or *Giai Pham* to see for themselves what the fuss was all about.

Looking back at the situation in 1956, all the anger and resentment of that period was directed at the 'American puppets' in the South who rejected the idea of nationwide elections as stipulated in the Geneva Agreements. Also, reports of anti-Communist massacres in the South gave rise to angry demonstrations throughout the countryside in the North as well as the cities, including one in front of the Hanoi office of the tripartite International Control Commission set up under the Geneva Agreements. But where the *Nhan Van, Giai Pham* affair was concerned, Ho Chi Minh went along with the action of the propaganda and security organs of the Party and the state. That was an irresponsible attitude.

Even so, people like Tran Dan and Van Cao, the musician who had written our national anthem, were treated with a degree of leniency compared with writers in China who had become victims of the Hundred Flowers campaign and were reported to be in a far worse position. Chinese intellectuals were paraded through the streets wearing dunces' caps, for the people to mock and spit at. They were abused and denounced at struggle sessions and then sent for hard labour, sometimes involving up to fourteen hours a day with only a cattle shed to sleep in.

I now believe that any violation of human rights, whether major or minor, is wrong. We cannot just happily say we were fortunate because we were less brutal than the Chinese at that time. Nor, in considering how the Pol Pot gang in later years massacred people and destroyed society in Cambodia, can we console ourselves with the thought that we dealt with matters more humanely so that it is unnecessary to acknowledge our own crimes.

The Vietnamese security forces – and there are many of them, both within the Cong An umbrella and outside it – have long made severe mistakes and continue to do so. There have been hundreds of political cases where people have been accused of 'opposing the Party' or 'opposing the leadership'. Others have been branded as spies in the pay of colonialist or imperialist secret services, like Nguyen Huu Dang who was sentenced to fifteen years' imprisonment in 1960 for talking to a Frenchman who remained in Hanoi with the Party's blessing. And who was Nguyen Huu Dang? He was none other than the Viet Minh official who made all the arrangements for the mass meeting on September 2, 1945, when Ho Chi Minh declared our independence. Even now, thirty years later, many of these cases, like that of Nguyen Huu Dang, have still not been fully explained and rectified, nor have many of the victims of this injustice yet been publicly rehabilitated. Instead, life for them continues to be a series of humiliations as described by Nguyen Manh Tuong in the memoirs he sent to be published in Paris in 1992 under the title *Un Excommunie*. A French-educated lawyer with a doctorate in literature as well, Dr Tuong was President of the Bar Association in Hanoi before deciding to join the Revolution in 1945. Although never a Party member, he participated in delegations representing the country abroad until 1956 when he showed sympathy for the *Nhan Van, Giai Pham* movement. As a result, he lived in Hanoi for the next thirty and more years, virtually excommunicated from the rest of society, and after being allowed out for a brief health check in Paris, continues to do so.

After the *Nhan Van, Giai Pham* affair and similar cases, such 'political reactionaries' were dealt with in secret. There were no judgements and no reports in the press or on the radio. Only the top leadership were informed through internal Party communications. The organs specialising in security, particularly those whose duty was to protect the Party and the army, acted according to their own whims without any regard for law. The social psychology of the majority of the population at that time was to entrust everything to the Party and the state. The mood of the moment was to agree to everything and toe the line. Even the families of those accused did not protest or react in a determined way because they thought it would be useless and could cause further harm. There are those who think the responsibility for political victimisation lies with the top leadership and naturally with Ho Chi Minh as well as Tran Quoc Hoan, the Minister of the Interior, and his subordinates.

I believe that this is the price we have had to pay for our blindness in going along with foreign ideology and worshipping it as the supreme truth. The whole nation (that is, the North of the country) abandoned its intrinsic values to embrace the concept of the pure peasant. And among the masses, the rights of freedom and democracy were obliterated. After 1954, there was a strict ban on every doubt, every challenging idea. Everybody had to submit to an invisible law, without daring to argue or put forward his own ideas. The price everybody has had to pay for this has kept on increasing.

After accepting Maoism, we also became subject to the influence of Stalin. His works which were printed and reprinted in Vietnamese long after he was discredited in the Soviet Union, became required reading for all middle- and high-ranking cadres. Then there were the pictures. Everywhere, in all offices and along the main roads, the faces of the world's leading communists looked down on us. But the people soon noticed that with the exception of Mao

Tse-tung, all of them – Marx, Engels, Lenin, Stalin and Ho Chi Minh – had beards or in Stalin's case a big moustache. So in popular parlance, Communism became equated with '*ong rau*', the bearded gentlemen, and not always politely.

Come 1956, another campaign was launched to accept planification of the entire economy according to the Stalinist model. There were times when the press went so far as to laud planification by publishing detailed statistics on the quantities of needles, pairs of underpants, condoms and boxes of toothpicks made of bamboo or wood that had been produced. Priority was given to heavy industry and collectivisation. Everything was implemented blindly without even a fraction of doubt about where the country was heading.

Misrepresentation became almost a way of life. Left without any counter-arguments, we felt ashamed. For a time the press reported production of over 100 tons of rice per hectare and then 200 tons, which was in excess of what China had claimed to achieve. Of course, these statistics were totally unrealistic and unrealisable in both countries, but in the case of Vietnam it was all part of the performance to praise China's increased harvests through competitive emulation of Mao Tse-tung thought. Agriculture was to become a science which made farming small plots seem derisory. Gardens, it was said, were for heaven, and nobody was allowed to express doubts or criticism.

This situation, if one looks back at it objectively, posed dangers for the leadership. There were many scholars and intellectuals outside the Party who had a far better understanding of the country than the Communists. There is a whole list of them who remained in the North, placing themselves in the hands of the authorities and accepting hardship as well as a poor but honest life. The very nature of their cultural background helped them escape the seductions of base materialism which motivated many high-ranking Communist cadres who, forgetting the ideals of the Revolution, embraced power for its own sake. Even within the Party, there were intellectuals who were sincere, upright and knowledgeable, but they were demeaned because they maintained high standards and refused to act as toadies.

The ideas of the 'professional' revolutionaries were becoming increasingly clear. Gradually the role of the intellectuals and technocrats within the Party and the government was eliminated by reducing them to impotence or to being symbolic and decorative. Many of them had already been abused, belittled and humiliated during the Land Reform Campaign by having to confess that they had been brainwashed by imperialist education. As a result they had to concede place to landless peasants. Then they were required to work for the Socialist and Democratic Parties which were said to rank equal to the Vietnam Workers' Party under the Fatherland Front. In reality these other parties were simply bodies organised for the purpose of propaganda. The upshot of all this was that real power slipped out of the hands of the capable men who remained in government. Instead they had to act under the auspices of their subordinates who were Party members.

Take Bui Cong Trung, for instance. As head of the State Science Committee in the 1950s, he said that we should not focus on increased rice production and food self-sufficiency as a formalistic aim in itself, but instead produce food and goods in line with the needs of the domestic market and world agricultural markets where requirements were very different. At that time, these two words 'goods' and 'markets' were completely forbidden and nobody listened. Then there were the ideas of Tran Cong Tuong in the 1950s and 1960s about building up a legal system and setting up a Ministry of Justice and a Law University. These too were ignored.

I had personal experience of this lack of legality. In 1961, as an officer of the 4th military region based at Vinh, I was chosen to be chairman of the local military council. The duties of the council were to represent the interests of the soldiers in matters of discipline, promotion and their material conditions. The council had to control expenditure, check accounts and supervise hygiene in the kitchens and mess halls of the barracks. For two years too, I was often designated chairman of the electoral committee to select candidates for the National Assembly and the People's Committees of the province of Nghe An and Vinh city. My task was to ensure that the committee acted according to 'orders from above'. A number of votes were distributed marked personal. That made some people in the province who were dissatisfied with the regime strike out the whole list of nominees before the first ballot. I knew this was contrary to the principles of the secret ballot and violated the rights of the voters, but

I let it happen thinking it necessary to protect the clean reputation of the army.

During the same period I was chosen to be a judge in the military tribunal of our zone. The chairman of the tribunal was usually the Deputy Commander of the military region, while advice was provided by legal cadres from the military committee. The tribunal dealt with cases of the embezzlement of state funds, manslaughter through the careless use of weapons, or accidents caused by military vehicles. There were also those who injured themselves in order to be discharged from military service. On the whole the verdicts were strictly according to law, only they were all decided beforehand and handed down to the council of the military region following the principles of the Party leadership which was absolute and supreme. At that time I thought it was only natural, but now, looking back, I realise that I myself played a part in allowing the Party to usurp the role of the state in violation of the constitution and the law, contrary to the principles of a truly democratic regime.

Instead the system of criticism and self-criticism was regarded as the peak of individual and social progress. I participated in hundreds, perhaps thousands of such sessions during the period from 1956 till 1964 when Maoism was popular and acceptable —in other words, before the extremism of China's 'Great Proletarian Cultural Revolution'. In every basic Party organisation, Saturday evenings were reserved for Party activities. Every cell or group would meet to read the Party newspaper and conduct criticism and self-criticism sessions. Our thoughts, our awareness, our actions, all were called into question. So too were our relationships with our superiors and subordinates, with our peers, friends, family and other soldiers. Our good points and shortcomings were all noted down in a record to promote self-improvement. The aim was to give prominence to the spirit and meaning of the Revolution. Everything for the collective, for the people and oneself for everybody.

In fact criticism and self-criticism was just something we had to cope with. There was no sincerity involved. You criticise me so I criticise you as strongly; you forgive me so I do the same. We divided into different gangs to compete with one another in arousing opinion. Hostile remarks were made, rumours were spread, there was distortion and slander to meet each situation. Then when we sat down around the table we said the right things. We were told we were helping each other for the common aim and being constructive in order to progress. In this context, mutual affection and respect contributed to our being straight forward with one another. But then when tempers blazed, feelings of friendship broke down and we turned round and addressed each other as 'comrade', instead of as brothers and sisters as usual.

For four years, from 1958 to 1962, I was responsible for political indoctrination in military Zone 4 which stretched from the province of Thanh Hoa down to Vinh Phu. Based in this area were the 324th and 325th Divisions as well as a brigade along the demarcation line dividing Vietnam. My duty was to teach political theory to a whole range of students including the major-general commanding this military region and his political commissar as well as numerous colonels and majors, in fact the entire officer corps which numbered hundreds. In the course of their duties, they attended my lectures about the basics of dialectical and historical materialism. For years I had studied the works of Marx, Engels, Lenin, Stalin, Mao Tse-tung and Ho Chi Minh either in the original or in translation. In my opinion, courses to study the works of Marx and Engels were extremely important. Above all, they provided abundant help in analysing and dissecting the nature of capitalism at that time.

To cover all this ground took two months of compulsory lectures comprising two mornings and evenings a week, studying documents as well as spending the morning chairing two sessions of debate and conclusions. In part that was because the advisers in the Army General Political Department responsible for political theory imposed a very tight schedule for the subject. The entire military region had only three instructors of political theory for whom I was responsible. And that was a time of comparative peace. The war in the South was only just beginning.

The decision to step up the struggle in the South was taken at the 15th Party Plenum held in 1959. That was when Le Duan asserted his pre-eminence. It was he who decided that revolutionary violence was the line to be pursued in the South based on his experience there after the Geneva Agreements. He remembered the months he had spent in Rach Gia, U-Minh and Ca Mau, the southernmost coastal areas, before returning to base in Cholon, the Chinese quarter of Saigon. There he drafted the fundamental concepts of the revolution in the South. They comprised armed struggle, which covered political struggle as well as tactical warfare, in three areas: the countryside, the urban areas and the mountains. It was to be a three-pronged campaign: political, military and agitprop against enemy forces. It was also to be carried on at three levels with main force units, district militia and guerrillas.

Being based in the area immediately to the north of the demarcation line separating the two halves of Vietnam, I soon became involved in the programme to infiltrate the South resulting from the decisions of the 15th Plenum. During 1959 and early 1960, we did not send whole units to the South, but instead secretly selected individuals from among those Southerners who had regrouped to the North in 1954. Initially this selection process was supervised by General Nguyen Chi Thanh. He was head of the Army General Political Department and the Politburo member assigned responsibility for the struggle in the South. Those chosen to go south had to be brave, physically fit and preferably unmarried. At that time they also had to volunteer to go. And before undertaking the trip south, they had to undergo an intensive course of training lasting a month and a half, carried out in a camp set up in the jungle close to a hill tribe area in the 4th Military Region where I was based.

All those who underwent the training were given increased rations to improve their fitness and then sent on exercises – running, crossing streams and climbing steeping hills carrying a rucksack on the back containing at first one brick and later up to six bricks. I was in charge of political training for these groups which at first comprised no more than thirty men, although by the end of 1960 the number had increased to 300 on each course. I had to explain to them about the directives of the 15th Plenum and the political situation in the South which, according to Le Duan, was changing rapidly as a result of this infiltration programme. He referred to the uprisings during 1960 in Tra Bong and Bac Ai in the central provinces as well as in Ben Tre near Saigon as a significant development in the people's armed struggle. Then at the end of 1960, the National Liberation Front was set up in the South.

Later, when he was a member of the committee drafting the Party history, Truong Chinh let it be known there was some blurring of the ideas of Le Duan with those of various other people. On another occasion, Truong Chinh stated more directly:

'Le Duan's ideas on revolutionary armed struggle were not the only ones, nor were they the first.'

Truong Chinh always referred to Le Duan as Anh Ba, Brother Number Three, his pseudonym within the Party leadership. This was also the name under which Le Duan's *Letters to the South* were later published. The volume was a heavily edited collection of the secret instructions he sent to his comrades in the South during the war. Le Duan's personal pride was very evident. On one occasion,* he boasted to his official biographers including myself: 'After the Geneva Agreements, Uncle Ho still went along with the idea of nationwide elections. What is that? An illusion. I knew better than him. I thought immediately about the use of violence. I told our brothers in the South to bury their guns. It was I who told them to leave forces in the South and not to regroup to the North.'

During these interviews Le Duan also exclaimed, 'As for me, I was far better then Uncle Ho. When he went to the Soviet Union and China, all he said was "Yes" to everything Stalin and Mao told him. As for me, I dared to argue with Khrushchev and Mao.'

In my opinion, Ho Chi Minh had a rather independent attitude towards both the Soviet Union and China. He realised that neither of them believed Vietnam could achieve military victory in the South, backed as it was by the United States, or wanted it. The Soviets just wanted to maintain peaceful co-existence, while China advised us to continue guerrilla warfare on the grounds that if we deployed battalion-size units, they would easily be destroyed by American firepower. But we campaigned to obtain modern weaponry from both the Soviet Union and China, whereas our struggle was eventually resolved through negotiations initiated under the guidance of Ho Chi Minh and the Party leadership.

However, although this was one of our strengths, Ho Chi Minh still showed weakness when he wrote rather a lot of articles praising China which were later published under the name of Tran Luc, one of his pseudonyms. They were characterised by

---

* In 1983 I was one of a group of journalists who interviewed Le Duan for biographical purposes. The group included Hoang Tung, then a member of the Party Secretariat responsible for ideology; Dong Ngac, the assistant to the Party General Secretary; and Nguyen Can who researched and wrote the introduction for *Letters to the South*.

a certain childish extremism in extolling the Great Leap Forward and accelerated production. He also praised the towering ability of the 'Great Chairman Mao' in encouraging the people to build iron foundries in every backyard, an idea which he introduced and publicised in Vietnam. Indeed, in such matters Ho Chi Minh, whose name means 'He who is Enlightened', was not enlightened at all. I recall that in 1950 he wrote an article along Soviet lines denouncing the Yugoslav leader Tito as a reactionary because he pursued an independent Communist line.

By 1960 a major struggle was emerging within the Communist world and the international workers' movement between pro-Soviet and pro-Chinese policies. It came to a head in November when the Soviet Union convened a conference in Moscow of leading representatives from eighty-one Communist or affiliated parties. Among those attending were Ho Chi Minh and Le Duan, who had just been formally endorsed as Party General Secretary at its Third Congress in September.

The 81 Party conference was a very heated affair which split the Communist movement into two factions. Who was its leader? The Soviet Union or China? Did it have one head or two? Khrushchev viewed the Chinese as dogmatic and conservative. On the other hand, Mao severely criticised Khrushchev with accusations of revisionism and the betrayal of Marxism-Leninism. Every morning Radio Hanoi and the network of public loudspeakers throughout the country broadcast lengthy Chinese Communist documents openly questioning whether the Soviet Union was compromising the essence of Marxism-Leninism and the very nature of proletarian internationalism.

Hence there were differing views among the Vietnamese Communist leadership. At first Truong Chinh was inclined to support Khrushchev's line approving peaceful co-existence, because that appeared to be the prevailing trend within the international Communist movement. Then Le Duan inclined towards China and gradually carried the whole Politburo and Central Committee along with him because nobody wanted to be labelled 'revisionist' or 'anti-Party'. According to Confucian tradition, those in a weak position try to appease heaven. So Truong Chinh did not react in any way when the Politburo tended increasingly towards the Maoist view.

General Vo Nguyen Giap also tried to remain neutral throughout the fierce clashes in this ideological struggle, but he kept finding

himself indirectly involved because many of his friends or rather
protégés had gone to the Soviet Union to study. Hence from
1962 onwards, despite his prominent position, Giap was edged
into a corner by Le Duan and Le Duc Tho. He was accused
of being pro-Soviet and in favour of Khrushchev's policy of
peaceful co-existence. There were even attempts to expel Giap
from the Politburo and the Party but thanks to Ho Chi Minh,
who was very fond of him, these were foiled.

A close associate of Ho Chi Minh has recounted to me how
Le Duan and Le Duc Tho kept on raising with the Party Chairman
the fact that back in 1957, General Giap had received a personal
letter from Nikita Khrushchev via the Soviet ambassador in Hanoi
who was widely believed to be a KGB agent. The two comrades
Le seized on this pretext to allege that General Giap was guilty
of maintaining 'unprincipled relations' with foreign nationals. But
Ho Chi Minh fully supported General Giap. He stated 'It is
true that Younger Brother Van [the name with which he always
referred to Giap] received this letter. He showed it to me and
cannot be blamed in this matter, because obviously if somebody
writes to him, it is not his fault.' But Le Duc Tho would not
let things rest there and continued to criticise General Giap, which
prompted Ho Chi Minh to ask 'Why do you keep on picking
holes like this? Younger Brother Van has discussed all this with
me and there is nothing more to say.' Still the two comrades
Le tried to involve the Prime Minister Pham Van Dong, but
since he always avoided factional strife he turned a deaf ear and
just laughed.

Against this background, a Chinese military delegation led by
Marshal Yeh Chien-ying visited Hanoi in December 1961 to
suggest that our southern comrades should only attack at section
or company level, never at battalion strength. That, the Chinese
said, was the way to defeat the American-backed regime in the
South. What is more, they advocated that our forces should restrict
themselves to guerrilla warfare in the mountains, where they would
not be exposed to attack by US planes and tanks. Peking's main
worry, as I heard its Defence Minister General Luo Jui-ching
explain during a visit to Vinh with this delegation, was that if
we provoked the Americans into counter-attacks close to the
Chinese border, they would have to intervene as had happened
in Korea.

Such views evoked a lot of debate within the Party Military Committee which was responsible for all the major decision-making in this sphere rather than the Ministry of Defence. The committee was headed by Le Duan, closely supported by Le Duc Tho, although neither of them had ever received military training or served as an army officer. Yet Le Duc Tho, particularly by virtue of his position as Party Organisational Secretary, intervened increasingly in the matter of military appointments and promotions with the backing of the other prominent members of the Party Military Committee. These were General Nguyen Chi Thanh, head of the Army General Political Department, To Huu, the poet in charge of the Party ideological committee, plus the Minister of the Interior, Tran Quoc Hoan, and the Chief of Army General Staff, Van Tien Dung. In fact this group of leaders, which specifically excluded General Giap, came to dominate all decision-making in connection with politics, military and foreign affairs throughout the period of full-scale war which was embarked upon following the 9th Party Plenum held at the end of 1963.

The timing of this plenum was apposite. On November 2 the two brothers Ngo Dinh Diem and Ngo Dinh Nhu, who governed the South, were killed during a coup d'état. Three weeks later President Kennedy of the United States was assassinated. After these events it was secretly decided to pursue the war in the South in earnest while condemning peaceful co-existence and revisionism in principle, but without attacking Khrushchev or the Soviet Union directly. In other words, at that time we tended towards the Chinese line in the Sino-Soviet ideological dispute.

3

WAR

While the top level of the Party was thus engaged in trying
to resolve its internal problems and decide on its relationship
with its two major fraternal backers, China and the Soviet Union,
I twice travelled south down the Ho Chi Minh Trail. The first
time was in 1961 when it really was a trail and we literally
had to hack or crawl our way through the jungle carrying only
a rucksack with our personal effects.

In early 1964 it was easier. The trail was still narrow and
only passable by bicycle, although it could carry a large load.
Nor was the trip as dangerous as it became during the early
1970s when the trail was intensively bombed. Even so, quite
a large number of deaths occurred. At each military staging-post
– and they were 20 to 30 kilometres apart – there was a cemetery
for those who had sacrificed their lives on the Trail. They died
from a variety of causes. Some soldiers lost their way in the
jungle and died of starvation. Small groups sleeping alone at night
were pounced on by tigers or attacked by bears. On one occasion,
I and three of my companions shot and killed a black bear staggering
drunkenly down a hill towards us after it had raided a beehive
and eaten all the honey. And in the rainy season there were
those who, unable to see clearly, stepped on poisonous snakes
and were bitten to death. Then there were stomach upsets and
severe attacks of yellow fever to contend with. Others swung
their hammocks up in the trees, only to be killed when the
branches were torn off in high winds. During such storms when
the water ran fast in the streams, it was also easy to lose one's
footing on a slippery bridge and fall in without hope of rescue.
Another hazard was jungle leeches; we encountered hundreds

and thousands of them on our march, and they attached themselves
not only to one's legs but also to certain vital organs, causing
a haemorrhage and threatening one's future family life. Sometimes
too, as one climbed mountains covered in moss on a rainy day,
the ground was as slippery as if it was covered with oil, so it
was easy to lose one's footing and fall into a deep hollow, rucksack
and all. Worst of all was eating poisonous mushrooms and leaves.
For that there was no cure.

The reason why we had to undertake this difficult journey
was the establishment under the Geneva Agreements in 1954
of the demilitarised zone along the Ben Hai river which marked
the division between North and South. The next year the
American-backed regime in the South reinforced its side of this
zone with barbed wire interspersed with landmines. Later it was
transformed into an electric fence stretching from the coast right
up to the border between Vietnam and Laos. Given the American
initiative in constructing this fence, it was dubbed the McNamara
Line since that was the name of the US Secretary of Defense
at the time.

Still no matter what it was called, the fence prevented us from
moving directly down Highway One. We had to circumvent
it by crossing into the mountains of Laos. Everywhere we slept
we set up hammocks. Seldom did we meet the local people
because we tried to keep clear of their villages. We were also
careful in crossing paved roads where passing cars or military
traffic might detect our presence. We used to stretch gunny sacks
across the road to avoid leaving any footprints, then the last person
to cross would pick them up while we made our way barefoot
into the surrounding jungle in order not to leave any incriminating
evidence of our passage.

On my first trip down the Trail in 1961, which lasted three
months, my task was to determine how difficult it was and how
to survive. I went as far as Quang Nam, travelling through Laos
near my old stamping-ground at Tchepone, then Quang Tri and
Thua Thien. In early 1964, following the death of the Ngo brothers
and Kennedy, the atmosphere was different. We felt a new opportunity was opening up to despatch larger units to the South.
We had already begun to send a few companies and even battalions,
despite the advice of the Chinese to restrict ourselves to guerrilla

warfare. Now we had to consider whether it was possible for whole regiments to travel south. The field of battle there had to be studied carefully. Could such units, which had no anti-tank weapons, contend with the very mobile and well-equipped army in the South?

By order of the Central Military Commission, the General Staff and the Political Department of the Army, I was assigned as a member of a group of twelve high-ranking cadres specially designated to go and study the situation in the South. Our task was to examine the nature of the terrain on the spot, the logistical ability of the enemy and the feeling of the people. What was the economic situation, and how could we attack the towns and big cities?

Actually we knew very little about what was happening in the South, apart from the picture painted by our propaganda, which was extremely black. There were no telephone links between the two parts of the country, no letters and little human contact. For instance, one of my sisters went south in 1954, and the first we heard from her was six years later when she managed to send word through a contact in Paris that she was well. Indeed in the North we felt almost totally cut off from the rest of the world except for the so-called fraternal countries which sent us delegations.

Obviously, however, if we were to pursue the war in the South, we had to look into the question of communications and how the Ho Chi Minh Trail could or should be expanded. In 1964 this was the subject of heated debate within the Army General Staff and its logistics department. There were those who argued in favour of maintaining the Trail as it was. They pointed out that some people could carry up to 70 or 80 kilos on their shoulders. There were even hill tribespeople in the mountains of the Quang Ngai region who could carry up to 90 kilos, which for the women was more than their own body weight. Then there were bicycles, particularly the Chinese-made Phoenix models which could carry up to 250 kilos up and down hill. All these methods of transportation were comparable to ants bearing food and building material back to their nest under cover of dense foliage and concealed from enemy attack. The opposing argument was to expand the trails to 6 to 8 metres wide to accommodate Chinese or Russian trucks. That would mean strengthening bridges and ferries, setting up a network of repair facilities and fuel dumps along the Trail, as well as anti-aircraft units.

This latter system was what we finally developed, and by the early 1970s we had constructed a network of oil pipelines along the trails. It was a tremendous logistical achievement with engineering units supported by volunteer youth groups not only building but also having to repair the roads and bridges destroyed by the enemy. There were also signals and medical units as well as, of course, defence forces deployed all the way along the trails to ward off ambushes and surprise attacks. In fact the Truong Son operation, as we called it, needed the equivalent of two entire army corps to maintain the trails as the strategic artery between North and South. Appointed head of this whole operation in 1963 was Dong Sy Nguyen, a native of Quang Binh province who was at that time head of the Military-Civilian Department of the Army General Staff.*

In order to prepare for our trip down the Trail in 1964, we went to spend two months in Xuan Mai in the North on a course of training which again involved carrying bricks in our rucksacks while climbing mountains – morning, noon and night. Then we returned to Hanoi where each of us had to learn to paddle a canoe around the West Lake which is 6 kilometres in diameter, at first once a day and then twice. To build up our strength for these exercises and our subsequent travels, our rations were increased, although as combatants we were already entitled to 18 kilos of rice a month compared with ordinary workers who only received 13 kilos. Also, they got no more than 200 grammes of meat a month, whereas our rations were higher. Sometimes on training courses, these even included half a chicken as well as eggs.

Our journey south at the beginning of 1964 started from Le Thuy district in Quang Binh. We crossed the source of the Ben Hai river and then Highway Nine in Laos before returning to Vietnam near Pleiku in the Central Highlands. We travelled the whole way on foot in stages of about 20 kilometres a day. Round

*   Dong Sy Nguyen, who adopted this name after being disciplined in 1947 for attacking Catholic villages, was rewarded for his work on the Trail in 1974 by being promoted over the heads of many other officers to major-general. Later he became a Politburo member and Deputy Prime Minister before being retired from all these positions in 1991.

our necks we each draped long sausage-shaped bags containing 10 kilos of rice. In our rucksacks we carried medicine, sugar, powdered milk, clothing, tents and mosquito nets. We were just like a gypsy family taking everything along with us—matches, torches, water flasks and, of course, guns.

During this trip through such difficult terrain, we rested only after every nine or ten days to wash our clothes. Otherwise we woke every morning at 4 o'clock to cook rice, which we ate with roasted sesame mixed with salt. Sometimes we were able to catch fish in the streams. We dried and salted them, although often there was more salt than fish. Then when we ran out of salt, we licked the banana leaves used to wrap the dried fish. What we really lacked was vegetables and fruit. Occasionally we would find an orange tree close to a deserted house and really treasured its fruit. In the same way, whenever we saw any edible leaves we stopped to pick them to make a soup for the evening meal, which we usually ate at about 4 or 5 before it got dark.

At night it was very cold in the jungles of Laos and the Central Highlands, especially in the winter months when we shivered in the damp and cloudy atmosphere. To keep warm, we tried to dig holes instead of sleeping in hammocks as usual. The worst thing was crossing streams. It needed the entire effort of one's mind to keep going because the rest of one's body was paralysed with cold. On the other hand, in summer a different discipline was necessary. We became so thirsty we began to see stars and had to drink very slowly whenever we reached a stream.

On this journey I even crossed Highway One in Binh Dinh province to survey the situation in the district town of Duc Pho and neighbouring strategic hamlets. They were supposed to be impregnable, but with the help of local guerrillas I was able to use a secret path to cross the so-called three rivers and three mountains, in other words the moats and fences, surrounding such fortified villages. I once had a narrow escape: I got into a village and started to preach politics, and then we were suddenly surrounded. At once my comrades turned off the light and we managed to escape through a tunnel.

Giving political lectures was another of the important tasks assigned to us on this trip. We had to explain to our comrades in the South the gist of the resolutions emanating from the 9th Party Plenum. There were several of them and it was I who had to tackle those relating to the international situation and where Vietnam stood when it came to the Sino-Soviet dispute. Since we were not allowed to carry any documents with us, that meant I had to learn the Party resolutions more or less off by heart before leaving the North. It fell to me to give an account of them to several people who have risen very high in the Party in recent years. They included the future Head of State, Vo Chi Cong, who in 1964 was Deputy Party Secretary in Military Zone 5 – the region encompassing the Central Highlands – and Doan Khue, the present Minister of Defence but at that time deputy political commissar in the same military zone.

This trip taught me a lot. I was able to study the economic situation in the South, and the organisation of the strategic hamlets and the possibility of attacking them. After I returned to the North at the end of 1964, we decided we could use big units in the South to attack important targets even in regimental strength in order to prepare for combat at divisional level. However, everything had to be well prepared from the lowest level upwards to eliminate the enemy progressively.

Ironically, given our ideological position at that time, our military ideas were very different from those of the Chinese. We stockpiled arms and ammunition in the South whenever possible and set up workshops to cope with repairs and any further damage caused by the Americans. But I have to admit that all my equipment from top to bottom, from my solar topee to my rubber sandals, and even my underpants – in fact everything I was equipped with –was made in China.

During this war we were quick to condemn the regime in the South for relying on the Americans as foreign interventionists. What we did not then realise in the North was that the Chinese and the Soviets were also foreigners. We always considered them as fraternal comrades helping us in a spirit of goodwill. All we could see was a puppet regime in the South relying on imperialist support whereas we in the North regarded ourselves as fully sovereign and independent in concert with the progressive world trend.

We were in fact completely lightheaded in the firm belief that victory was ours. We did not even worry about the disastrous floods which swept the Central Highlands in 1965, swallowing up houses, cattle, pigs, chickens and numerous human beings

The author at a land reform course, 1956.

Preparing to go down the Ho Chi Minh Trail at the rear base in Military Region 5, 1964. The author is second from left.

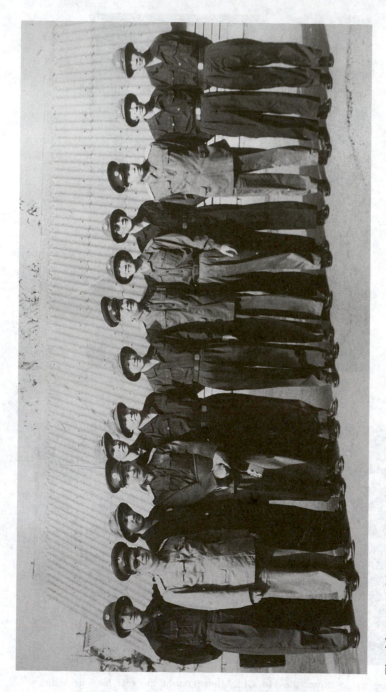

The delegations of the Democratic Republic of Vietnam and the National Liberation Front of South Vietnam at Camp Davis, February 1973. Fourth from left, the author; seventh from left, General Tran Van Tra; eighth from left, General Le Quang Hoa.

in their wake. We always thought that to be young at a time of war meant we had to be at its forefront. To seek peace, to try to save one's life and leave sacrifice to others, was for us shameful cowardice and selfishness.

When I returned to the North in October 1964, I became a journalist. I had already written some articles for the army newspaper, *Quan Doi Nhan Dan* when based with the 4th Military Region. Now General Nguyen Chi Thanh, the head of the Army General Political Department, assigned me to work on the paper. General Thanh originated from a poor peasant family in the same area of Quang Tri where Le Duan and the poet To Huu were born. That was why they worked closely with one another. But that was not the basic reason for General Thanh's prominence. Having joined the Party early, he was imprisoned by the French, but used the time to educate himself. As a result, in 1945 he became Viet Minh leader in Central Vietnam and three years later was transferred to the Viet Bac region to take over as head of the political section of the *Quan Doi Nhan Dan* editorial board. There he made a name for himself in 1950 by exposing a case of military indiscipline in which a colonel fighting the French in the border region had misappropriated equipment and funds for his own personal use. On the insistence of Nguyen Chi Thanh he was sentenced to death in order to set an example to the whole army.

Partly on the basis of this incident, General Thanh was considered to be one of the most dynamic and clear-minded of our senior officers. He rocketed to prominence, becoming the second highest-ranking general in the army after Vo Nguyen Giap. And he was proud of the fact that he had skipped quite a few ranks to achieve that position. Yet he was also to be seen wearing peasant clothes, riding a bicycle out of Hanoi side by side with his bodyguard to go and sit in a roadside café to talk to the people there. On the other hand, despite the nature of his education, he read assiduously and studied the political, social and military situation as well as cultural matters. He spoke well, quoting from the works of famous strategists such as Sun Tzu, Clausewitz, Napoleon and Zhukhov. And in articles written under his pen name Truong Son, General Thanh crisply analysed the question of whether we could ever hope to defeat the Americans who were so rich and had so much modern weaponry at their disposal.

These articles in fact became required reading throughout the
People's Army.

Nevertheless when I joined *Quan Doi Nhan Dan*, it was a
time of considerable tension for the newspaper. Its editor Major-
General Van Doan, who had gone to Moscow for higher political
studies in 1962, did not return home. Instead, together with Colonel
Le Vinh Quoc, the political commissar of Military Region 3,
he requested political asylum in the Soviet Union at the beginning
of 1964 because he did not approve of the resolutions of the
9th Party Plenum. For the same reason, the new editor, Lt.-Col.
Hoang The Dung, was suspended from work together with at
least four members of his staff after several visits to our office
by secretive cadres who arrived in cars with their windows obscured.
While we dared not refer to the fact, we came to realise that
our former colleagues had been taken into detention together
with many other people on the suspicion that they were pro-Soviet
revisionists. Much later when they were eventually released, although we were still afraid to contact them directly, we discovered
that they had been intensively interrogated. Among the questions
usually asked were: What about Giap? When and where did you
meet him? How many times did you visit his house? What did
you talk about with him? Who else was present? What did Giap
say, particularly about the Soviet Union and the conflict within
the international Communist movement? Did he talk about
Khrushchev or Mao? Did he mention Marshal Stalin? And what
was his attitude towards Hungary and the presence of the Red
Army in Budapest? Did Giap have anything to say about Le
Duan and Le Duc Tho or those officers who chose to remain
in the Soviet Union?

But who was empowered to ask such questions relating to
the Minister of Defence, who was not even accorded his proper
title during this series of interrogations? According to General
Kinh Chi, who is now retired, the order came from Tran Quoc
Hoan, the Minister of the Interior, with the approval of Le Duc
Tho. But certainly the latter was the guiding light in this case.
And how did Kinh Chi know? From 1958 to 1976, before being
promoted, he was the colonel who headed the department known
as *Bao Ve*.

Even to this day, few people are aware of the existence of
a security organisation called *Bao Ve*, which simply means

'protection'. Its duty is to the guarantee the total loyalty of every military officer and unit towards the Party, and to investigate and deal with those who deviate from its policies. Formally, the *Bao Ve* is a section of the Army General Political Department, with a network of its own within all military bodies from the Ministry of Defence and General Staff at the top, right down to regimental level. In reality its cadres, who have absolute authority over the political existence of every single member of the armed forces, no matter what their rank, have close links with the Ministry of the Interior and the Party Organisational Committee. So, under this system, the *Bao Ve* could question the attitude of the Minister of Defence, even though in theory he was in charge of all our armed forces.

General Giap's lack of authority became apparent when suddenly in 1964 Do Duc Kien, the head of military operations, Nguyen Minh Nghia, the director of Military Intelligence, and Le Minh Nghia, secretary to the Minister of Defence, were arrested. Apparently they too were regarded as 'revisionists'. In fact all three of them were outstanding intellectuals from the French colonial period. They were knowledgeable, as well as good and close friends of General Giap throughout the Resistance. After that they went to study in the Soviet Union, where they did extremely well. For instance Kien, who was originally an agricultural engineer, graduated from the Soviet military academy at Frunze with a Red Star. Following these arrests, several dozen other military officers were detained – most of whom were educated men of urban origin rather than peasant stock.

I once asked General Giap why he did not intervene to demand justice for those who had worked under him and become the victims of injustice, suffering long terms of imprisonment and loss of freedom – quite a lot of people blame him for this. He replied that he certainly would have done so, but that he was powerless once the Party Organisational Committee and the *Bao Ve* usurped power and became supreme. General Giap said he had to be careful not to make matters worse for his colleagues who were in danger of being detained even longer if he had intervened.

Another casualty of this period was Hoang Minh Chinh. Like many other members of the Hanoi élite, he was French-educated but had abandoned school to join the Resistance and become a leader of the Communist youth movement. He added to his reputation by leading an attack against the French military airfield near Hanoi when he was badly wounded. On the strength of all that, Hoang Minh Chinh was eventually sent to Moscow to study social science, and when he returned in 1962 he became head of the Institute of Philosophy in Hanoi. Then, having already helped draft the speech that Ho Chi Minh delivered in Moscow at the 81 Party Conference in 1960, he was asked by Truong Chinh to prepare the documents for the 9th Party Plenum at the end of December 1963. They were hotly debated and finally rejected as revisionist, after which Hoang Minh Chinh was committed to long years in prison.

A similar fate was suffered by Nguyen Kien Giang. With good Resistance credentials from Quang Binh province, he had risen high to become deputy head of the Party's publishing house *Su That* and was then sent for two years' study at the Higher Political School in Moscow. On his return home in 1964, he found himself regarded as a 'revisionist' and was detained for many years.

Of course none of this was ever reported in the press. In Western countries, journalists play a special role in society. Their ethic is to compete with one another in digging out the most sensational stories. So they enjoy a secure place in public opinion and the authorities think twice before offending them.

By contrast, when a correspondent in Vietnam writes an article, it has to be corrected and signed by the deputy head of his office. Then the head of the office reviews the work, makes further amendments and places his signature of approval on it. This process of correction and approval continues on up through several more stages of the hierarchy until it finally reaches the editor of the newspaper. By then it has become a mass effort with cuts here and new ideas inserted there, so much so that the original author often does not recognise the fruit of his creation, because every trait of his own individual style of writing has been eliminated in the process.

A chronic sickness of the Vietnamese press is its stridency and tendency to use hackneyed phrases which are 'full of sound and fury, signifying nothing'. For instance, certain adjectives like 'heroic', 'gigantic', 'infinite' and 'absolute' have to be used, while there are various stylistic formulas for writing editorials depending on the subject. We all know them off by heart.

My responsibility when I joined *Quan Doi Nhan Dan* was to write articles about current domestic and international issues. I also wrote for the army and Party monthly journals. That meant reading quite a lot of foreign newspapers, and I also met foreign journalists who came to Hanoi after the United States launched its bombing offensive to destroy the North.

Both then and later, I was asked so many questions about the war and how we won it. In my opinion, it depended on a large number of factors: the people, history, culture and the complex international situation linking Saigon with Washington, while we had close relations with the Soviet Union and China. The struggle in fact had so many aspects to it, that it is impossible to cover them all.

First, there was the attitude of the Americans for whom South East Asia and Indo-China did not constitute an area of vital strategic interest until they got drawn into it step by step. The process started with their providing support for the French and then after the Geneva Agreements, the Saigon regime. To deal with the guerrilla war, the Americans developed special warfare tactics by sending in advisers, weapons and technical experts. When that failed, they had to resort to all-out war, but they wanted to win it as quickly as possible with the minimum number of troops. However it kept on escalating to the point where over half a million men were committed to Vietnam, and the bombing of the North was progressively expanded and intensified until it reached Hanoi.

In my opinion, the organisation and equipment of the American forces were formalistic and cumbersome, and therefore totally unsuitable for contending with conditions on the ground in Vietnam, its climate and above all the nature of a struggle that was rooted in the people. The same was true of the Saigon army. Under American influence, its organisation and weaponry lacked any flexibility. Even its uniforms were too heavy, as I discovered in 1975 when I met many high-ranking Saigon officers and we compared the weight of our respective equipment including boots and rucksacks, only to conclude that what had been supplied by the Americans and before them by the French was unsuitable for either jungle warfare or the heat of the lowlands.

As for the Americans actually fighting in Vietnam, I was able to gain some specific insights into their attitude. Most of them had signed up for one- or two-year tours of duty because it was compulsory. But that was their major weak point. Because they were fighting a long way from home, their main concern was to serve out their term as safely as possible in order to return to their families. The same mentality prevailed in the Air Force where pilots were required to carry out 100 missions before returning home. Accordingly they became increasingly cautious. I reached this conclusion after interviewing over 200 of those who were captured. They included pilots who had been shot down on their first mission. A great many more had carried out between thirty and sixty missions. But there was only one who was on his ninety-seventh with just three more to go before returning home safely.

Talking to these pilots as well as other captured officers and marines, I found them highly trained with good technical knowledge. Some of them were also quite well educated with degrees in science, technology, history and law. But their understanding of Vietnam and Indo-China was very cursory. In my opinion, the psychological training of the American forces was not good. There were many gaps and even misinterpretations in their awareness of reality. Their greatest mistake was to put too much faith in weapons and firepower while disregarding the human element.

This was very evident in the way the Americans dealt with the Saigon regime. Their greatest problem was to find a political structure and leaders with the ability to represent the South. Although Lyndon Johnson hailed Ngo Dinh Diem as the 'Churchill of Asia', he had many limitations. Southern intellectuals viewed him as a traditional mandarin who was outdated. He was also a Roman Catholic in a population where the large majority of people are Buddhist. And his style of ruling through his family, the most conspicuous of whom was his brother's wife Madame Ngo Dinh Nhu, was taking things too far. Hence in 1963 the Kennedy administration changed horses in midstream and brought about the downfall of President Ngo Dinh Diem and his brother. I believe the Americans considered this necessary in order to move from special warfare to all-out war and the intervention of US ground forces in Vietnam, which the Ngo brothers would have opposed.

We were aware of this because of Vu Ngoc Nha, known to us as Hai Nha (Nha no. 2). In Saigon he was referred to as 'His Excellency', the adviser to Ngo Dinh Diem and later Nguyen Van Thieu. In fact he held the post of presidential adviser from 1957 until 1968 when he was disgraced.

Nha was a native of Thai Binh province in the North and served as a political commissar there, having attended the national conference of guerrilla fighters held in the Viet Bac liberated zone in 1951. Then three years later, after the Geneva Agreements, he was personally assigned by Premier Pham Van Dong to join one of the military units the French were transferring to the South. On arrival in Vung Tau, thanks to his knowledge of Catholicism, he was able to make contact with several influential priests who had fled from the North, and it was they who introduced him to the Ngo brothers.

During all the years he spent working in Independence Palace, the centre of power in Saigon, observing what was happening, gathering news and documents, Nha passed on to Hanoi some very accurate, valuable and up-to-date intelligence. This did not emerge fully even in 1968 when he was arrested and put on trial. He made a 'confession' which left everybody uncertain about whether he was really a Communist cadre or just a devout Catholic following the new Vatican line which was sympathetic to the 'third force' in Vietnam. He was simply adjudged to be unreliable. Indeed after Nha was imprisoned, he received a high decoration, the equivalent of a Purple Heart, from the Vatican!

Much later when I published his story in the Sunday Magazine of *Nhan Dan*, Nha told me a lot about life in Independence Palace. He said that on one occasion President Ngo Dinh Diem was called upon by the Americans to sign a lease ceding Cam Ranh Bay – the ideal naval base in South East Asia and the Western Pacific – for a period of ninety-nine years in return for a massive amount of aid. Diem discussed this with his adviser. According to Nha, he pointed out to Diem that a century earlier, just after the French arrived, the great mandarin of the Nguyen dynasty, Phan Than Gian, signed away three provinces in the southern Mekong delta to them. The people were so dismayed that he was conscience-stricken and committed suicide by taking poison. Nha then went on to remind Diem that he was a devout Catholic and his faith forbade him to take his own life, hence any agreement he concluded with the Americans would not benefit either the nation or his religious belief. Later when the US administration

pressed Diem to allow American ground troops to be based in
the South, he turned to his adviser one evening and said, 'Nha,
this question is very important. If we let the troops come here,
they are foreigners and in no time they will be shooting and
bombing. They will be taking military action on our soil and
staying here. So if there are ever talks about reunification, what
could we say to Ho Chi Minh?'

In fact, although we criticised Ngo Dinh Diem publicly as
an American puppet, Ho Chi Minh adopted a more sober appraisal.
He realised Diem was a patriot like himself but in a different
way. Later many other people came to accept and value Diem
as a leader who was imbued with the spirit of nationalism, and
who lived an honest and clean life and, like Ho Chi Minh,
was unmarried.

In getting rid of the Ngo brothers, the Americans thought
the situation would improve to their advantage. Instead it got
worse still. First there was political chaos after General Duong
Van Minh staged a coup against Diem. Then he was ousted
by General Nguyen Khanh who only survived for a short period
before Nguyen Van Thieu, together with Nguyen Cao Ky, came
to power. Their regime was marked by growing economic chaos
and widespread corruption as well as the repression of Buddhists
and humiliation of intellectuals, youths and students in the South.
In addition, prostitution and drug-peddling around the US bases
developed into a major social crisis.

In this situation, the Saigon army naturally degenerated in every
way. That was the heavy price which was paid for having over
half a million American troops in their midst. They were used
to a high standard of living at home, but when they went into
battle they had no clear understanding of what it was all about.
Coming to live in that small country with its consumer society,
they were just like easygoing tourists with guns. They did not
know that they were destroying old traditional values and breaking
down the basic foundations, no matter how frail, which prompted
them to enter the war and save Vietnam in the first place. In
other words they did not establish the national consensus they
had hoped to create. Rather they eroded it.

More ironically still, after this American military presence – and
over 2 million men served in Vietnam at one time or another–caused
such chaos, the United States undermined the basic foundations

of the war still further with its Vietnamisation programme. The Saigon army only knew how to fight American-style. It had forgotten its basic roots and lost its self-confidence.

The basic foundations of the United States were also shaken through the damage caused by the war to its long-standing values of democracy, social justice and public morale. Television brought home very graphically the horror of My Lai and the sight of General Nguyen Ngoc Loan, the chief of police, shooting one of our patriots in cold blood on the streets of Saigon during the Tet offensive in 1968. The Americans were also able to see for themselves the cowardly free-fire zones and the panic of their own soldiers at Khe Sanh. All of this had a strong influence on their thoughts and feelings.

The Tet Offensive was largely the brainchild of General Nguyen Chi Thanh, who went south in 1964 as the special envoy of the Politburo to become head of what we called R Base and was known to the Americans as COSVN (the Central Office of South Vietnam). From there he was able to take close note of the situation, even before the Americans started to send in ground troops and transform the nature of the war. Consequently, as the fighting escalated, he came to believe that it might be possible to win. He realised that the US troops were engaged in what was to them an alien environment. Rather than let them learn about it and choose where they fought, General Thanh's idea was to stick tight to the Americans and hit them where it hurt. In other words we had to seize the initiative, hit hard and reach a swift conclusion.

To explain these ideas, General Thanh returned to Hanoi in 1967 but not along the Ho Chi Minh Trail. Instead he went from R Base, situated in the Vietnamese-Cambodian border area, to Phnom Penh where he was able to acquire Chinese travel documents and board an ordinary commercial flight to Hong Kong. From there he slipped into China and travelled comfortably back to Hanoi to take part in a long series of meetings with the Politburo and the Army Party Committee to plan the Tet Offensive. Once everything was finally decided, these two bodies held successive farewell parties on July 6. General Thanh was preparing to return to the South by the same route the next day and he drank heavily. Then he went back to his home in Ly Nam De Street, took a bath and, having previously suffered from a weak heart, collapsed and died. That same evening I was immediately ordered by General Le Quang Dao, the deputy head of the Army General Political Department, to write an obituary for the press. At the same time, a major investigation was launched into the facilities at Military Hospital 108 in Hanoi which was responsible for the health of the top leadership. None of this was revealed publicly. Instead the rumour started to circulate that Nguyen Chi Thanh had died the victim of an American bombing raid in the South.

In fact, the Tet Offensive launched on January 31, 1968, turned out to be a great victory for us, at least psychologically. Playing on the over-confidence and arrogance of the American commander, General Westmoreland, we achieved total surprise with a smart and bold move to launch simultaneous attacks on more than forty cities, towns and military bases; the targets included the US embassy in Saigon. Thanks to the media, which exaggerated the damage caused by this offensive, the American public was bedazzled, and under strong pressure the US administration had to agree to negotiations in Paris with the participation of the NLFSVN (National Liberation Front of South Vietnam) which it thus implicitly recognised. At about the same time it began the process of de-escalation leading to the Vietnamisation of the war.

On the other hand, during the Tet Offensive we suffered heavy sacrifices and made many military mistakes, the consequences of which continue to be debated in Hanoi. For example in Saigon we planned to create a 'big bang' by occupying the US embassy plus the Presidential Palace and taking over Saigon Radio, but none of these objectives succeeded. In fact, of the two groups sent with pre-recorded tapes to put on the radio, one lost its way and the other was attacked and captured *en route*. Then there was the situation in Hue where the fighting continued for well over a month and resulted in the massacre of thousands of people. Quite how many thousands nobody knows because they were buried in various places. Possibly it was the biggest massacre of the war, bigger even than My Lai about which the Americans have been so obsessed. So who was responsible? Was it General Tran Van Quang who was in charge of our forces in this military region at the time? Or were the Americans partly to blame because of their fighting tactics? These are questions

I have often asked because I have a personal interest. I spent nine years of my life, from the age of seven, going to school and growing up in Hue from where many of my friends and classmates later disappeared.

When our forces from the North, backed up by local units, first moved into Hue, they arrested hundreds of officials and sometimes whole families. The former imperial capital was regarded as a nest of feudalism, a den of enemy thugs. Special units had to be set up to detain all these prisoners as well as the many Saigon troops who were captured. Then when the Americans counter-attacked in force by sending in the marines, a confusing series of orders emanated from Hanoi. First, at the beginning of March, the General Staff instructed our troops to stand firm at all costs. This was followed shortly afterwards by an order to withdraw west into the mountains. Panic ensued and it was compounded by American bombing raids on our lines of retreat when both our troops and some of the prisoners they were taking with them were killed. Undoubtedly, however, many other detainees who could not be evacuated in the confusion of the withdrawal were massacred in an attempt to cover up the reality of what had happened in Hue during our temporary occupation of the city. These efforts clearly backfired when some of the sites of the massacres were discovered and there was a tremendous outcry both in the South and internationally. Even the leadership in Hanoi had to pay attention. General Tran Van Quang, the overall commander of operations in the attack on Hue, was criticised, as were several of the senior officers serving under him, but typically they were allowed to continue working in other positions rather than being severely disciplined.

Nor did we learn from the military failures of the Tet Offensive. Instead, although we had lost the element of surprise, we went on to mount further major attacks in May and September 1968 and suffered even heavier losses. This too has continued to be a subject of controversy in Hanoi. Our side also suffered seriously from the subsequent pacification plans dreamed up by the Americans, such as Operation Phoenix and the Chieu Hoi campaign which was designed to induce our troops and supporters to defect.

Yet it has to be acknowledged that in the North, although we were constantly counter-attacked and suffered heavy destruction from over five million tons of bombs, we still stood surprisingly firm in contending with the bombers of the Rolling Thunder operations and the Phantom jet fighters. Factories collapsed, bridges were broken, roads torn to bits, schools and hospitals razed to the ground. But all this only raised the level of bitterness and hatred at being attacked so inhumanely, and conveyed new purpose to our combatants. Our traditional patriotism was strengthened. It inspired us to affirm our fundamental sense of nationhood.

At that time, the leadership and the authorities were at one with the people in being morally and ethically dedicated. Therefore the people were at ease. It was almost as if there were no thieves and no bribery. There was also a feeling of affection and mutual self-help between the towns and the villages, with evacuees being welcomed with open arms. And mothers of families which remained in Hanoi or other towns in the North were prepared to queue up for hours without complaint to get something to eat for their children who were becoming severely malnourished.

The author Duong Thu Huong who was expelled from the Party in 1990, was right when she wrote: 'The Party was able to draw upon an invaluable source, like mining a rich vein of gold. That being the eternal love of country felt by a nation whose moral values have been forged through a long, long tradition of resisting foreign aggression. Communism, socialism and Marxism–Leninism did not directly affect the broad mass of the people. To speak of these theories is a blatant way of trying to prove one's own case.'

In my opinion, to follow stubbornly such policies as class struggle and democratic centralism in order to implement such extremist programmes as land reform, with its denunciations and death sentences, or the repression of democratic tendencies in the *Nhan Van, Giai Pham* affair and the anti-revisionist campaign this is like carrying a stone only to drop it on one's own foot. To change the basic foundations which underpinned the struggle during the war belittled the spirit of the people and all they contributed.

To put it more clearly, the Americans aimed through their war of destruction to cause such enormous losses that their enemy would be brought to its knees. But the enemy was poor and had little to lose. He was like the poor man who, when he goes off to war, thinks only of saving his own life because the possessions he loses matter little. If he survives, he can then work to build up wealth. Therefore since he does not have to calculate material losses, it is easy for him to enter into a life or death struggle with the enemy. More important in this situation was that our heroic and indomitable tradition of opposing foreign aggression continued to prevail, and in modern times it developed even more strongly in order to gain freedom and independence for Vietnam. This was appreciated by Ho Chi Minh, but not until 1966 did he coin his famous saying: 'Nothing is more precious than freedom and independence.'

During 1964 and 1965, according to the people close to him, the health of Ho Chi Minh declined markedly. So he was not consulted about the routine, day-to-day decisions taken by Le Duan and the Politburo. They used the pretext 'Spare Uncle Ho the worry. We should not bother the Supreme Leader.' In fact Ho Chi Minh began writing his will in May 1965. After that, he revised and added to it every year in May, around the time of his official birthday. In a book about how the will was drafted, his long-time secretary Vu Ky has also revealed that Ho Chi Minh made several lengthy and secret visits to China during the last years of his life, although this was the period of the Cultural Revolution. What is more, despite the fact that China was bitterly critical of Vietnam for entering into negotiations with the Americans in 1968, it was Chinese and not Soviet doctors who nursed Ho through his last illness.

To look back on Ho Chi Minh's career is to realise that he was a sincere patriot who sacrificed his whole life to the pursuit of the Revolution. He played an enormous role in the struggle for independence. He was a symbol of heroism for the people in the North as well as many in the South, including intellectuals, and faith in him created a basis for solidarity and our struggle against foreign aggression.

But there are some who question whether the liberation struggle was really necessary and whether we would have been better off without it. All the great powers have granted independence to their former colonies as a matter of course, so did we make a mistake in embarking on armed struggle, thus losing a lot of time and sacrificing many lives to gain our independence? Many other countries achieved the same end without a single shot being fired. Such hypotheses are not justified. The collapse of the colonial system was brought about through many forms of struggle coinciding with one another.

One friend has also suggested to me that initially Ho Chi Minh regarded the liberation struggle as the main goal which could only be achieved thanks to the support of the Communist world. But later he regarded the primary aim of the struggle as a proletarian revolution to advance the cause of Communism throughout the world. In fact many articles have been written about whether Ho Chi Minh was a patriot or a Communist or both. In his will he stated that when he died he would be going to meet Marx and Lenin, but that has to be seen in the historical context of international proletarianism, which was the cornerstone of Party policy in Vietnam, while class struggle was viewed as the thread guiding the development of our society. Yet these factors which were intended to bring about national unity have led to our present state of backwardness. These are issues which still need to be carefully considered.

I believe that Ho Chi Minh's ability to develop democracy and legality, and his understanding of the need for it, were limited, not to say greatly defective. When the North embarked on building itself up, Ho was already old and in poor health. He was also out of touch with the situation which needed people of a newer generation. He ought to have cultivated such people earlier. Given these limitations to his awareness and historical outlook, he never paid attention to developing a significant measure of democracy for the country. Bureaucracy and family feudalism still weigh heavy, so creating a major political burden for Vietnam to bear. The Party engulfed and set its mark on everything in order to take power.

One person who was ready to express his views on this subject, albeit off the record, was Le Duan. I remember extremely clearly how he talked about his own exploits compared with those of Ho Chi Minh. In very elated fashion, Le Duan said 'As for me, well, I am better than Uncle Ho. He opened his mouth and talked along the lines of the Confucian code of morality, like human dignity, loyalty, good manners, wisdom and trustworthiness. What is that? It is outmoded feudalism. As for me, I am for collective mastery by the workers.'

Such subjectivity and arrogance were unrestrained. If it was true that Le Duan was greater than Ho Chi Minh, then it was to be welcomed as a sign that the younger generation was an improvement over the older one. However Le Duan was deluding himself. The way he promoted the idea of collective mastery cost who knows how much paper and ink as well as hours of debate and discussion. But it did not make things any better or more democratic.

Just as the date of Ho Chi Minh's birth has been falsified (and remains a subject of controversy), it is now known that he did not die on September 3, 1969, as originally announced. His death occurred a day earlier, but the date was changed and the news delayed in order not to mar the celebration of Vietnam's National Day. Nor was Ho Chi Minh's will, as read out at his funeral by Le Duan, the full and final version.

All this came to light twenty years later when Ho's secretary Vu Ky decided that he had to set matters straight and correct the Party for the sake of the peasants. One section of Ho Chi Minh's will that was concealed was his wish that all agricultural taxes be suspended for a year as his gift to the people at the time of his death. Vu Ky also described what really happened to the will.

On the evening of September 2, 1969, after Ho had died, one of his closest comrades, Pham Van Dong, the prime minister, came to pay his respects. Vu Ky then tried to give him a folder containing all four drafts of the will but Pham Van Dong drew his hands away exclaiming 'No, Comrade, I will not take it. This is an important matter. Leave it until tomorrow morning when there is a meeting of the Politburo, then hand it over.'

The next morning Vu Ky did as he was told. Immediately Le Duan took charge of the matter and called on Hoang Tung, the editor in chief of the Party newspaper *Nhan Dan*, to accompany him to a small side room. There Le Duan decided which bits of the various wills should be published and gave them to Hoang Tung for that purpose. All the rest of the documents were handed over to Tran Quoc Hoan, the Minister of the Interior, for safe-keeping in absolute secrecy.

Vu Ky, however, did not forget how the public had been deceived about the contents of Ho Chi Minh's will and tried in vain to recover the original documents when Tran Quoc Hoan was dropped from the Politburo and lost his position as head of the Cong An in March 1982. Only on his deathbed was the former Minister of the Interior prepared to reveal that the folder containing Ho Chi Minh's wills was hidden 'at my house in the second compartment of an iron safe on the ground floor'. And that was where Vu Ky discovered it.

On the twentieth anniversary of Ho Chi Minh's death in 1989, I persuaded Vu Ky to write about this story for publication in the Sunday magazine of *Nhan Dan* of which I was then editor. The reaction of the leadership was very strong. Several members of the Politburo denounced the pair of us for committing *lèse-majesté* in daring to publish secret documents about Ho Chi Minh without top-level permission. Confronted with the serious eyes of four members of this body as well as the head of the Party Committee for Ideology and Culture,* Vu Ky was very composed. He said: 'Where did I publish Uncle Ho's will? I simply wrote an article about how he came to draft it. The article was written at the request of Bui Tin who works for *Nhan Dan*, and I was happy to do so because for the past twenty years I have been unable to sleep or enjoy food since the people were unaware of all that Uncle Ho's will contained.'

After that, the Politburo had to meet twice to discuss the matter. Finally it handed over to the National Assembly the task of announcing the complete will as well as the decision that agricultural taxes would be reduced, but only by 50 per cent spread over two years. Vu Ky and I were delighted. We clinked glasses of beer together, thinking of our dear peasants who had sacrificed more than anyone else in terms of human lives and material losses during the war. For the next two years things would be slightly better for them.

Vu Ky's revelations about Ho Chi Minh's will also raised questions about the construction of his mausoleum. Many intellectuals, cadres and compatriots say that one should not act contrary to the wishes of a person who is about to take leave of life, since those wishes are sacrosanct. Ho Chi Minh did not want a lavish and costly funeral, like that stage-managed by Le Duan. He had stated in his will that he wished to be cremated and his ashes divided into three to be interred eventually in the north, centre and south of the country to become the focus for the creation of national parks. His wish did not materialise. He was not even buried in his native soil, according to Vietnamese tradition. He

---

*   The four Politburo members who interrogated Vu Ky were Nguyen Thanh Binh, Dao Duy Tung, Nguyen Duc Tam and Dong Sy Nguyen as well as Tran Trong Tan, head of the Party Ideological Committee.

still lies in a cold and gigantic mausoleum, costing who knows how much in building material and human labour. At least it was not constructed until after 1975.

Many foreigners expected there would be a power struggle in Hanoi after Ho Chi Minh's death. We knew better. Le Duan had already long asserted his dominance over the Politburo. In any case, nothing could be allowed to impair the pursuit of the war against the Americans and it was now on two fronts, the battlefield and the negotiating table.

Our chief negotiator in Paris, initially in secret, was Le Duc Tho, head of the Party Organisational Committee since the late 1950s. He had the air of an educated man but he was an extremist and very devious. Although he had worked for many years in the South as a 'professional' revolutionary, he was a northerner from the area of Nam Dinh, just south of Haiphong, where his family were quite well known among the local bourgeoisie. In fact, one of his many brothers had graduated from a French high school, although he always felt himself superior because he was 'prison educated'.

When he went to France, Le Duc Tho did not seem to be inquisitive or anxious to learn. He scarcely watched television and was even less interested in sightseeing. Vietnamese living in Paris who worked or had contact with the delegation headed by him at that time all had this feeling.

Many people say that Le Duc Tho lived simply, but mentally he remained a mandarin and a family feudalist. On many occasions I heard him talk of the decisions issued by the Party Central Committee on organisational matters. He spoke very strongly and passionately, but always clearly in a way that sounded as if he was scolding and admonishing other people. During the period when I attended the Nguyen Ai Quoc Party School in 1969, some of my classmates described him as 'a master whose aim was to teach morality'. Whenever he talked, he loved to lecture and disparage the work of the organisation in a determined way. But never once did be acknowledge any shortcomings, no matter how small, on the part of himself or the Organisational Committee for which he was responsible.

Yet everybody knew that the organisational work of the Party and the state was extremely important for the choice of cadres. However, it was very badly done and caused a lot of damage.

There was prejudice against intellectuals under the criterion 'red rather than expert'. Younger cadres were not trained to take over. They were simply despised, and that still remains a problem. Le Duc Tho continued to be responsible for the organisation of the Party for nearly thirty years, but he always maintained that he could not be brought to book for any mistakes or shortcomings. It was always other people who had committed them.

The negotiations between Le Duc Tho and Henry Kissinger, which began in secret in February 1970 and were only revealed to the public two years later, dragged on into 1972. So too did the war.

After the military setbacks we suffered in 1968 following the Tet Offensive, it took us a long time to recover. We had lost the initiative because we were over-confident and had not safeguarded our existing gains. There were even units which destroyed their base areas before advancing to attack, only to be forced to retreat with nothing to fall back on. Indeed it was not until mid-1970 that we regained our strength in the South, although we continued to manipulate public opinion in the United States to our advantage. We were then able to repulse the attack into southern Laos by the other side in 1971 which aimed to cut through the Ho Chi Minh Trail. Hence we were ready in February 1972 to launch a new series of offensives in three areas: Quang Tri, just south of the demilitarised zone, Pleiku in the Central Highlands and Loc Ninh, west of Saigon.

Once again I returned to the battlefield in the South, this time as a journalist. Although the Americans knew that the war would become more brutal, they deployed massive modern weaponry like the Abrahams tank, Frog missile-launchers, new armoured personnel carriers, Phantom and Thunderchief fighters, B52 bombers and a whole range of mines.

Still, I packed my knapsack lightly and set off on my way to Quang Tri. On this and similar journeys, I went as a volunteer. Feelings of victory, the struggle for national independence, the right of the people to live freely, the devotion of our combatants and above all my professional pride as a journalist motivated me. I came to know a lot of foreign journalists as diverse as Wilfred Burchett, Walter Cronkite, Peter Arnett, Nayan Chanda and Tiziano Terzani. Why should they report the latest news or carry out investigative journalism to earn themselves a reputation, but not a Vietnamese?

During some battles, it is true there were times when I was scared stiff and particularly during our 1972 offensive when the B52s were carpet-bombing us. The atmosphere was like living through a typhoon with trees crashing down and lightning transforming night into day.

After returning from Quang Tri, I was seconded by the Politburo from the army newspaper to *Nhan Dan*, the official organ of the Party, because the situation in the South was reaching boiling point. My task was to liaise between the Ministry of Defence, the General Staff, the Army General Political Department, the army newspaper and *Nhan Dan*. With a special pass issued by the Security Command of the Defence Ministry, which had to be renewed every three months, I was able to enter all of its departments including those responsible for logistics, training, anti-aircraft warfare, artillery and the navy. I also attended top-secret briefings and read the military reports of the General Staff. Because the destructive air war carried out by the Americans in the North was very drastic, I participated in the meetings of the Chiefs of Staff on some mornings and then went back to report to the editorial board of *Nhan Dan* to discuss how we should cover the situation. We had to decide whether to report the facts, comment or publish pictures. We also had to select members of staff to go and do on-the-spot reporting. Such work was really strenuous. Sometimes we slept in the office and some nights in the bomb shelters because of the prolonged American night-time raids.

During this period in 1972, I wrote more then eighty articles covering the war in both the South and the North, and about the American pilots imprisoned in what became known as the Hanoi Hilton. I interviewed the first pilots to be shot down and captured. Some of them had taken part in the Korean war. Then there was the crew of one plane which had tried to attack the Yen Phu power plant but had been shot down and then parachuted into one of the lakes in the centre of Hanoi. One of its members, who was lucky to survive with a broken shoulder and leg, was Major John McCain. It would never have occurred to me even in my wildest dreams that I would meet him again many years later in 1991 as a US Senator in his office on Capitol Hill.

During December 1972, the cities and towns of the North were remorselessly bombed by the Americans. Then suddenly they stopped, negotiations were resumed and the Paris Agreements were signed on January 30, 1973.

We were overjoyed at this outcome and I still think that Le Duc Tho was churlish in refusing to accept the Nobel Peace Prize that he was subsequently awarded together with Henry Kissinger. Such an attitude was both too tough and too short-sighted. It alienated international opinion, particularly that of the progressive forces. Instead Le Duc Tho appeared to be pretentious and condescending towards our enemies. That did not reflect well either on himself or on Vietnam.

4

VICTORY

In the midst of our joy at the conclusion of the Paris Agreements, I was appointed a member of our delegation to travel to Saigon. Its task was to take part in quadrilateral negotiations with the Americans, the Saigon government and representatives of the Provisional Revolutionary Government in the South about the exchange of prisoners of war and the departure of all American forces from Vietnam within the next sixty days. Ceasefire lines also had to be agreed between the areas controlled by the Saigon forces and the liberated zones.

Early on the morning of January 29, 1973, we went out to Gia Lam airport just outside Hanoi, where the craters made by the recent B52 bombings had been filled in. There was an atmosphere of happiness at our historic victory coupled with a feeling that a new phase in the struggle was about to begin.

At 9.30 a.m., the loudspeakers announced that two American planes had requested permission to land to pick up our delegation. The officer tracking their path on radar commented on what a difference the Paris Agreements were making. It was the first time that the Americans had ever asked to enter our airspace and provided flight plans in advance. The two Hercules aircraft landed within ten minutes of one another and their pilots introduced themselves. In return we offered them orange juice, coffee and cakes. It was all very polite. Then at 11.25 we took off for the two-hour flight to Saigon.

As soon as we touched down at Tan Son Nhut, three Saigon immigration officers came on board and asked us to fill in entry forms as if we were arriving in a foreign country. But one of our delegation protested that according to the Paris Agreements we did not need to complete such formalities. After all, we had

73

not asked the American aircrews to fill in entry forms when they had disembarked at Gia Lam that morning. The point was accepted by the Americans but not by the Saigon authorities. So we remained on board the Hercules, as the afternoon turned into evening and then night.

Obviously by this stage the Americans were highly embarrassed and their ambassador took the matter up directly with President Nguyen Van Thieu, but to no avail. Instead all the Americans could do was offer us some food and drink. However, we refused it on the grounds that we wanted to disembark and get on with our work. Actually there was a happy atmosphere on the plane because we knew we were in the right and were once more able to prove the stubborn intransigence of the Saigon authorities. The leader of our delegation, General Le Quang Hoa told us that only the day before, he had been received by the Prime Minister, Pham Van Dong, who had warned him that the Saigon regime would do everything possible to sabotage the Paris Agreements, so we must be on our guard.

This particular incident ended at 11.20 the following morning when we were finally allowed to disembark without completing formalities. We were then driven straight to Camp Davis, an enclosed area within the periphery of Tan Son Nhut airport. The camp comprised about eighty buildings, large and small, which had previously served as an American communications centre. There was still evidence of this in the graffiti written on the walls. Nevertheless the Americans had prepared beds for us with new sheets and pillows. They also brought us orange juice and milk and cooked us a meal of roast chicken with cream cakes to follow. We just wanted to get on with our work.

Saigon seemed hot. The temperature was 30 degrees compared with 20 in Hanoi. It was also noisy. Planes and helicopters were taking off and landing all through the day and night. We wondered whether such activity complied with the Paris Agreements. Then we heard the sound of gunfire coming from the direction of Cu Chi to the north-west of Saigon. That raised further doubts about the cease-fire which was supposed to have entered into force.

On February 1, General Tran Van Tra arrived to head the delegation representing the Provisional Revolutionary Government of South Vietnam. He was flown in by American helicopter from

Loc Ninh, which was liberated during our offensive in April 1972. General Tra, who had studied mechanics in Hue during the time of the French, was an active and intelligent man. He knew how to combine principles with flexibility. He had been operating in the South since 1945 and was currently commander of what we called B2, encompassing the entire war zone in the Mekong Delta including Saigon. In effect that meant he was militarily in charge of most of the South.

General Tra was greeted on arrival at Tan Son Nhut by General Hoa. The two men embraced each other warmly. They were united in victory. American and Saigon officers stood by and watched astonished. Here were two of their arch-opponents celebrating their reunion publicly on the tarmac in the middle of Tan Son Nhut, no less.

The next day was the eve of Tet Qui Suu, the Year of the Buffalo. A meeting was held of the heads of all four delegations to discuss procedural matters relating to the joint inspection teams which were to travel around the South to monitor the cease-fire and check on the American withdrawal. As usual there were lengthy wrangles about flags, designations etc., so the Americans proposed the talks be continued the next day. Here at least, all three Vietnamese delegations were unanimous. They pointed out that the first day of Tet was celebrated as a holiday by the entire Vietnamese nation, and that the Americans obviously knew nothing about local custom.

That evening we held a party at Camp Davis and listened to Radio Hanoi, which broadcast a poem by To Huu hailing the Paris Agreements and looking forward to greater victories. We were also celebrating the forty-third anniversary of the founding of the Party. However the Saigon authorities staged several provocations with helicopters hovering low over Camp Davis, against which we lodged a strong protest. Still the first day of Tet passed off amicably enough with everybody exchanging greetings, although it soon became apparent that the leaders of the two delegations on our side were very different in character.

General Tran Van Tra, whom I got to know quite well during the sixty days we spent at Camp Davis, was a very outgoing and broad-minded person. He enjoyed reading and listening to music. He was also good company and often told stories and cracked jokes even with the other side, including the Americans.

By contrast, General Le Quang Hoa was extremely dour and taciturn. He had previously been political commissar in Military Region 4 in central Vietnam and this was his first visit to the South. He read little and had no sense of culture since, having been a landless peasant, his education was rudimentary. He was therefore ill at ease both at the negotiating table and at the formal receptions to which we were invited. In fact all of us in the delegation from Hanoi were privately worried that such an unsuitable man had been sent to lead a diplomatic mission. On the second day of Tet, the talks got underway in earnest with our first trip into Saigon.

Since our arrival in the South, the foreign press corps had been denied all access to us. That particularly irked me as I had been nominated official spokesman for our delegation. But now we were on our way through the streets of Saigon to the International Control Commission where the foreign press were waiting for us. General Tra took the lead in greeting the assembled journalists, cameramen and TV crews. We even managed to exchange telephone numbers with some of them before the Saigon police intervened to stop any further contact.

From then onwards we no longer felt totally isolated at Camp Davis. Thanks to the telephone, we could always contact the foreign press whenever the Saigon authorities staged another provocation. On the other hand, some journalists called us to check on reports appearing in the local press. The work of the joint inspection teams also got underway and I made several trips on American aircraft and helicopters to various towns in the Mekong Delta as well as elsewhere in the South to check the cease-fire arrangements. Sometimes the planes were fired upon, although from which side it was impossible to tell. Anyway, we protested as we did about all sorts of other incidents. We also monitored the withdrawal of US forces, but of course we realised that some Americans were simply swapping their military uniforms for civilian clothes in order to stay on as 'advisers' to the Saigon forces.

What mattered even more to the Americans during this period was the release of their prisoners of war. I flew back to the North on March 4 to observe the hand-over of the first group of American pilots who had been captured and detained in Hoa Lo prison, the 'Hanoi Hilton'. I believed and stated publicly then, as I still continue to do now, that we also handed over all the rest of the Americans we held captive at that time in other camps scattered around the country. Le Duan and Le Duc Tho issued firm orders on this matter because they wanted all our people held by the other side in the conflict to be returned as swiftly as possible without any bargaining.

As well as acting as spokesman for our delegation, I was also writing numerous articles on what was happening for *Nhan Dan* and the army newspaper under my penname, Thanh Tin. Of course these articles were very propagandist, as was the book I subsequently wrote about this sixty-day period covering the exchange of prisoners and the departure of American forces from Saigon.

The last of them left on March 29 and it just so happened that I was the officer designated to bid them farewell as they boarded their planes. Sergeant-Major Max Bielke from Oregon was the last of all. I shook his hand and presented him with a picture of the Hoan Kiem lake in Hanoi printed on a piece of bamboo. In wishing him good luck and happy reunion with his family, I also expressed the hope that he would revisit Vietnam but as a tourist. He seemed to take the point, thanked me and smiled.

Then, two days later, our delegation returned to Hanoi. We were warmly greeted on our arrival and went straight to the Ministry of Defence to report to General Vo Nguyen Giap. He congratulated us on the success of our mission. So too did the Prime Minister when we called on him at Government House on April 1.

Like many cadres, I had long admired and respected Pham Van Dong. He was a cultured man who led a simple and sincere life. He also had to endure a great deal. He had married a beautiful girl who lived at the Zephyr ice-cream parlour across the road from the restaurant pavilion on the bank of the Hoan Kiem lake in the centre of Hanoi. She used to help revolutionary soldiers at the time when they were operating underground. Then in 1949, when she accompanied her husband to the Viet Bac military zone, she became very ill with some sort of mental disease which left her ravaged and debilitated for the rest of her life.

Feeling duty-bound as a faithful husband, Pham Van Dong usually went to have dinner with her every Saturday evening. Otherwise he lived alone with his work, reading and listening

to the radio a lot. But in later years his eyes grew dim beyond
any cure. He kept himself amused by listening to someone reading
from the work of Victor Hugo or Anatole France. He also went
for a long stroll every morning and evening. His one consolation
was his only son Duong, who turned out to be a good student
and spent some time in the army.

Pham Van Dong was an intellectual who thought a great deal.
He was devoted to country and became very emotional about
it. There were times when tears came to his eyes when considering
the fate of the people, particularly the women and children. He
also wrote several books, like that marking the 600th anniversary
of the birth of Nguyen Trai, an outstanding nationalist who is
universally respected.

Some intellectuals have suggested that it would have been better
if Pham Van Dong had restricted himself to the sphere of culture.
He would have achieved more. Instead, he was naive as Prime
Minister and was often blamed for the weak-willed way he worked
within the system. He was aware of such criticism. On several
occasions, I heard him point out that he was the longest-serving
prime minister in the world, having held the position for almost
forty years. By the time he retired in 1986, he was also the
oldest prime minister in the world. But he lamented that he
was also the most powerless prime minister. He even said, 'I
can do nothing. When I say something, nobody listens. If I propose
changing a deputy minister, it turns out to be impossible. I cannot
even choose my own ministers.'

One example of his powerlessness was when his personal
secretary, the scientist and poet Viet Phuong, was unjustly labelled
as a revisionist simply because he had written some outspoken
poems mockingly pointing out how we had a tendency to brag
unreasonably about our achievements. Our moon, for instance,
was always rounder than that of the enemy. Yet although Viet
Phuong came close to being sentenced to death, Pham Van Dong
just kept quiet. He neither joined in the denunciation, nor provided
any support for his secretary. Only when matters died down and
Viet Phuong returned to work at the Institute of Economic Administration, did the prime minister get in touch again and offer
to write a letter of recommendation. That was typical of Pham
Van Dong. Perhaps his long experience had taught him that having
a lot of knowledge and intelligence can be dismissed as meaningless

by a system which is so rigid that it has no regard for a person's ability or for any other human considerations.

There are still those who reproach Pham Van Dong for not struggling harder and raising the question of his responsibility as prime minister. After all, if he could not establish his authority, who could? But then everybody sympathised with him because of the nature of the system. The Party had set itself up as the supreme and absolute power. It was the Party Organisational Committee which made all official appointments. The government could only nod its head in approval.

Within the Politburo, Pham Van Dong was the person who had the least to say. Maybe it was because he felt humiliated and preferred to remain aloof from the power struggles between the different cliques. He only spoke when he thought it was really important to do so.

One instance was at the end of 1974 when the Politburo was discussing the military campaign to be carried out during the forthcoming spring. Here Pham Van Dong said: 'For over a week I have been thinking about the ability of the American administration to react and I have come to the conclusion that even if we offered the Americans a bribe to intervene again, they would not accept it. So let's go ahead with the campaign in the South. Yes, even a bribe cannot induce the Americans to return again.' Then he laughed. Very often when he had finished speaking, Pham Van Dong would laugh in a very natural and relaxed manner.

At that time Le Duan was pressing for the application of iron fist tactics in preparation for a major offensive. Four army corps had already been formed and trained in the previous two years. Now he wanted to seize the opportunity for action. According to the proposals he put forward, the aim of a Spring Offensive in 1975 was to start a process which would lead to the end of the war within two years. In later years, Le Duan claimed that at the end of 1974 he also had the idea of drafting a supplementary plan to take advantage of any new opportunities which might arise to end the war as quickly as possible.

A lot of people have their own ideas about what happened in 1975. When we were interviewing Truong Chinh for his biography, he remarked: 'Don't write anything like the articles by Thep Moi about our victory over the Americans. They are not correct. It is a bad habit. They are fabrications and embroidery. The authors are opportunists whose writing may damage Anh Ba [Le Duan]. And don't write anything like the book entitled *Our Great Spring Victory* which was ghost-written for General Van Tien Dung by Hong Ha. It contained many mistakes. When it was published, it had to be corrected in at least thirty places and everybody laughed.'*

That was true. The way General Van Tien Dung rushed into print, claiming a large measure of personal credit for the victory in 1975 was extremely controversial. Everybody knew he had been Chief of the Army General Staff since 1954 as a result of the reputation he acquired during the war against the French as political commissar of the famous 320th Division, which waged a very successful campaign in the Red River Delta provinces. But after that he did little to justify his position. Instead he enjoyed the patronage of Le Duan and Le Duc Tho in their attempts to outflank the more intelligent generals appointed to senior positions by General Giap.

The fact was that Van Tien Dung was a tailor's son from a village on the outskirts of Hanoi who joined the revolution at an early age and so had very little education. Nor during his entire career had he ever set foot in the South until he arrived in the Central Highlands to assume charge of the campaign there in early 1975. This evoked some sarcastic comments from General Tran Van Tra, the commander of the National Liberation Army in the South, who had been in the thick of the fighting ever since 1960, making only occasional visits to the North during all that time. He utterly despised the arrogance of General Dung.

General Tra has also written a book about the Spring Offensive in 1975. Indeed I encouraged him to do so. We often had occasion to exchange ideas about all sorts of topics like the state of the press, literature and music. He was a cultured man and his memoirs about the 1975 Spring Offensive, published in 1982, were much appreciated by people in the South.

Then the General Political Department issued an order banning the circulation of this book. Le Duc Tho also criticised it as

---

* Hong Ha, who is currently a member of the Party Secretariat, served as editor of *Nhan Dan* from 1982-6 when I got to know him well. The most significant thing about him is that he is a diligent and secretive official totally committed to his work, just like his older brother Thep Moi. They always acted like clerks.

a book that was wrong from start to finish. Likewise he condemned
Ha Mau Nhai, the director of the publishing house in Ho Chi
Minh City which issued it. In my opinion, the main weakness
of Tran Van Tra's memoirs is the way he neglects all the massive
efforts the North made to help the South. Even so the banning
of his book was wrong. Shortcomings should be discussed and
corrected, not just rejected out of hand. The ridiculous thing
about some of our leaders is that they want every book to reflect
their own views. Instead they should realise that autobiographies
are a valid form of self-expression.

Actually, as General Tra makes clear in his book, he and his
close associate Pham Hung, the Party Secretary in the South,
also took part in planning the offensive. In late 1974 they felt
it essential to make their way to Hanoi because they were aware
of the real situation on the ground and how rapidly it was changing.
They knew too that decision-making at the top did not always
run smoothly. As Minister of Defence, General Giap did not
enjoy full power. Le Duan was head of the Party Military Commission and claimed ultimate authority. From the early 1970s,
Le Duc Tho had also been a member of this body with responsibility
for the South and considered himself to be Number Two. Then
there was the Army General Staff whose members, especially
General Van Tien Dung, were regarded as bureaucrats by General
Tra. They lived relatively comfortably in Hanoi, remote from
the daily hardship and dangers of the battlefield. They only knew
in theory about what was happening there. And yet if a single
irresponsible move had been made during the planning stage,
it could have resulted in tremendous losses and perhaps even
defeat. That basically is why the accounts of the Spring Offensive
written by Generals Tra and Dung are so different.

According to General Tra, the offensive really began at the
end of December 1974 when troops under his command, who
were in a high state of combat readiness, embarked on a series
of attacks in Phuoc Binh province close to the border with Cambodia but considerably north of the Mekong. These battles were
hard-fought, yet ended in victory. This could however, have
evoked a strong reaction from the Ford administration in
Washington. When it did not, the way was open for General
Van Tien Dung to travel south to spearhead what he describes
as the beginning of the Spring Offensive with the attack in early

March on the town of Ban Me Thuot in the southern Central Highlands.

The version of events given by Le Duan and Van Tien Dung has also been firmly rejected by some generals I know. In books not yet published, they claim that it was actually General Giap who did all the planning. They have evidence to prove that Giap was always in direct command throughout the 1975 offensive and that it was he who really led it to victory. They have even produced the daily command diary of the Operations Department of the General Staff which clearly and carefully recorded every order made by Giap right down to the very minute and second when it was issued. These records also show how rapidly and daringly he reacted to developing situations. Every moment counted and most of the orders are written in his own hand. Giap was always present at the command post in the Citadel in Hanoi to follow developments, make corrections if necessary and issue immediate orders. A general from the operational staff told me that even if he was threatened with having his head chopped off, he would swear this was the truth.

I have also exchanged ideas with officers on the General Staff about the reason why Le Duan later tried to claim that General Giap was chicken-hearted and afraid of the Americans at the beginning of 1975. Apparently it was because, when weighing up the situation, Giap hesitated to commit all fifteen of our infantry divisions to the South and decided that the First Army Corps should stay back to act as 'goalkeeper' to protect the country's great rear base. Indeed, in March General Giap instructed the anti-aircraft units and the air force to be prepared to prevent the Americans from resuming their bombing raids on the North, since the High Command was aware of a report from the United States that the Americans might react to developments in the South with a new round of bombing. He raised this possibility and insisted that it was essential for us to be on our guard.

Many more arguments ensued after the capture of Da Nang on March 29, when the Politburo passed a resolution to complete the campaign in the South within a month. General Giap claimed there were already enough divisions in the South to attain this objective, but Le Duan insisted that the whole of the First Army Corps based in the Ninh Binh/northern Thanh Hoa region should move south with the exception of the 318th Division. In the end General Giap agreed.

That was the point when I too went south again as a journalist reporting for the Party newspaper *Nhan Dan*, of which I was then actually Deputy Editor. Together with twenty-three other journalists, I was on the first of our planes to land at Da Nang after its liberation at the end of March. From there I flew on by helicopter to Ban Me Thuot and then made my way by jeep to General Tra's headquarters at Loc Ninh. There I again saw a lot of General Tra whose antipathy towards General Dung was by then very evident. As the fighting around Saigon intensified, the senior command staff moved forward to a position hidden deep in the rubber plantations of Song Be province, where they were joined by Le Duc Tho who had travelled south by plane, car and motorbike to be present at the moment of victory.

As a correspondent reporting on the war, I moved around in tanks, armoured cars and command jeeps often feeling frightened when we came under enemy fire. But then for me it was strange to sit in a tank in the midst of a battle and hear its commander give orders to fire at our opponents only a couple of hundred metres away. My previous experience of battles had always been on my own two feet. However, my fears were only transitory. Towering above all else was a feeling of imminent victory and enthusiasm at being able to witness such significant developments.

During this campaign, it was an enormous advantage that the delegation of the Provisional Revolutionary Government of South Vietnam continued to maintain a presence at Camp Davis. It acted, so to speak, as an observation post in the heart of enemy territory. We could evaluate the feeling of the people in the capital and collect accurate information on the conflicts of opinion within the Saigon regime. We also received a lot of help from the Poles and Hungarians on the International Control Commission. They were able to keep a finger on the pulse of the social and psychological atmosphere in Saigon. So too did some of the foreign journalists who attended the weekly press conferences we were allowed to hold at Camp Davis. They also served as useful points of contact, although we had other channels as well.

Pham Xuan An, known to us as Hai Trung, had studied journalism at an American University and worked for the Time-Life group for many years. He was a confidant of Tran Van Don and Tran Kim Tuyen, who worked hand in glove with the CIA. He was also close friends with American, British, French and Japanese journalists based in Saigon. He accompanied them into battle on American helicopters and then spread all sorts of stories on Radio Catinat, in other words the rumour mill which stretched the length of the bars and cafés of Saigon's main boulevard. At the same time, he despatched numerous valuable documents and photographs to Cu Chi for transmission to Hanoi. This intelligence network consisted of only two people, Pham Xuan An and a woman who acted as a courier. Amazingly, both of them were able to carry out this task for twenty years without once being exposed, and they were both honoured as heroes in 1976.

Some foreign journalists have remarked that I too was always in the most important place at the right time. Perhaps it was because of my professional sense of responsibility. I was not out to enjoy myself. Anybody else wanting to cover a story I was covering would have been welcome and thus to have enhanced his reputation.

Early on the morning of April 30, 1975, the day the war ended, I was in Cu Chi and it was simply by chance that I ended up at Independence Palace in Saigon. When I arrived there I saw a tank commander who had been wounded. I was told there had been fighting near the An Quang and Xa Loi pagodas which were the most militant in Saigon. Then Lt.-Col. Nguyen Van Han, the chief of security of the Fourth Army Corps with whom I had previously been closely associated, and Bui Van Tung, the political commissar of the 203rd Tank Regiment, informed me that Duong Van Minh – Big Minh as he was known – who had become president of South Vietnam two days earlier, was sitting inside the palace with all his cabinet, waiting. However there was nobody present of a rank high enough to go and talk to him. In the People's Army of Vietnam, only officers of the rank of colonel or above were considered to have sufficient authority and seniority to make decisions. Lt.-Col. Han said he had been ordered to wait for such an officer to arrive before entering the building. He then asked me to go in and talk to the president because I held the rank of colonel. I replied that I was only a journalist now, but Lt.-Col. Han persisted. Eventually I agreed.

To reduce tension, I asked two young soldiers to leave their

AK47s outside. Then Lt.-Col. Han entered the room where Big Minh was waiting and announced that a high-ranking officer had arrived. Everybody stood up as I walked in with Lt.-Col. Nguyen Tran Thiet, another journalist from the army newspaper in Hanoi. As soon as we appeared Big Minh said 'We have been waiting for you all morning.'

By then it was mid-day and I did not know that much earlier that morning Minh had already announced a cease-fire over the radio, so I replied it was time to stop the war and avoid further sacrifice on both sides. At that time I believed our policy was to achieve reconciliation between all Vietnamese; at this point, seeing a lot of anxious and tense faces around me, I went on to say that all Vietnamese should consider this a happy day because our victory belonged to the whole people and only the American foreign invaders had been defeated.

Some of those present in the room, particularly Vu Van Mau the prime minister-designate, began to smile when suddenly there was a burst of gunfire outside which broke one of the window panes. Everybody ducked but I told them not to worry. Our soldiers were simply firing in the air to celebrate. One had raised the National Liberation Front flag over Independence Palace.

Once everybody had got up again, I tried to calm their nerves by asking Duong Van Minh whether he still played tennis. I then talked about his orchid collection. He was reputed to have over 600 species, some of which he had brought back from Thailand when returning from exile there. I also asked Vu Van Mau why his hair was so long, since he had vowed to wear it short for as long as Nguyen Van Thieu remained President. Thieu had resigned and left the country two weeks earlier. At this Big Minh laughed and said it was no wonder we had won the war because we knew everything.

What actually transpired on that occasion has now become a subject of controversy. On April 28, 1991, *Quan Doi Nhan Dan*, the army newspaper, claimed that it was really Lt.-Col. Bui Van Tung who accepted the surrender of South Vietnam. He was certainly present and wrote the statement which Duong Van Minh then read out. All these proceedings were recorded on a machine we borrowed from Boris Gallach, a German correspondent for the magazine *Der Spiegel*, who had managed to get into Independence Palace. So too had Frances Starner of the *Far Eastern Economic Review* who took a lot of photos, copies of which she later passed on to me. Official photographers from the National Liberation Front also filmed the scene and then Lt.-Col. Bui Van Tung escorted Big Minh to Saigon Radio to read out his statement on the air.

Meanwhile, I adjourned to what had been the presidential office, occupied until only two weeks earlier by Nguyen Van Thieu, to write my report on all these developments. The problem was how to despatch it to Hanoi. All communications out of Saigon had been closed down. So I made my way out to Camp Davis where some of the comrades I had known in the communications division agreed to send it in Morse code. This report, which was addressed in the first instance to General Le Quang Dao, Deputy Head of the Political Department in the Army, appeared under my pen name in the army newspaper on May 2, 1975. It was the first eye-witness account of the surrender of Saigon to be published anywhere in the world. The only trouble was that in describing the menu of the last meal that Big Minh ate in Independence Palace at lunchtime on April 30, the Morse became somewhat garbled. True, we Northerners cook in a different way from people in the South, but the dishes as described in my report seemed weird indeed.

I was lucky in being able to get my report out, while those foreign journalists still present in Saigon fumed in frustration at their inability to communicate with the outside world. Among them was Tiziano Terzani, who though an Italian was correspondent for *Der Spiegel*. On May 1, he was very downcast and close to tears on this account and begged for my help. Since his colleague Boris Gallach had been helpful in recording the surrender of Big Minh, I smiled and said maybe it was possible because that afternoon an Ilyushin 18 was arriving from Hanoi and would be returning the same day. I added that I had friends at the Vietnam News Agency who could forward the article to East Berlin for transmission to the West. And that is what happened, to the relief of Tiziano who was immensely grateful.

Those first days in Saigon after our unexpectedly easy victory were extraordinary. To celebrate this historic event the commanders of all the forces involved assembled at Independence Palace. They included the generals in charge of the four army corps and one special mixed corps which had participated in the campaign. Also

The author writing his report on the defeat of the Republic of South Vietnam at the desk of ex-President Nguyen Van Thieu at Independence Palace, April 30, 1975.

In front of the Chinese Embassy, Phnom Penh, January 9, 1979, with General Le Trong Tan (fourth from left).

With General Vo Nguyen Giap at the Sixth Party Congress, December 1986.

The first edition of *Nhan Dan's* Sunday Magazine, Tet 1989.

Meeting Senator John McCain on Capitol Hill, October 1991.

present were the commanders of the Air Force, the Navy and those branches of the armed forces responsible for armoured, anti-aircraft and chemical warfare as well as propaganda and special operations. All these senior officers had been present twenty-one years earlier at Dien Bien Phu when, holding junior commands, they had been put to the test. Clearly the war against the French had been a sort of university, a stage on which to rehearse and learn about military theory and practise it as an officer. If it had not been for that war, the struggle against the Americans would not have turned out in the way it did.

Then on May 7, 1975 or thereabouts, General Vo Nguyen Giap arrived at Tan Son Nhut and was taken to Independence Palace which had just been transformed into an official guest house. There he was greeted by General Tran Van Tra, who had become the head of the Military Committee administering Saigon. I still recall that evening. An officer said that he had acquired a good-quality piano from a military base in the South which he would send to General Giap's home in Hanoi. I have never seen Giap so angry. With his eyes blazing and uttering obscenities, he replied that it was impossible for him to accept such booty: what would everybody else who had participated in the campaign expect?

After that I respected General Giap even more. However, when the Fourth Party Congress was held in 1976, it was apparent he had more or less been replaced as Minister of Defence by General Van Tien Dung whose book had by then been published. Ignoring the role of General Giap, this book virtually claimed that its author had himself masterminded what had become known as the Ho Chi Minh campaign, leading to our 'Great Spring Victory'.

5

ARROGANCE

In early 1975 I was nearly fifty years old and had spent the major part of my life serving the Revolution. I had fought against the French and the Americans in various different capacities. On several occasions I had fallen ill and thought I would die. Like so many other soldiers, I had suffered from persistent dysentery and malaria, and I bore the scars of blisters and boils. I had also been wounded three times by mortar shells and artillery. So the first days of May that year were overflowing with the elation of victory. Then I began to ponder and became uneasy.

Various questions troubled my mind as I tried to comprehend the fate of my compatriots. It was strange. During our hard struggle, life had seemed so simple and easy, but now there was much that was difficult to understand. The war had wasted so many Vietnamese lives on both sides and they were all our blood relatives. And for what? We were told it was to liberate the country.

At first there were many people who did not realise the implications of our victory. They saw it simply as the end of a long war and believed that immediately thereafter we would rebuild the country for the next generation. What they did not realise is that fighting a war is easy compared with reconstruction. They thought that with continuing help from our international friends, our towns and cities would soon become beautiful. Only gradually did they come to realise that coping with an economy in times of peace is far more difficult than waging a war. Besides, Communist propaganda is good at painting one-sided pictures. It never depicts the real problems, and in 1975 we were much too shortsighted to look at the rest of the world objectively and learn from others. We were drunk with victory.

That attitude was disastrous. We were arrogant in our ignorance. The Party claimed to be the servant of the people but it did not listen to them at all. Just like during the land reform campaign in the 1950s, policy was handed down from above. National reconciliation, which had been one of the cornerstones of our policy before our victory, soon turned into recrimination.

One of the members of the former Saigon regime with whom I spoke at Independence Palace on April 30 was Nguyen Van Hao. He had been Deputy Premier in charge of economic affairs as well as responsible for the National Bank of South Vietnam. I asked him why he had not fled like so many other people associated with the Saigon regime. He replied that he was a Vietnamese and felt he could contribute towards the reconstruction of our country. He went on to tell me that he had advised his staff to do likewise. After all, we on the Communist side had been trained in China and the Soviet Union while experts in the South had experience of the Western financial system, particularly that of the United States. Therefore we could constitute a good combined team to reconstruct the country.

But it did not happen. Hao met with difficulties and became discouraged. A few years ago, he obtained permission to go to France and subsequently worked as an economic adviser in Haiti. Why treat people like this, especially Nguyen Van Hao who had rendered considerable service to Vietnam?

On April 30, 1975, he told me that South Vietnam's gold reserves, which Nguyen Van Thieu was rumoured to have transported out of the country, in fact remained intact and under guard in the national treasury in Saigon. Hao claimed he had firmly resisted any idea that this gold be sent abroad on the grounds that it should contribute to national reconstruction.

As soon as I learnt that there were 16 tons of gold sitting in Saigon, I telegraphed the information to Hanoi. Two days later a couple of officials were sent down to take custody of it. The advice of Hao was that if this gold were invested wisely, it would help finance the reconstruction of Vietnam. That idea was rejected as capitalist. But a couple of years later when I was accompanying Truong Chinh on one of his travels and asked him what had happened to this gold, he said that most of it had been used up in coping with various emergencies.

Soon after our victory, I also talked to a lot of other high-ranking officials and officers of the former South Vietnamese regime. At first our discussions were amicable. They had been led to believe they were being sent for courses of re-education lasting several days. Then it became several months and the period was progressively prolonged. What had happened was that the Defence Ministry initially assumed responsibility for dealing with its former opponents, but within a short time the Ministry of the Interior took over the task. It already had a network of detention camps in the North under the administration of General Le Phu Qua, and soon a similar system was established in the South. As a result, men who had been regarded as prisoners of war became transformed into political criminals, needing to be punished.

In my capacity as a newspaper correspondent, I went to visit re-education camps at Thu Duc, Long Thanh, Quang Trung, Ba Ria and Tay Ninh. I also saw camps in the North in the Tuyen Quang region. All this worried me. There seemed to be no explanation. Communists generally consider themselves to be compassionate. So why pursue a policy of such harshness towards hundreds of thousands of people?

For example, at the re-education camp in Thu Duc I saw numerous young women who had served in the Saigon army having to sleeping on a cement floor covered only with a thin sheet of plastic without any mats or mosquito nets. In Tuyen Quang in the North, many of those detained in the camp were in their seventies. The food they were given was insubstantial and lacked nutrients, and this caused blindness and weakness. I became aware too that some detainees who were considered particularly recalcitrant were kept for long periods in solitary confinement, chained and fettered. But why? Was this the way to re-educate them to understand the reason for our struggle or did it simply discourage them and make them more bitter towards the new regime?

I was able to peruse the re-education syllabus for high-ranking Saigon officers and see the way young instructors were trained for the task. I realised that this whole re-education programme was hopeless. It was just a formality which would never achieve its aim. I raised this matter with Pham Hung, the Minister of the Interior, and his deputy Vien Chi who was responsible for security matters in the South. I asked Pham Hung specifically about the case of Nguyen Huu Co who had only been Chief of Staff in Saigon for thirty-eight hours. In reply he smiled and said: 'Time in office means nothing. Co and his friends would have killed us if they could, and therefore he deserved no mercy.'

I never did find out from whom or from where the idea of re-education had originated or whether it had been properly discussed, and its pros and cons weighed up. It was after all a national policy affecting the lives and psychology of tens of thousands of people and families as well as millions of their friends and relatives – in fact the whole of society in the South. People were sent to what were called re-education camps, which in reality were prisons.

Because of the number of people involved, the situation in the camps was terrible. The way the camps were administered was bad and even old-fashioned. Some detainees were used to control others, contrary to modern techniques used to reform juvenile delinquents, murderers and persistent drug addicts.

I still shiver when I think about the hundreds of camps set up along Stalinist lines after 1975. Yet there are those who argue that re-education was necessary. It was better than shooting, beating or abusing war criminals. What else was one supposed to do with them? In fact there were those who said that these war criminals were responsible for the deaths of millions of our compatriots and comrades, so why should we feel compassion for them? War is war and the victors have the right to decide on its aftermath. Compassion should be saved for oneself. Why waste it on the enemy, those who stood on the firing line directly opposite us?

Other people said I lacked true conviction and did not view matters objectively. They pointed to the fact that out of the million and more soldiers and officials of the Saigon regime, only about 100,000 were sent for long-term re-education. The other 90 per cent were granted full rights as citizens. For example General Nguyen Huu Hanh of the Saigon army even became a member of the Fatherland Front in Ho Chi Minh City, while Nguyen Xuan Oanh, who had been Deputy Premier of South Vietnam and acted briefly as Prime Minister, was elected as a representative to the Assembly in Hanoi, so why make a fuss?

I still think differently. Should we not concern ourselves about the unhappiness of other people? Are such feelings unworthy? Should we attribute different values to the suffering of people on different sides of a war, especially after that war has ended? Is pain simply a one-sided affair? Why should we use stories of past massacres carried out in other countries such as the Soviet Union during the Stalinist era or Cambodia under Pol Pot to defend our own policies as more humane and lenient? After all, we detained many prominent and respected intellectuals like the former civilian Prime Minister of South Vietnam, Dr Phan Huy Quat, who was left to die in Saigon's notorious Chi Hoa prison.

I believe that to impose strict political views as well as heavy and lengthy punishment on so many members of the former regime was unnecessary and contrary to our proclaimed policy of national concord and reconciliation. This is a topic which arose especially in discussions I had with Father Chan Tin and Nguyen Ngoc Lan, also a former Catholic priest, both of whom I had known since early in 1973. At that time they were active in providing aid in the form of money, clothing and medicine to political prisoners of the Saigon regime as well as 3,000 of our combatants from the North held captive on Phu Quoc island. Now after 'Liberation' they were equally concerned about all those people we had imprisoned. They claimed it was unjust and contrary to all the policies we had proclaimed during the war. I believe it was also contrary to the generosity of victors after the end of a war. In fact it simply increased resentment and pain for many people, and for no good reason. Such a policy lacked compassion according to our national tradition. More than that, it lacked wisdom by belittling the ability of those people like Father Chan Tin, who were not anti-Communist and had the potential to contribute to national reconciliation after the war.

I remember an incident which happened in September 1975 when the Khmer Rouge crossed the border from Cambodia and attacked an area near Ha Tien. They were repulsed and withdrew into a small forest. At the request of the 9th Military Region, the General Staff ordered the Air Force to bomb the forest. Three F5 fighter-bombers were placed on stand-by, but because we had nobody trained to fly them, we had to use aircrew from the Saigon air force. It was a very successful mission. On their return to Tan Son Nhut there were celebrations. The men involved were congratulated for having wiped out the enemy. General Vo Nguyen Giap was particularly pleased. But several weeks later an order arrived from the General Political Department in Hanoi forbidding the deployment of any 'puppet' officers in future operations because they were dangerous and unreliable.

To apply policy on the basis of a primitive and childish conception of class struggle is to damage the nature of politics and the strength of the nation. Why does one person make disparaging comparisons with the bad deeds of somebody else in order to protect his own lack of understanding and knowledge, rather than learning to deal with the matter humanely, truthfully and intelligently? During the Tran dynasty in the thirteenth century, our forefathers, after crushing the invaders, adopted a policy of reconciliation, proclaimed an amnesty for those who had consorted with foreigners, and burned all files in order to create a new era of peace and prosperity. From then onwards, everybody who committed a crime was brought to justice.

Previously I have maintained that if only Chairman Ho Chi Minh had lived until 1975, the epidemic of arrogance which spread after our victory would soon have been stopped because he always reminded us not be discouraged in defeat or proud in victory. He also said that if we did win we would have to guard against acquiring the spoils of war to an excessive degree, as this could only lead to corruption. Also, the harsh and extensive measures taken against those detained in what were called re-education camps would probably not have occurred because Ho Chi Minh was compassionate and had a deep sense of human values. He was also very decisive and capable of overturning existing policy. However, in this case we cannot use the word 'if'. It is not possible, nor is it scientific. Ho Chi Minh had died more than five years previously.

After 1975, even those people who were known to have been neutral during the war or actively opposed to the Saigon regime without being Communist were expected to comply with the measures thoughtlessly applied by the state and the Party. One person who complained to me on this score was the Most Venerable Thich Don Hau, the head of the United Buddhist Church of Vietnam, which had been founded in Hue during the 1950s. As such it was the organisation which was at the forefront of the demonstrations in 1963 against the religious repression instigated by Ngo Dinh Diem and his brothers, as well as of the protests three years later against the subsequent military regime.

Consequently Thich Don Hau came to be regarded as a patriot, and when I visited Hue after liberation I often called by at the Linh Mu Pagoda to talk with him. I found him a very lively and erudite old man, well versed in classical poetry in addition to Buddhist doctrine but totally disillusioned with politics. He told me that the State Commission on Religious Affairs regarded the Buddhist clergy as children to whom everything had to be dictated, even the choice of ordinands.* Many so-called 'patriotic' Catholic priests felt the same way.

Another victim of blind and rigid official attitudes was Truong Dinh Du, a respected Saigon lawyer, who sought to stand as opposition candidate to the military in the 1967 presidential elections. Because he gained a lot of support among students and intellectuals by campaigning against official corruption, he was later detained and imprisoned on a charge of slandering the government. Ostensibly that earned him a special status. Soon after the liberation of the South, I met him at a seminar of 'patriotic intellectuals' held to discuss the establishment of an economic and legal research group under the sponsorship of the Ho Chi Minh City People's Committee. There was therefore considerable surprise when he was suddenly arrested in 1978 without any explanation. On making enquiries with officials from the Ministry of the Interior, I discovered that several reactionary elements who had recently been detained and interrogated stated that they had intended, if they had been successful, in 'ousting the Communists from power' to install Truong Dinh Du as President of Vietnam. On this basis, the Cong An concluded, he had to be a CIA agent. So without any corroborating evidence, let alone a trial, Truong Dinh Du was taken north where word has it that he died of ill health caused by his imprisonment.[†]

Even the dead were not allowed to rest in peace. In 1978,

---

*   Thich Don Hau died in May 1992, when the state tried to stage-manage his funeral, much to the dismay of his disciples, many of whom were already subject to house arrest or have since been detained.

[†]   Ironically Truong Dinh Du's son, Truong Dinh Hung (known as David Truong), who had been sent to the United States to study and become an anti-war activist, was also detained in 1978. He was accused by the US authorities of passing state secrets to the Vietnamese mission to the UN and was subsequently deported.

the Ho Chi Minh City People's Committee passed a resolution on the problem of 'overcrowding' and removal of remains from the Mac Dinh Chi cemetery where many of Saigon's élite had been buried, including the families of some Party members who had rallied to the North during the war. The Committee members wrote to the army newspaper complaining about the move and we, on the editorial board, passed these letters on to the relevant authorities with the comment that there could be long-term consequences because of our traditional respect for the graves of the dead. But it was to no avail. In the eyes of our Communist leaders, an 'enemy puppet', whether alive or dead, was always a puppet – a second-class citizen or somebody who had no citizen's rights at all. They therefore had to be removed from the cemetery to provide room for first-class citizens. Thus many city-dwellers had no choice but to see the remains of their loved ones banished to rot in the so-called New Economic Zones: the places were in barren or otherwise uncultivated land, often deep within the jungle, where there were no facilities for either the living or the dead.

However, among those buried in Mac Dinh Chi cemetery were a former President, ministers, generals and officers of the Saigon regime as well as businessmen and ordinary citizens. All had to be removed within the space of two months. Then the site was bulldozed to create a childrens' park, so that the children themselves were dragged into this violation of Vietnam's traditional respect for the graves of the ancestors.

All this stemmed from a lack of moral values, the inhumanity and blindness of a Communist leadership which had become arrogant and lost touch with the people. Many members of this leadership believed they were the only people who merited spacious burial grounds with flowers and pine trees. The rest of the people did not matter and if the graves of the 'puppets' disappeared, so much the better.

I was well aware that the person chiefly responsible for implementing this policy was Le Duc Tho's younger brother Mai Chi Tho, who became Chairman of the Ho Chi Minh City People's Committee after it was set up. His immediate assistant was Muoi Tuong who went on to acquire an equally notorious reputation in Hanoi by destroying historic sites and burial places.

I once met a professor of pharmacology at Saigon University

who told me he had decided in 1975 to stay and contribute to the task of building the country. But he became discouraged and by 1980 could stand the situation no longer, so he asked to emigrate to France legally. For him, liberation had seemed more like occupation or annexation. Cadres coming from the North had shown no concern for the maintenance of medical equipment in order to raise the educational level of the students. They just took over all the most important positions without having the ability to administer and soon envied, criticised and denounced one another while despatching all the best medical equipment to the North. This was not a matter of sensibly sharing resources between the haves and the have-nots. The equipment was broken up and sold for the benefit of the individuals concerned.

The professor confided to me, 'In observing this situation over the past five years, I can see that there are true revolutionaries and 'fake revolutionaries', just as on our side there are true 'puppets' and puppets with a revolutionary spirit. Your mistake is that you have never looked at this question properly. You just put everybody in the same basket: puppets are all worthless and untrustworthy and must be totally discarded, while revolutionaries are all good and better than anyone at all from the previous regime. And you view their offspring in the same rigid way. You are imbued with a firm class viewpoint. So how can you stabilise society, make the people feel at ease and help the country develop?'

When somebody's class background is investigated, it is as if a theoretical framework is publicly applied to his whole life. Every relationship is noted down in a dossier. Naturally people have had to be careful about what they reveal to avoid difficulties.

Before 1975 it was dangerous for people living in the North to admit that they had relatives abroad, let alone family members in the South who worked with the Saigon regime. Such 'political connections' simply fuelled suspicions about one's own loyalty, so it was better to keep quiet about them. But after April 1975, there was a trend in the South to acknowledge one's family in the North and appease one's native village. Indeed it became evident that almost every family had relatives on both sides, although this had previously been hushed up. But the system of political discrimination and insinuation continued. The way in which punishment was meted out and accusations were made without any reason gave rise to further concealment and falsification within society. In fact, history was repeating itself.

After the North was liberated in 1954, thousands of children from families designated as national capitalists were singled out for maltreatment, because although their standard of living was not as high as capitalists in the West, they were regarded as 'bad elements', exploiters who had to be punished. It was really hard for these children. As people say, one can choose one's friends but not one's parents.

These 'capitalist' children were forced to go and work either in factories or in the countryside. It was difficult for them to get higher education, even though many of them wanted to do so and had the necessary ability. The educational process was weighted against them because those who got the best marks were not 'bad class elements'. They knew they had to wear this yoke without ever being able to lift their heads. Very few of them went abroad to study, they could not be trusted to work and usually they occupied menial positions. The fulfilment of these young people's potential was always postponed until tomorrow. A similar situation awaited young people in the South who were classified as children of puppets, so wasting a great deal of the nation's talents. This injustice carried out for the sake of extremist and pointless class struggle has brought hardship and misfortune to our youth as well as harm to the whole of society.

Take the case of the young Vietnamese pianist Dang Thai Son who won the Chopin International Competition in Warsaw in 1980. He was subjected to all kinds of brazen tricks. His mother and sister told me he was taught and encouraged from childhood by his parents, but because his father was the well-known musician Dang Dinh Hung who was associated with the *Nhan Van, Giai Pham* group, his son got nowhere until he was discovered and taken to Moscow by a Soviet professor. Then when the competition took place in Warsaw, Vietnamese officials provided no help at all and left Dang Thai Son, together with his Soviet tutor, to arrange everything on their own. But once the competition was won, things were very different. The embassy in Moscow called in the press, as did the Ministry of Culture in Hanoi and various official committees of artists, to announce shamelessly that Dang Thai Son's success was the result of our socialist system of education which, despite millions of tons of American bombs, had discovered and cultivated young talent so that it could flourish in the Soviet Union and win competitions in Warsaw etc.

Professor Ta Quang Buu, for many years Minister of Higher Education in Hanoi, was removed from his post because he protested against the method of using family background for assessing the work of students and whether they should go abroad for further studies. This system, he indicated, had led to a great loss of intellectual talent, and he was much admired by his staff as well as by students and young professors throughout the North. But the leadership always considered it had the right to decide and there was no need to listen to the ideas of anybody else!

The basic fact is that in 1975 the leadership became lax, intoxicated and dizzy with victory. Most of the top leaders were in their sixties and thought increasingly about their families, their children, their homes and property. That is easy to understand. They were human beings not saints. Few of them could resist the lure of materialism because they lacked the education which forms the basis of human dignity. Therefore, there was nothing to control them and they let themselves go. But this was the beginning of our real cultural crisis.

During the war, the morale of the people was good because they believed in the struggle and in ultimate victory. I recall that during the bombing raids carried out by the Americans, goods were unloaded beside the roads and railway stations. There was rice, tinned meat, sugar and milk but nobody touched it. People left their homes to evacuate to the countryside without bothering to lock the door. They just secured it with a piece of wire and it was not burgled. At night women used to cycle up to fifty kilometres through the darkness to fetch food for their children. They came to no harm. In the countryside, the peasants helped all the evacuated families to settle in. I think most people had a good and loving heart, particularly when the country was subject to foreign aggression. And, to put it bluntly, it was due to basic tradition. It had nothing to do with Marxism–Leninism, socialism or class struggle, as some people dare to say. They even claim that the system of criticism and self-criticism created such a situation.

But after April 1975 the situation changed rapidly. People became far more pragmatic and interested in profit and at the same time less trustworthy. Was this a case of the ideology of the South spreading to the North or just good relations? As the popular saying goes, 'The relations came south and the goods went north'. I entirely disagree.

There had always been special shops in Hanoi for the top leadership or *Nomenklatura* as it was known in the Soviet Union. In particular when food was in extremely short supply in the North and severely rationed, with many children suffering from malnutrition, there was a store on Ngo Quyen Street in Hanoi where the families of the Politburo and their cronies could always obtain top-quality fragrant rice. It was carefully grown without the use of fertilisers on 100 hectares of collectivised farmland near Hanoi specially reserved for the 'old men' of the Party, just as in former days certain fields were earmarked for royalty. There were other special shops in Hanoi too – in Hang Trong and Ton Dan Streets – providing clothing and international goods for the *Nomenklatura*. What is more, all these shops were managed by the younger sister of Le Duc Tho as part of his Party organisational network. It also involved one of his brothers, Dinh Duc Thien, who having managed the steel manufacturing complex at Thai Nguyen north of Hanoi with no professional qualifications, was transferred to the army with the rank of general in charge of supplies during the Ho Chi Minh campaign. After that he was appointed to head the department responsible for the oil and gas industry, of which again he had no knowledge. Meanwhile Le Duc Tho's youngest brother Mai Chi Tho had became Chairman of the Ho Chi Minh City People's Committee, also without any prior experience of administration.

By comparison, the system we took over in the South in 1975 was completely different. In the military field alone, we inherited a great quantity of aircraft, helicopters, warships, tanks, artillery pieces and just plain guns, and when logistics experts from Hanoi arrived at the base at Long Binh, for instance, just after our victory, they found so much equipment that they thought it would take fifteen to twenty years to cope with it all. The base was enormous with a network of watchtowers and roads neatly set out on a grid pattern and named after American states. But we had no idea how to manage it. We had no computers, only notebooks and pencils. Soon unit after unit, as well as the military from different regions, were coming to ask for equipment. So too were provincial and district authorities. There was no proper system of distribution. Much of the equipment – uniforms, mosquito nets, tents, water flasks etc. – was then sold on the market with the profits going into the pockets of corrupt individuals. A lot also disappeared to the North while heavy equipment, such as artillery and electronics, was damaged or deteriorated through lack of maintenance. So within a few months, Long Binh was a worthless shambles. To me that seemed totally irresponsible, betokening a peasant mentality. It also showed no respect for people who had sacrificed so much. On the contrary, it became apparent that all we knew how to do was to destroy as we had done during the war. We had no idea how to use things constructively and how to build. If only we had made good use of all that equipment instead of wasting it, maybe the situation would be different now.

I spent the years 1976 and 1977 in the South, where I was responsible for reporting on the situation for the army newspaper, *Quan Doi Nhan Dan*. I wrote not just about the re-education camps for former officers and officials of the Saigon regime. I also covered the suppression of 'dishonest traders', the reform of the bourgeoisie and the movement for the socialist transformation of agriculture. All these policies were carried out hastily on the basis of administrative orders rather than persuasion. As a result, the people became uneasy and the economic performance of the South failed to develop. That made me dispirited and at times very angry. I recall a profound remark by an American journalist. He said: 'You have won the war, but you cannot win the peace because you act like a conquering army!' It was not totally like that, but it is a matter worth considering.

The person appointed by the Politburo to supervise the 'socialist transformation' of trade and industry in the South was Do Muoi. He first made a name for himself towards the end of 1956 when, as Party Secretary in Haiphong, he was transferred to Hanoi to help with the anti-bourgeois campaign – also billed as the transformation of trade and industry. That was his big opportunity because he was classed as an artisan. From the age of about fourteen, he had travelled around mending and repainting doors. So if he were to be asked who exploited him, he would have difficulty answering. Nevertheless, because Vietnam had no big industry in the classic Marxist sense, Do Muoi was regarded as a worker with the correct criteria to become a member of the leading class, even though he has little education.

As soon as he arrived in the South after April 1975, Do Muoi set himself up as commander-in-chief with six aides to help him carry out his designated task. Then in Saigon alone, which was the most important and complex area, he formed eleven action groups, six of which were from the army under the command of Nam Tran.* The other five groups comprised Cong An cadres with Cao Dang Chiem, known as Sau Hoang, a Deputy Minister of the Interior in charge.

I first met Sau Hoang on April 30, 1975. To be fair I have to say he was the person officially designated by the Provisional Revolutionary Government of South Vietnam to enter Saigon and accept its surrender. But he was late and only reached the Presidential Palace at 3 p.m. when I introduced him to Big Minh and the rest of his cabinet who had surrendered several hours earlier. I well remember that Big Minh then drew me aside and asked whether Sau Hoang was Cao Dang Chiem, the man who had led the Viet Minh para-military forces in Saigon way back in 1945. I replied in the affirmative.

Soon afterwards Sau Hoang installed his office in what had been the former Saigon Police headquarters. I often talked with him there, particularly in early 1978 when the major campaign against capitalist traders was launched. He frequently told me stories about the 'kings' of the rice, fertilizer and metal trades. On the other hand I tried to point out, albeit in vain, the lack of leadership control in this campaign. A vast quantity of money, gold and jewels was simply disappearing, much of it going into the pockets of those conducting the campaign.

At the same time, over half a million people were forced to leave the country under what was known as Plan 2, so that the authorities could lay their hands on the property of these families. Their homes were then allocated to the 'new class' taking over. Nor were all those departing of Chinese origin, as was then claimed. Almost half were Vietnamese.

When the Ministry of the Interior gave the green light to

---

* Nam Tran (Tran Van Danh) was deputy head of the delegation led by General Tran Van Tra at Camp Davis in 1973. Originating from military intelligence, he later became Deputy Minister of Public Works and was put in charge of the construction of the Tri An hydro-electricity plant west of Saigon. This was another major project built with Soviet aid which turned out to be less than a success.

carry out Plan 2, the exodus of boat people was so organised
that they all had to contribute gold to the national treasury. Each
person leaving had to hand over from 3 to 5 taels of gold. But
in Bien Hoa province, the price was more than double that amount.
The province had also organised the interception of these people
at their point of departure, where they were stripped of any
further gold, silver, jewels or dollars they might be carrying and
dispossessed of their vehicles which they had intended to hand
over to relatives or friends. All this property was then distributed
between the gangs carrying out the searches and Muoi Van, the
former land reform commissar from the North, who had become
head of the Cong An in Bien Hoa and was later sentenced to
death for organising this network. But who knows how many
others took advantage of it and still remain unpunished?

And who was responsible for the death and suffering of tens
of thousands of boat people who had to endure thirst or attacks
by pirates? Who indeed, if not those Communists holding power
who let production decline, reducing the people's standard of
living to a pitiful level while corruption flourished and theft,
prostitution and gambling spread throughout the whole country!

They talked hypocritically of the old morality but allowed
themselves to live somewhat differently. At first the difference
was small but it gradually grew larger. There are no limits to
the time and scope of corruption. Party cadres could argue that
they no longer needed to fear prison, the death sentence or bombing.
They had sacrificed nearly their whole lives to the struggle, so
it was only right for them to enjoy a little comfort. They deserved
it. But how much?

Members of the Politburo closely observed the Party Secretary
General. Members of the Central Committee watched the Politburo
and so on down the pecking order. This kind of watching spread
rapidly almost like an epidemic. There was no need to organise
courses to teach anybody. The habit of giving presents became
automatic. A grand mandarin was given a small packet but it
contained dollars, gold and silver of great value. The small mandarin
got a large packet with goods of lesser value. The big shots were
driven around at first in small cars. The lesser ones acquired something more showy. It was the same with houses, and this sort
of thing became acceptable.

The overall impression made by the Vietnamese leadership

was that it was composed of professional revolutionaries dedicated to their aim. They were proud of their work. They had achieved victory and they lived simply, at ease with their surroundings following the example set by Chairman Ho Chi Minh. Those were their strong points. But they also had weaknesses leading to mistakes. During the tension of the war all decision-making was concentrated in the hands of a few men and they had become over-confident. They simply assumed that since the people had always supported them in opposing foreign aggression, they them-selves were immune to criticism. In fact they had never been challenged. The Party Central Committee had rarely met during the height of the war. Nor had the National Assembly, and for years afterwards it never debated anything seriously except whether or not to change the national anthem to something less bellicose. Even that posed a problem for Truong Chinh, the Chairman of the National Assembly. He in particular was Confucian, that is he belonged to a tradition whereby everybody kowtows and agrees. But overall our leaders were unaccustomed to handling diverse opinions. Above all, they could not tolerate economic and technical advice. Previously everything from sophisticated weaponry down to basic food supplies had been provided by either the Soviet Union or China. Now in the time of peace after 1975, the leadership failed to study matters clearly and scien-tifically.

For instance, Le Duan would not listen to experts about the construction of the Hoa Binh hydro-electric power station. He said it was a political decision and insisted that channels be tunnelled through rock to avoid nuclear attack. As a result, the project was wasteful and extremely expensive, taking over fifteen years to achieve any results. The same was true of the Thang Long bridge over the Red River near Hanoi. Le Duan wanted it to be the longest bridge in South East Asia, but it became a white elephant and hardly anybody used it.

Very few of Le Duan's initiatives in rebuilding the country were actually worthwhile. People still complain to this day about two of his policies in particular. One was the amalgamation of a large number of provinces and the other was the transformation of districts into strategic economic units. These ideas are referred to as 'the sudden whims of the Party General Secretary'. After 1975, he thought that by creating provinces of one or two million

people, they would become construction units. This idea was
not carefully discussed by the Politburo or the National Assembly
to weigh up the pros and cons. The former provinces of Ha
Dong, Son Tay and Hoa Binh were joined to form Ha Son
Binh, while Quang Binh, Quang Tri and Thua Thien in the
South were forged into Binh Tri Thien. There are various other
examples as well, and they were all very costly because the process
caused a long-term loss of unity.

Provincial Party Secretaries and their deputies, Chairmen of
the People's Committees and directors of various local offices
all squabbled with one another about who would take over what
position in the new provinces. The result was a great waste of
time and effort. It also created provinces covering hundreds of
square kilometres, like Binh Tri Thien, and were completely
unmanageable. So in the early 1990s most of these composite
provinces were dissolved and reverted to their original component
parts.

Many cadres still acknowledge that the worst disaster relating
to the amalgamation of the provinces and districts occurred in
1983 when Le Duan excitedly proposed raising the districts to
a strategic level in contrast to the previous system where they
had occupied the intermediate level between province and village.
According to Le Duan's idea, 400 districts would become full-blown
'units for the reconstruction of the economy', each comprising
thirty or forty different specialised agencies. As a result, a lot
of new staff were required and the cost of salaries kept escalating
without producing any obvious results.

This expansion progressed for nearly three years, but after Le
Duan died in 1986, nobody was interested in the districts any
more. Given the state of the economy at the time, trying to
achieve so much without resources and money was regarded as
wasteful and only created more difficulties. So personnel levels
at the district level were reduced, this organisational adventure
came to an end, and the country became poorer and continues
to do so – all because of the sudden whim of the top leader.
People still complain that after the 'old man' died, it required
a lot of time, money and effort to clean up the mess he left
behind him.

I once heard Le Van Hien, the former Finance Minister, try
to explain a new tax system which would allow private traders

to pay on a sensible basis. The idea was immediately rejected by Le Duan. 'No, that is impossible. We cannot operate like the capitalists. Comrades, please calm yourselves. Taxes in our country will be levied on the basis of the pre-eminent production of our state enterprises. They are the source of the abundant and dependable wealth of this socialist country of ours.' In reality, all these state enterprises had long been heavily in debt. They are still very backward.

Le Duan scarcely ever seemed to write anything down. He just said what he thought on the spur of the moment. He also stammered a lot and was difficult to listen to. That was what everybody felt. They all became weary trying to understand what he was saying because he also spoke ungrammatically. In his relations with cadres, Le Duan rarely had any sincere and intimate conversations, and he also showed little concern for other people. There were journalists who met him many times and interviewed him, but when he met them again he did not recognise them.

When Le Duan visited India in 1985, for instance, he only spoke to members of the Politburo and Central Committee who were part of the delegation. He paid no attention whatsoever to the photographers, film crew and journalists, or to the protocol and security officials who accompanied him. He never chatted with them. In this respect his attitude contrasted markedly with that of Ho Chi Minh and other top leaders. Every morning he would just breakfast with an assistant to discuss the day's programme. Then I would give him a summary of the overnight news and he would outline to his interpreter what he was going to say. Everybody who accompanied him had the impression that he had little regard for those people who worked for him.

Following our victory in 1975, our leaders had virtually no experience of democracy because they had never lived in such a society. If they had travelled abroad, it was mostly to Communist countries. They had escaped from a feudal and colonialist society to become revolutionaries, but their conduct clearly remained Confucian, given the way they deferred to one another to preserve harmony and discipline as was done within a traditional village or family hierarchy.

The office of the Party Central Committee is located in what was formerly the Albert Sarraut School on Ba Dinh Square. There the Politburo and the Party Secretariat have a large conference hall. But the members of the Politburo still all work in their own homes which are often quite far apart. Each home consists of a private villa which has been expanded to accommodate the family, offices, secretaries, chauffeurs and security guards. The office usually contains six to twelve people. There is a *chef de cabinet* and his deputy, an official secretary and a secretary in charge of appointments and activities, as well as those responsible for correspondence, the press, economics and foreign affairs. Then there is the personal photographer and majordomo who organises the domestic household, the cook and the servants.

Given the way in which Politburo members live and work in Hanoi, senior Party bureaucrats face many difficulties. If they want to consult the view of the Politburo, they have to visit thirteen or fourteen different homes, make numerous notes, circulate their ideas, and try to form some sort of consensus out of all the various opinions expressed. A member of the Central Committee Office once complained to me that nowhere in the world was there a ruling Party whose Politburo members worked with such lack of co-ordination. It was an old habit which had become senseless. They were used to working as guerrilla leaders and could not adapt, as some Party officials began to realise once they looked realistically at the situation in other socialist countries after 1975.

Consequently there was a move to try to ensure that all Politburo members had offices close to one another in the Quang Ba area on the bank of the West Lake in the suburbs of Hanoi where the Tortoise Conference Hall is situated. Its name derives from the roof which is shaped like a tortoise, and according to the office of the Central Committee, it is the meeting place of the Politburo. The surrounding area, particularly the housing complex reserved for Le Duan and his family, used to be a forbidden zone which was closely guarded, with the village's allocated to the Politburo members attracting special vigilance.

Le Duan also had a big house on Hoang Dieu Street which was often being enlarged. Then there was his three-storey house on Tran Quoc Toan Street in Hanoi where his first wife from Quang Tri province resided. His second wife Madame Nga, officially known as Bay Van and a member of the provincial committee of An Giang in the southern part of the Mekong delta, owns the largest house in the district capital. But after 1975 she moved to Ho Chi Minh City where she was allocated a spacious villa by virtue of her position as deputy editor of the newspaper *Saigon Giai Phong*, which she occupies only nominally since she has no journalistic training.*

In 1975, the Party committee responsible for its financing and administration collected a lot of data about public buildings and villas in the South. The most luxurious of the villas in Ho Chi Minh City, Dalat, Vung Tau and Nha Trang were allocated to the members of the Politburo and their families. But these houses belonging to 'Brothers Three, Five and Six' were usually locked up and silent except for the cleaners and guards since the owners only lived there for a few days each year. However when they did want to go on holiday, even for a weekend at the northern seaside resort of Do Son, they would happily commandeer a helicopter or a plane to fly them there, particularly after our victory. General Dao Dinh Luyen, who headed the Air Force at that time, once told me how onerous this task was because every time one of the senior leaders flew anywhere, he would insist on being accompanied personally by an officer from the Air Command Staff.

There was another form of privilege which became common, stemming again from Confucian custom whereby gifts are conveyed upwards in the hope that power and prestige will subsequently

---

* The issue of multiple wives was raised at the Third Party Congress back in 1961 when some delegates who had regrouped from the South and wished to get married in the North were forbidden to do so on the grounds that it was unclear whether the wives they had left behind were alive or dead. If they disregarded this ban, they risked severe punishment and even being expelled from the Party, because Party discipline prohibited bigamy and adultery. However, by that time both Le Duan and Le Duc Tho had secretly acquired two wives, one in the North and the other in the South. Here Ho Chi Minh himself had to intervene. He ruled that in the case of these two gentlemen, both marriages were legitimate because they had been contracted before the Party enacted a Marriage and Family Law which would in future be strictly enforced. That left many delegates wondering about double standards and whether there was one law for the upper echelons and another for the lower. Indeed while Le Duan continued to maintain one wife in Saigon and the other in Hanoi, Le Duc Tho was even bolder. There was a time when both his wives lived under the same roof at his home on Nguyen Canh Chan Road in Hanoi and ate at the same table in a spirit of North-South harmony. This was truly a masterpiece of Party organisation!

flow downwards. Hence when the Party General Secretary and his entourage, numbering over thirty people, established the habit of visiting the mountain resort of Dalat during the hot summer months, a ritual came into being. On their departure, the provincial committee of Lam Dong usually presented each of them with a rather large package containing Bao Loc tea, coffee from Ban Me Thuot, medicinal liquor and herbal balm. The ladies, the sons and daughters, and even the grandchildren of only three and four years old also all received packages. What is more, while in Dalat the sons of the 'revolutionary mandarin' and his daughters, commonly referred to as the princes and princesses, no sooner had to say the word that they would like to taste some wild game than the provincial committee would send out a team to hunt day and night through jungle and stream to bring back a deer.

Special personal privileges became very evident. To the north of Ho Chi Minh City, the Tan Uyen area in Song Be province has a lot of rubber plantations intermixed with cashew trees. This became a hunting ground favoured by officials from the Ho Chi Minh City administration. Whenever guests from the Central Committee travelled south, the whole area started to bustle. The director of the rubber plantations had to mobilise two to four production brigades to abandon their work in order to drive wild game into a 'trap' for the 'old men' to shoot. The high-ranking officials sat in small huts providing shelter from the sun and raised their guns between sips of expensive liquor and puffs of fragrant cigarette smoke to kill wild boar, sambar deer, civet cats and monitor lizards. Around these shelters are natural streams crossed by plank bridges which can be raised to protect the security of the 'marksmen' once their guns fall silent. It is a very aristocratic way of hunting. One can imagine how the workers in the production brigades felt when they lost their earnings in order to serve those who style themselves 'servants of the people' and act in this way among their poverty-stricken comrades and compatriots.

The Vietnamese leadership still continues to maintain that under the doctrine of collective mastery, it is the people who are the masters while Party cadres are simply their servants. This jargon has long sickened those who realise how different the situation actually is, although they are not free to say so. Instead since the leadership belittles public opinion, the people, having no shame, respond in a popular verse which says mockingly:

> *The servant travels in a Volga,*
> *The families of the masters wait at the station for a train.*
> *The servant has a nice villa,*
> *The families of the masters use oil paper to keep out rain.*
> *The servant attends banquets, noon and night,*
> *The families of the masters eat greens and pickles every day.*

The higher the rank of the cadre, the more privileges, both conspicuous and discreet, he enjoys. They include housing and transport as well as food and drink, plus priority medical treatment at hospitals such as the one equipped in Hanoi by the Soviet Union where the most modern techniques and drugs are available. What is more, these privileges extend to wives, children, grand-children and in-laws of the *nomenklatura*. All these people benefit from the policy of 'making allowances'. Then there are the gifts, presents and appropriate rewards like travelling abroad on duty or even within the country itself.

When Truong Chinh became Chairman of the National Assembly and toured various provinces in the South after 1975, I sometimes accompanied him. No longer was he 'Brother Cautious' who had cycled around during the Resistance to visit his network of contacts and eaten boiled sweet potatoes washed down with green tea like everybody else. Now he travelled in a motorcade of Volgas to be greeted everywhere by official reception committees, speeches and banquets. True, his health did not permit him to be as adventurous as before. But his pronoun-cements became progressively more formalistic and rigid.

Then, when I was working on Truong Chinh's biography, there was an incident which I shall never forget. He had gone to spend three weeks' holiday in Dalat with his family and invited me to join him there. He was living in Villa No. 1, which had previously been a residence of the Emperor Bao Dai and his family. One day after he had finished recounting his memoirs and while we were waiting for dinner, Truong Chinh asked me to come to his bedroom. There he pointed out the bed with sheets of gold brocade embroidered with dragons and phoenix. The pillows were the same. Speaking softly as if he wanted to awe and impress me, Truong Chinh invited me to take a close look and asked whether I was aware that the bed and the bedclothes

had belonged to Emperor Bao Dai and Empress Nam Phuong.
I looked and also saw Truong Chinh's wife sitting there as if
she were on the throne.

I was half amused and half surprised to the point of amazement.
I had discovered a diehard Communist leader who had been
determined to get rid of the royal family. Yet here he was now
being so proud and emotional about sleeping in a room where
he could use sheets and pillows embroidered with the symbols
of royalty!

By contrast, I am acquainted with Mrs Trinh Van Bo who
lives in Nguyen Gia Thieu Street in Hanoi. She was a property
owner who felt very 'patriotic' back in 1945 when she contributed
over 3,000 taels to the 'gold week' proclaimed by the Revolution.
She also loaned many houses to the state on condition that they
would ultimately be returned to her family. In fact it was at
one of her houses, No. 46 Hang Ngang Street, that President
Ho Chi Minh sat and wrote the Declaration of Independence,
so it has now become a national museum. Naturally since then
her family has grown with the birth of children and grandchildren,
so now Mrs Bo feels really cramped and in need of space. She
has requested the return of one of her houses and has gone to
great lengths but without any success. Recently she made an
appeal to the head of the State Council, but received no more
than a formal acknowledgment. Yet from the story she tells, Mrs
Trinh Van Bo was in effect the Minister of Finance back in
1945 at the time of the provisional revolutionary government
and played a major role. But nobody has ever thanked her for
her contribution. Such ingratitude, drawn out over such a long
period, while people in positions of authority talk about virtue
and justice, is really beyond belief.

I also knew a president of the law tribunal in Hanoi. He
too was not a Party member but was highly regarded in legal
circles as conversant with the law and with being impartial. He
graduated in the old days and once worked with my father in
Hue. When he was nearly eighty years old, he told me 'Your
father taught me and so many other people in the legal profession
to be honest. But recently when I have judged cases, I have
had to contend with many letters from the top leadership. These
letters bear the heading "Office of Brother Number Three" or
of the other brothers, Sau Tho [Le Duc Tho], Anh To [Pham

Van Dong], Anh Nam [Truong Chinh], Muoi Cuc [Nguyen Van Linh] and Sau Dan [Vo Van Kiet] and the rest. There is no stamp, just a signature. We have had to comply with the orders of the *chef de cabinet* or the secretary of these men. These letters are always considered to have so much more value and to be more effective than official state correspondence.'

Demands for housing, salary increases, promotions, children to go abroad to study, all these matters were resolved through such unofficial and inappropriate channels. The country lacks a legal system. The Ministry of Justice was set up only recently and there is still no Law University. There is just a course in legal studies. But clearly a state has to be built on the basis of law.

In the old days, the Party was clean and the people had a high sense of self-respect. But when greediness ran riot and the whole system became rotten from top to bottom, morality became non-existent and there were no laws to exercise restraint. Since 1945, legal experts like Phan Anh, Tran Cong Tuong and later Nguyen Huu Tho have stressed that the development of a legal system is very urgent. But these ideas have been ignored, since the Party has been regarded as all-important, 'the necessary and appropriate prerequisite' for constructing the administration. But this concept of Party rule has been a source of chaos and social degeneration.

6

ADVENTURISM

When he was recounting his memoirs, Le Duan became very passionate about the period from 1977 onwards. He said, 'These Chinese hegemonists and expansionists have always been our enemies. I have known that ever since Nixon went to Peking in 1971. After our victory in 1975 I said that we had to be on our guard and watch out. The Chinese have long been our enemies and will remain so for hundreds of years to come.'

As a result of such attitudes, about half a million people of Chinese origin, many of whose families had lived in Vietnam for generations, were forced to leave the country in a campaign carried out by the Cong An on the orders of the Ministry of the Interior. They were not just the businessmen and craftsmen, the 'comprador capitalists' from Cholon, the Chinese quarter of Saigon, whose economic influence had to be curbed for ideological reasons. They were also coal-miners from Quang Ninh in the North as well as 100,000 fishermen from the Gulf of Tonkin and the famous pottery workers in Mong Cay, all of them of Chinese origin. In other words this campaign was motivated by xenophobia rather than anything else, a mistake admitted in a secret Politburo circular issued in 1982. Even Party members of Chinese origin were expelled. So too were Vietnamese with Chinese wives. This was extremism of a rightist variety which had turned leftwards.

When this campaign was launched in 1978, the security forces were startled. It was realised that the Cong An was spread very thin, so a decision was taken to increase its strength. The security force in each urban ward was increased from six or seven men to forty or more, and now every ward has somebody with the rank of captain in charge of security.

That gave rise to the joke about the foreigner who visited Vietnam and asked why the Cong An always went around in groups of three. The reply was that one could read, another could write and the third was there to control these two intellectuals. And it is true that many of the people who joined the Cong An were poorly educated. Some of them, from peasant families, considered it an honour to be chosen to serve the Party in this way. Others like Le Trung, the son of Le Duan, who neglected his studies, found service in the Cong An a convenient way of avoiding military duty on the battlefield. But there were also some Cong An cadres who were very intelligent and clever, like Hai Tan from the Mekong Delta region who was honoured as a hero because he foiled a plot to infiltrate arms from abroad with Chinese support. During 1981 and 1982 nearly 700 guns were captured and more than eighty people were arrested, many of whom were placed on trial. The security forces had good co-ordination with the Lao authorities too in capturing several armed groups which crossed the Mekong from Thailand with the aim of infiltrating Vietnam.

However, I have to mention that there were times when because of their arrogance our security forces blundered badly, as in the case of Vo Dai Ton which I followed closely. He was a colonel in the Saigon army who fled to Australia in 1975 and tried to return home six years later to overthrow the government. But he and his whole group were intercepted in southern Laos and taken to a secure location near Hanoi, where he was interrogated and ended up making a confession a hundred pages long detailing his organisational support in Australia, the United States and Thailand. His confession culminated by stating that thanks to re-education, he now appreciated his guilt and wished to learn more in order to serve Ho Chi Minh better. This statement delighted the security forces and because they were anxious to make the most of it, the Minister of the Interior Pham Hung was informed and he agreed to meet Vo Dai Ton. This interview went so well that arrangements were made for Ton to visit Ho Chi Minh's mausoleum and then speak to both the domestic and international press. Some officials questioned Pham Hung's judgement but he brushed all fears aside. He was confident that Vo Dai Ton would perform as required. Indeed when I was taken to talk to him at the 'safe house' where he was staying outside Hanoi, he seemed genuinely contrite about his past and grateful for all the care he was now receiving. At the formal meeting organised with Vietnamese journalists at the end of June 1982, he expressed the same sentiments and everything went exactly as planned. The security officials involved were so delighted that afterwards they treated Ton to a first-class meal including Hanoi beer.

Then the foreign press corps in Bangkok, as well as those few journalists who happened to be in Vietnam already, were invited to a press conference on July 9, 1982 at the International Club on Hung Vuong Street within a kilometre of Ho Chi Minh's mausoleum. Here Vo Dai Ton, dressed in a smart new beige suit, began his speech exactly as rehearsed beforehand until he suddenly announced that his organisation intended to liberate his compatriots from a cruel Communist regime. He was immediately hustled out of the room to be confronted by a furious Duong Thong, head of the Counter-Espionage Branch. At that Ton simply smiled and said that the Vietnamese authorities did not understand the mentality of foreigners. They would not believe him if he did not first condemn Communism in order to prove how much he had now benefited from re-education. After some discussion the press conference was allowed to resume, but when an American correspondent asked a question, Vo Dai Ton seized the microphone and shouted 'Our mission is a struggle to overthrow a dictatorial regime. We believe in victory.' That was the end of the proceedings although some of the foreigners present did not grasp the significance of what had happened. Vo Dai Ton had tried to use the occasion to denounce our Communist regime. Straight away he was stripped of the clothes he was wearing and on the order of Duong Thong, taken to a prison in Ha Dong, where he was severely punished.*
He had fooled everybody from the Minister of the Interior downwards. They knew this was the case, but nobody was prepared to admit any mistakes or draw any lessons from experience.

In Hanoi, if one takes a walk around Yet Kieu, Tran Binh Trong, Tran Hung Dao, Nguyen Du and Nguyen Thuong Hien

---

* Vo Dai Ton was eventually released on condition that he would say nothing about his detention, and he was allowed to return to Australia in late 1991 in the hope that this would improve relations between Hanoi and Canberra. However, he has subsequently travelled around the world talking and writing a book about his experiences in Vietnam.

Streets, one will see that the security forces are spread wide, occupying a lot of very good and even splendid property. These offices are well-equipped with high-class technology. Then there are conference halls and guest houses. Indeed for many years the tallest building in Hanoi was the six-storey Ministry of the Interior on Yet Kieu Street, where the office of the Minister on the second floor is far more magnificent than any other in the country. It was built in 1973 with Soviet aid on land originally belonging to the School of Fine Arts. The latter has a tradition stretching back to the beginning of the century, but it continues to be housed nearby in a squalid building near to collapse, where the professors and students are cramped and uncomfortable.

The state of our security forces owes a lot to the East German Stasi and the Soviet KGB. These two organisations, more than any others, trained our cadres in various specialised subjects, and exchanged experience about methods of detection and investigation as well as the techniques of counter-espionage. So the Cong An has numerous sections dealing with politics, economics, culture and foreigners. As such, it became just as over-manned as the armed forces.

After 1975, there were plans to demobilise a large part of the army, but instead many units were sent to carry out economic work in the areas which needed to be developed, especially the Central Highlands. Then the disagreement erupted with the Overseas Chinese followed by the conflict with Cambodia, all of which led to an increase in the size of the army.

This decision was unreasonable and taken without any proper consideration. It played into the hands of the enemy who were trying to reduce the strength of Vietnam to a low ebb through having to carry a heavy military burden and a large defence budget for a very long time. It was even more ironical that the concept of 'All People's Defence and All People's Security' was developed and repeated to the point of becoming trite and boring; given the realities of society it could not be applied.

In 1978, it was not just the Chinese towards whom we were arrogant. We had almost established diplomatic relations with the United States when Phan Hien, the Deputy Minister of Foreign Affairs, demanded the $3 billion in war reparations which had been promised by the Americans at the time of the Paris Agreements. How stupid! Neither side had respected these agreements. The

North sent big units to the South, so how could we expect the South to abide by the agreements? Thus there was no justification for demanding reparations at this juncture. Nor was there any apparent appreciation in Hanoi at that time of the relationship between the American President and Congress. So this issue simply created more difficulties in the way of normalising relations between Washington and Hanoi.

On top of all that, there was the Cambodian problem. Even to this day, few people are aware of why we had to take military action against Cambodia. Having remained in the South, I knew that immediately after our victory in 1975, clashes broke out along the border between Vietnam and Cambodia. This fighting became progressively more severe, especially following a massacre which occurred in Chau Doc on the night of April 30, 1977, the second anniversary of our victory.

From then onwards, the Khmer Rouge became more reckless and bloodthirsty along the border with the provinces of Minh Hai, An Giang, Long An and Tay Ninh. In September that same year, I saw with my own eyes Vietnamese victims of the Khmer Rouge with their skulls smashed, their eyes gouged out, their stomachs slit open and their genitals ripped off. For a whole week that horrific sight obsessed me so much that I did not dare look at a piece of meat, let alone eat it.

For us it was very difficult to hit back. In February 1978 I took part in a meeting of high-ranking cadres convened by the Ministry of Defence at the military base within the Tan Son Nhut compound about how to respond to these Khmer Rouge attacks. At that time we were not permitted to cross into Cambodian territory, but later we could carry out hot pursuit for up to 10 kilometres as long as we returned the same day.

The Khmer Rouge troops were good at enduring all weather. For food, they simply had a parcel of rice wrapped in leaves. They waded through the marshy terrain along parts of the border, which they knew well, and where they carried out guerrilla warfare, appearing and disappearing suddenly. In addition, their feelings of hostility towards us had long been built up. As a result, Vietnamese losses were quite high and there were many months when we suffered many more deaths and injuries than during the war against the Americans and the Saigon army.

To investigate how this situation came about, I was able during

1978 to visit camps set up in Ben San district of Tay Ninh province for refugees who had fled from Cambodia. There I talked to more than a hundred people including Buddhist priests, journalists, schoolteachers, doctors, workers and some peasants. After that I wrote a long article about what had happened in Cambodia since the Khmer Rouge seized power in Phnom Penh on April 17, 1975. For the first time, too, I used the word 'genocide'.

I sent this article to *Nhan Dan* in May 1978, but the paper's editorial board hesitated to publish it because Pol Pot was still regarded as head of a 'fraternal Communist party'. I had to go to Hanoi personally with four notebooks that I had filled with my interviews with Cambodian refugees to explain what they had told me. There were stories of barbarous mass killings and of people slain with hoes, then buried collectively. Other stories told of strange mass weddings and a country with no towns, no markets, no schools, no hospitals, no money and no colours. All clothing was black which quickly faded to grey. But there were blood, tears and despair in plenty.

Finally in August 1978, my article was published together with some photos I had taken. Then towards the end of the year, a decision was reached to launch a major military offensive, almost as big as that in 1975. Its aim was to strike direct at Phnom Penh and liberate the whole of Cambodia in co-ordination with some Khmer Rouge units which had recently defected and been re-organised. This decision was taken very secretly in order to create the maximum surprise.

The offensive was launched on Christmas Day, December 25, 1978, under the leadership of General Le Trong Tan, Chief of the General Staff, and General Le Duc Anh, commander of Military Region 9 on our southern border with Cambodia. At first we met with quite strong opposition in places like Svai Rieng, Kampot, Kratie and Prey Veng. But after we had advanced about twenty kilometres, it seemed as if there was no more resistance. Most of the Khmer Rouge had fled westwards. So on January 7, after only twelve days of fighting, we succeeded in capturing Phnom Penh.

I accompanied the southern prong of the Vietnamese attack which swept through Ta Keo province towards the capital and on the night of January 6, I had one of the most hair-raising experiences of my whole career, one which I shall never forget.

Five of us, all military correspondents, were travelling in a Soviet military jeep driven by 1st Lt. Quy. In addition there were Captain Xue, the photographer of the army newspaper, two radio propaganda officials from the Army General Political Department, and myself. Our press vehicle set off on the evening of January 6 at the end of a military convoy comprising two divisions. They were the 4th and the 8th from Military Region 9. In all there were about 400 vehicles in the convoy. They comprised army trucks, artillery vehicles, armoured cars and tanks as well as jeeps carrying the command staff, signals equipment and the engineers. Then there were the ambulances.

Our vehicle pressed forward, and near midnight we reached the head of the 4th Division's convoy, while the 8th Division had moved on even further. I therefore decided to make a break for it and try to catch up with the 8th Division, but during this operation all headlights had to be switched off. The Khmer Rouge were well known for conducting ambushes in tricky mountainous terrain. So we travelled carefully for about ten kilometres through the darkness until suddenly Captain Xue whispered in my ear 'Dear commander, if we keep moving in this way, it will be dangerous.' I kept quiet. We had only two AK47s and three pistols between all five of us and our vehicle was still moving forward. Then I felt something let go inside me. I thought about my responsibilities towards my comrades. Bravery is a necessity but we should not be excessively adventurous. So I instructed the driver, 'Stop here, Quy, we had better wait for the 4th Division.'

About twenty minutes later the 4th Division caught up with us, and its leading tank passed on its way. We followed. Less than ten minutes afterwards, there was a loud explosion which shattered the air around us. Later we discovered that immediately ahead of us was a crossroads where the Khmer Rouge had stationed a brand-new Chinese tank with its 75mm. cannon trained in our direction. It fired at us, killing one soldier and wounding another two, whereupon the rest of our troops jumped out and opened fire.

At that the black-uniformed Khmer Rouge fled and we were able to take over the Chinese tank to replace the one we had lost to continue the operation, while the body of our dead comrade was collected by an ambulance, swathed in a white shroud and taken away for burial.

The Khmer Rogue were very daring and brave when fighting face to face with the Vietnamese, but when their defence network was massively penetrated and shattered they lost heart and just fled in total disarray as if they could no longer organise any resistance. As for the five of us, we felt as if we had returned from the dead. If we had kept on moving ahead, we would certainly all have been killed and become heroes. Therefore every year on January 7, we met at my house to commemorate our memorable escape.

We reached Pochentong airport just before dawn on January 7 and the royal palace in the centre of Phnom Penh by mid-day. Then that evening we got into the Chinese embassy, the biggest and most imposing building in the capital. All the Chinese diplomats had withdrawn to Thailand on the evening of January 5 together with those of North Korea, Romania and Yugoslavia. Only the staff of the Lao embassy in Phnom Penh had remained. They had received orders from Vientiane to stay put and I met them on the morning of January 8. The Lao ambassador Vinachit, an elderly man who could speak Vietnamese, told me that he and his four staff members had just come through a nightmare. They had been scared stiff that at any moment the Khmer Rouge would burst in and kill them during the panic of the withdrawal from Phnom Penh. Therefore they hid under a bed until the Vietnamese arrived.

As for the Cambodian people, they were at a very low ebb. Those remaining in Phnom Penh were weak and ill. There was no end to the welcome they gave the Vietnamese forces. Then for the next few months, hundreds of thousands of gaunt and diseased people, dazed as if they were returning from hell, wandered shoeless along dusty roads, regardless of blistering sun or driving rain, trying to get back to their homes. So many families had been separated and forced to go to different parts of the country.

At first when we went through Svay Rieng and Ta Keo provinces, the towns were completely empty, just like Phnom Penh. Grass was growing everywhere. Houses had no numbers, streets had no names. There were no markets, no money, no goods for the people, no paper and no identification cards. One cannot imagine a country without schools or hospitals. The people were reduced to a state where they did not speak or smile any more. We met Doctor Ich Kim Seng who had studied in France and

was at one time Cambodia's Minister of Health. He had walked
barefoot from Ta Keo. His skin was so wrinkled that although
he was a little under sixty years old, he looked like an old man
of eighty. Under the Khmer Rouge he had been forced to tend
buffalo so that their soldiers could sometimes eat meat.

Then we found the mass graves, fields filled with the bones
and skulls of people who had been beaten to death. The sight
of them haunted me for endless days and nights. And all of these
ghastly sights stemmed from the policy of constructing 'an extremely
clean, fair and pure Communist society'. I was absolutely amazed
to read, thanks to some Cambodian friends, various editions of
the Khmer Rouge theoretical journal *Red Flag* produced during
1977 and 1978. It enabled me to understand the high-handed
and brutal way that theory had been applied to the detriment
of ability and so degenerated to the point of mental illness.

I was assigned to help in the formation of SPK, the Cambodian
national news agency, as well as the country's military newspaper
and then the journal entitled *Kampuchea* published weekly. I also
helped *Pracheachon*, a newspaper originally established back in the
1960s, to re-appear and become the organ of the People's Revolutionary Party of Cambodia.

Together with some of the Cambodians responsible for the
press, I also organised the reception of several delegations of foreign
journalists visiting Cambodia in early 1979. They were taken
from Pochentong airport to Phnom Penh on a large bus with
loudspeakers which had been repaired by Vietnamese soldiers.
We then took them down the Mekong to see a Khmer Rouge
collective kitchen and flew them to Siem Reap to visit the famous
Khmer temples of Angkor Wat and Angkor Thom.

Among these journalists was Takano, a correspondent for the
Japanese communist newspaper *Akahata*. He spoke Vietnamese
very well, having graduated from the University of Hanoi. But
he was to die soon afterwards when he returned to Vietnam
and was shot in Lang Son by the Chinese during their invasion
across our northern border in February 1979.

I stayed in Cambodia for almost three years, returning to Ho
Chi Minh City and Hanoi only occasionally. During that period
I collected quite a lot of documents. Some of them came from
the Chinese embassy in Phnom Penh. One was the text of an
agreement signed on July 17, 1976 for Chinese troops to come

and build the biggest airport in the whole of South East Asia at Kompong Chnang in Cambodia. Then there were congratulations from Mao Tse-tung to Pol Pot welcoming his historic (and bloody) feat in completely eliminating capitalists, exploitative landlords and reactionary lackeys in such a short time. But that was a revolution achieved through staves and mallets shattering a million skulls for the sake of socialism and a pure form of Communism and Marxism-Leninism in order to achieve international proletarianism!

From the Khmer Rouge documents that I found, it was possible to study their genocidal policy. In reality it was much more cruel and lethal than that carried out by the Nazis during the Second World War. But it was beautifully cloaked under the form of Communism, pure Communism, the purest form of Communism, with a regime that was absolute because it was led by a Communist party that was clear-sighted, in fact so clear-sighted that it was a model for all other Communist parties throughout the world, so it was claimed.

Khmer Rouge rhetoric actually created quite an impression because it kept on repeating adjectives. But in reality it was carrying out a Cultural Revolution along Chinese lines which was even more thorough and widespread and offered no compromise. The Cambodian leadership were absolutely self-confident that they could look after 'their own house' when the rest of the world shut the door on it.

Consequently I approved of our policy of attacking and liberating Cambodia. We had a right to defend our country against Khmer Rouge atrocities. At the same time, it was an emergency operation to rescue a whole people who were being reduced to misery and gradually killed off. Senator McGovern of the United States had previously called for military action to save the Cambodian people from being massacred but nobody responded. Then when the Vietnamese moved in, maintaining strict discipline, enduring hardship, bringing with them rice, salt, meat and vegetables, stationing troops out in the jungle, sharing food, clothes and medicine with the people of a neighbouring country, we received a lot of gratitude and respect. Clearly it was a very magnanimous action.

This feeling would have lasted much longer if we had not subsequently committed many mistakes. One was that we remained in Cambodia far too long. I believe we should have withdrawn much sooner and unconditionally. After the liberation of Cambodia, the disease of subjective arrogance took over again. Within the Party, it was explained that we were carrying out our international proletarian duty in strengthening the Revolution and expanding it to other countries. But among the people it was regarded as the equivalent of inviting oneself into a house belonging to some-body else.

The person primarily responsible for our policy towards Cam-bodia was Le Duc Tho. He had been assigned by the Politburo to oversee its liberation and the construction of its new Party and state apparatus. Even before our forces reached Phnom Penh, he presided over a meeting held near Snoul in what is known as the Fish Hook area of the border to set up a Cambodian government to replace that headed by Pol Pot. Among those he chose was Pen Sovan, who became Minister of Defence and later emerged as General Secretary of the Cambodian Communist Party. His appointment came as little surprise to many Cambodians because for several decades he had been a broadcaster with the Voice of Vietnam as head of its Khmer language service. Then there was Chan Si who was also a member of the Vietnamese Communist Party and had been responsible for an electricity sub-station in Vinh Phu province. Yet he eventually rose to become Prime Minister in Phnom Penh before his sudden death in 1983. As for Bou Thuong, who became Cambodian Deputy Prime Minister with the rank of general, before 1979 he was a captain serving in a remote district in the Central Highlands. Le Duc Tho even chose a twenty-six-year-old female medical assistant from Tra Vinh in the Mekong delta region to become a member of the Cambodian Party Secretariat with responsibility for educa-tion. She far outranked Vandy Ca-On who had a doctorate from the Sorbonne and was in charge of science teaching.

Le Duc Tho usually lived in a villa behind Chamcar Mon, the royal palace on the bank of the Mekong in Phnom Penh, and often convened meetings of key cadres including the Cam-bodian Party General Secretary, the Prime Minister and his cabinet. I once saw him talk to a group of Cambodian cadres at the palace during 1981 and again in Thu Duc at the beginning of 1982. Had I not been personally present, I would never have believed such scenes were possible. They all quivered with fear when Le Duc Tho scolded them very outspokenly as if they were naughty children. I just sat and listened to this speech, hoping that the interpreter was mistranslating and softening its meaning, otherwise it would have been appalling for the audience.

'You comrades must study assiduously. You must work seriously. You have to polish up your morals as Communist officials in order to be worthy of the faith placed in us and the Revolution. You have to understand that cadres must be carefully chosen and anybody who shows weakness will be replaced. As for alcohol, you can drink but not too much. And for any comrade to allow his wife to lead him by the nose to go trading is impermissible.'

The removal of Pen Sovan from his positions as Party General Secretary and Minister of Defence in 1981 was also the work of Le Duc Tho acting together with General Le Duc Anh. On their recommendation, the Politburo in Hanoi accepted an 'appeal' from several members of the Cambodian Communist Party. The Cambodian people had nothing to do with the rise and fall of Pen Sovan. So what was his mistake? According to a Vietnamese adviser in charge of training Cambodian cadres, Pen Sovan sometimes opposed Vietnam and sometimes his own Party. He also expressed dissatisfaction with his lack of power as Party General Secretary and the way his military authority was ignored by General Le Duc Anh. Such an attitude was intolerable in the eyes of our leadership, so Pen Sovan was taken back to Vietnam to spend the next ten years under house arrest near Hanoi. He was only released and allowed to return to Cambodia after the Vietnamese forces withdrew and the United Nations took over responsibility for the country.

Another of our mistakes was to consider the Khmer Rouge as crippled – remnants which would soon be eliminated completely. We ignored the fact that they were likely to receive sympathy and support from the Thais and Chinese. We also totally ignored the role of Prince Sihanouk. Nobody thought it worthwhile to reply to the letters he sent to Pham Van Dong in Hanoi, although they had previously been good friends. So the Vietnamese army got bogged down and stuck. Narrow-minded nationalism and xenophobia caused resentment as well as many difficulties for us.

Together with several other Vietnamese and Cambodian journalists, I visited the battlefields in the provinces of Battambang and Siem Reap in western Cambodia as well as spending some time living with Vietnamese 'volunteers' along the border with Thailand. They even had to decant drops of stagnant water from banana leaves or from the barrels of their rifles into aluminium plates in order to drink, wipe their faces or cook their rice. They suffered a lot and we should not have sacrificed 52,000 dead plus over 200,000 wounded, many of whom lost arms and legs due to mines.

I interviewed some of these amputees and on one occasion travelled back to Ho Chi Minh City with them on a Soviet Antonov 24 aircraft. For ten long years, this plane made two flights a week to Phnom Penh to pick up between ten and thirty Vietnamese war wounded each time. It was really heart-rending.

While we were waiting for the plane at Pochentong airport, I talked to some of the wounded. Most of them had lost one or both legs as a result of mines made in China which had been placed along the border with Thailand. But only rarely were they Party members or the sons of officials as in previous conflicts. They were mostly the children of peasant families from the South or ordinary townspeople, the small fry of society who had been forced into military service.

That discovery left me astounded and harassed by doubts. It turned out that the burden of this war was being borne by a section of society beyond the fringes of power. Our system of military conscription was just as it had been in old feudal times. In Cambodia this 'noble international duty', as it was called, was not for the children of the mandarins, whether high or low. Instead, like the children of Le Duan, they went abroad to study or work irrespective of qualifications in order to send back money and goods for the family. And at home it was also the sons of the political 'élite' who got the easy jobs and the perks. In their eyes, they had the 'courtesy to concede the glory of war' to others. What they were really doing was to make the little people in society bear all the hardship and suffering while Party members looked after their own interests. This sort of social injustice became very widespread.

I would really like to see the National Assembly convene a session on the war in Cambodia and openly discuss who was personally and collectively responsible for its consequences. Why was it so long-drawn-out? The people and the Assembly have never been told why Vietnam became stuck in this international mire and above all why the country wasted so much blood, money, time and resources in Cambodia. The consequences have been enormous and the debt has to be liquidated.

From 1982 onwards, in my discussions with Ngo Dien, the Vietnamese ambassador to Cambodia and an old friend, as well as General Le Hai, the officer responsible for political work among the Vietnamese 'volunteer' army, I expressed the view that this was a very uneasy situation. I said, 'Our soldiers are bogged down. We must withdraw quickly without any reservations or lingering regrets. Otherwise the situation will have an even worse effect on our country. We should leave it to the United Nations and the international community to find a solution to the Cambodian problem. Judging by their many appeals, they are prepared to accept responsibility for negotiating between the various factions in Cambodia. What is more, Vietnam would be able to participate in this process together with other countries.'

I also pointed out that Vietnam did not have sufficient strength or a good enough reason for maintaining such a large army in a neighbouring country when the question of the complete elimination of the Khmer Rouge was out of its reach. For ten years in succession during the United Nations annual debate on the Cambodian issue, Vietnam remained very much in the minority, receiving only twenty or thirty supporting votes, but still carried on regardless.

Ironically Le Duc Tho also became critical of the decision to allow our troops in Cambodia to get bogged down. In a speech he gave to a limited audience at the Army History Institute at the provincial Party headquarters in Dalat, he described the supporting structure of the expeditionary force as a sick and skinny cow that could not produce milk. Then he went on to say that the Vietnamese army had three achievements it could boast of.

---

* In this speech, Le Duc Tho also criticised certain aspects of the Tet Offensive and the 1975 campaign but when some of the cadres present took notes and circulated them, they were summoned to Army Intelligence for interrogation and detained on the charge of distributing 'enemy intelligence'. One of them was Colonel Ngoc Bang who was responsible for history in Military Region 7. Eventually he was able to prove that it was the ideas of Le Duc Tho he had circulated and then only to a meeting of the Cong An in Ho Chi Minh City. As a result he was allowed to return home but with no apology or explanation of why he had been expelled from the Party and forced into retirement.

These were the best heroics, the most hardship and the most indiscipline.*

A very serious incident took place in western Cambodia – in April 1984, if I remember correctly. The province of Siem Reap was swept by rumours that the Khmer Rouge were preparing to mount a major offensive. They were said to be infiltrating weapons with the help of local officials who worked for them at night while ostensibly carrying out their official duties for the government in Phnom Penh by day. These rumours naturally reached the ears of Vietnamese military intelligence, which was also supplied with more concrete evidence of Khmer Rouge intentions by a young Cambodian informant. Then our forces, or volunteers as they were called, managed to capture a Khmer Rouge unit commander near the Tonle Sap lake. Under 'professional' methods of interrogation, he produced a list of provincial officials who were collaborating with the Khmer Rouge. This was passed to the Vietnamese High Command in Phnom Penh which authorised the making of arrests. Not only district officials but also government experts working in the province were detained and interrogated by Vietnamese military intelligence.

The climax of what was seen by the Cambodians as a reign of terror occurred when a Vietnamese officer, escorted by armed bodyguards, went to detain the Party Secretary of Siem Reap province. The latter, having in vain attempted to point out the sovereign status of both Cambodia and its Party, managed by a ruse to commit suicide. After that the whole affair could no longer be hushed up. Both the government in Phnom Penh and the Vietnamese High Command sent investigators to Siem Reap, where they found that interrogations by Vietnamese military intelligence were reminiscent of Stalinist methods employed by the KGB and the East German Stasi. There were widespread demands that Le Duan should visit Cambodia to apologise. Instead General Chu Huy Man, one of the military members of the Politburo in Hanoi, was delegated to perform the task. But the damage had been done. Although there were many high-ranking Vietnamese officers who were disciplined and demoted as a result of this incident,* their overall commander General Le Duc Anh

* One of those disciplined after this incident was General Hoang Hoa. A protégé of Le Duc Tho, he had served as military adviser during the Paris peace talks and became a member of the Party Central Committee at the 5th Congress

kept quiet while numerous Cambodians viewed their so-called brotherly relationship with the other countries of Indo-China with increasing scepticism.

In my opinion, the determination to create a federation of Vietnam, Cambodia and Laos was another of our major mistakes. Since all three countries of Indo-China had been part of a single battlefield, there was said to be a special feeling of friendship between their peoples, governments and three fraternal Parties. These relationships were characterised as comradely or fraternal, hence a 'special alliance' had to be formed. But what was so special about this relationship? Among the three countries, Vietnam had a population of over 60 million while Cambodia had barely 6 million and Laos just over half that total. So what sort of equality was that?

Without question Vietnam was the big brother and Laos was the smallest of nephews, with Cambodia just a poor relation. Hence the idea of equality was in reality very difficult. As a result, Vietnam's sincerity became suspect. It was criticised by the members of ASEAN and scorned by the world at large. But on the international scene, Vietnam had a habit of regarding itself as a centre of influence, particularly in Indo-China. Thus it did not consider that it had any need to take into account the views of other countries or international opinion at large. It was prepared to go to any length to maintain its own views, despite isolation and difficulties.

For example when the Committee for Social Science organised a seminar in the lecture hall of the Hanoi polytechnic in 1985 on the subject of the 'special alliance' between the three countries of Indo-China, I protested that the title was inappropriate. There could be no special relationship between three such countries which were so unequal in every way. It was in vain.

There were some very strange manifestations of Vietnam's relationship with its fraternal partners. For example there were annual meetings between their Ministers of Defence. In 1982, this meeting took place in Chamcar Mon, the former royal palace in Phnom Penh on the banks of the Mekong. Representing the Vietnamese Ministry of Defence was General Chu Huy Man,

in 1982. Le Duc Tho took him to Cambodia as Chief of Staff, but after the Siem Reap incident he was demoted to Colonel, dismissed from the Central Committee and given a staff job in southern Vietnam.

the head of the General Political Department of the army and a member of the Politburo. This general, whose background was that of a landless peasant from a very poor village near Vinh, was the last to speak after the Defence Ministers of Cambodia and Laos. Without any notes or preparation, General Man said, 'Now it's my turn. We are brothers linked by special emotional bonds. We belong together. I speak with a...a...voice. We agree with one another, don't we?' Then he cleared his throat and said, 'Dear comrade, General...Bou Thuong, Minister of Defence of ah? the People's Republic of...Mongolia!'

At that I saw the Vietnamese officers present become very startled. General Man had forgotten he was in Cambodia. This is not a joke. It is true. The fact is that a week earlier in Hanoi, General Man had made a speech welcoming a delegation from the Mongolian Ministry of Defence. But now, having drunk a cup or more of local toddy, he was tipsy and confused, and so his improvisation became a calamity.

The behaviour of senior leaders like Le Duc Tho and Chu Huy Man, both of them Politburo members, had a considerable influence on many Vietnamese experts sent to Cambodia. True, there were some who were well-informed, dedicated and helpful. As such they were valued and respected, but unfortunately there were very few, too few of them. There were far too many experts who were false or venal or had been appointed as 'privileged experts'. In other words, they were cadres with 'long-term achievements' and therefore close to retirement age. As such they were accorded the privilege of going to Cambodia for several years to work as experts, irrespective of whether they could carry out this difficult task or not. In Phnom Penh they could purchase goods from Thailand without paying taxes and transfer them to Vietnam with scarcely any control. They were said to be 'investigating the market' or 'studying the goods'. It was a way of storing up a little something in preparation for a slightly more comfortable retirement.

Many Cambodian intellectuals told me frankly that a lot of Vietnamese economic, planning, banking and financial experts had no education and could not be considered as experts. Even so these so-called experts presented their views without any reservations. They acted as if they were dealing with Vietnam or the Soviet Union, which was nonsense in relation to the particular circumstances of Cambodia. Some defence and security experts also carried out their work subjectively and imperiously. They acted high-handedly without any regard for national sovereignty. The consequences of the bad feelings engendered by such behaviour can hardly be estimated.

I wondered why we did not leave matters to the Cambodians to teach one another. The official reason was that what we did had been a necessity for Vietnam – those responsible were all new Party members. Nevertheless, this was a matter of relations between two nations with differing concepts of nationalism.

In 1985, after I had returned to Hanoi, an expert from the Party newspaper *Nhan Dan* became adviser to the journal *Kampuchea*. On one occasion, he showed me an article written by the editor of that journal which had been translated into Vietnamese. The expert was almost in tears. He said 'Look! This article is hopeless, I have to pull it apart and start over again.'

I found this attitude difficult to take and said 'The best thing would be not to correct a word of it. Just let the writer correct it himself, if it is really necessary. If you do as you suggest, they will have to listen because they are afraid of our advisers, but in their hearts they are full of hostility towards us.'

There was even a case where a Cambodian couple who applied to join the Party were disciplined by Vietnamese experts because they wrote love letters to one another! I think that the basic trouble stemmed from the top experts. They spread the contagion and it caused endless harm.

Another aspect of our continuing presence in Cambodia which caused me concern was the size of our armed forces. According to figures produced by the International Institute of Strategic Studies (IISS) in London, the armed forces of Vietnam amounted to over one and a half million men with a further 300,000 in the security forces. I came to realise the implications of these statistics when I accompanied the Vietnamese Defence Minister, by then General Van Tien Dung, on his visits to India and Indonesia in 1985. During our talks, the Indian Defence Minister explained that his country had 700 million people and had experienced border wars with both China and Pakistan, but its armed forces numbered less than a million. He said that India's economy and budget could not support any increased spending on defence.

I sat and listened in amazement, silently comparing these statistics with those of Vietnam.

Several months later when we went to Indonesia, General Murdani, Chief of Staff of the armed forces there, stated that his country had a population of 180 million, in other words three times larger than that of Vietnam, but its armed forces only amounted to 700,000 men, although it had a vast territory consisting of over 3,000 islands which created many security problems. Then there is China where the size of the armed forces is even less in proportion to the total population.

According to IISS statistics, in most countries throughout the world, the armed forces comprise less than 1 per cent of the population and the security forces less than 0.1 per cent. If those proportions had been applied in Vietnam, we should have had an army of 650,000 and security forces numbering a mere 65,000. And if we want to develop our economy rapidly, we have to reduce these figures even more.

The fact that our armed forces were so large was yet another example of bureaucratic incompetence, lack of attention and law-lessness. Decisions were made according to personal whim, without any proper consideration or scientific analysis. This question of disproportion arose because decisions were taken by the Politburo without consulting the government or the National Assembly, let alone the Fatherland Front.

Because the army and the security forces were so big, the military budget expanded but life for the troops became difficult. Their morale deteriorated as did their sense of discipline, so they became less effective than before, as I found when I paid a visit to the 304th Division, my former unit. The battalion commanders let their men return home for long spells on condition that they brought back with them a few kilos of rice and a couple of chickens. The financial allocations to army units have to be im-proved. The same is true of security men patrolling the roads who are so poor that they have to resort to reckless methods. There are times when they blow their whistles to stop vehicles and check their papers simply in order to obtain a couple of cigarettes or a few *dong*. One cannot really blame them. They are unable to live normally because the administrative system is so conservative and irresponsible. Social injustice has spread everywhere.

I also visited the camps of army veterans and the severely war-wounded in Nghe An and Ha Nam Ninh provinces. These people were deeply demoralised. Clearly society had a huge debt to pay to almost a million people who had shed their blood and sacrificed most if not all of their youth for the country. It really makes my blood boil when I see people in power using their positions in the Party and the state to profiteer, coin money and build large houses where they live extremely comfortably with crowds of children and over-indulge themselves day and night, even getting drunk, while the war-wounded are left to survive in destitution. It is gross ingratitude, a crime.

This situation cannot be laid at the door of General Vo Nguyen Giap, who finally lost his post as Defence Minister to General Van Tien Dung in 1980. Nor did Giap approve our ten-year-long occupation of Cambodia and despite numerous invitations he refused to visit Phnom Penh. Maybe that was why in early 1982 at the 5th Party Congress he too was dropped from the Politburo. Quite a lot of cadres and Party members believe that the move was an 'initiative' by Le Duan and Le Duc Tho and that to avoid it attracting too much attention four other long-standing members of the Politburo were also made to lose their positions, ostensibly on the grounds of old age.* In other words it was just like the children's game 'Hand in hand, one, two, three and we all jump out!'

The demotion of General Giap was a cause of concern both inside the country and abroad. At the time, the leadership explained that because of his age and his health he was making way for the younger generation. However, since Le Duc Tho, Pham Van Dong and Truong Chinh were just as old and poor in health but did not step aside, that explanation did not hold water.

There are those who, from personal motives, previously feared the aura surrounding the commander of the battle of Dien Bien Phu and then started to worry that it was far brighter than that of those who claim to have masterminded the Ho Chi Minh campaign in 1975. In fact the whole of Hanoi, particularly in military as well as intellectual circles, knows that Le Duan always

---

* They were Le Thanh Nghi, Minister for Economic Planning, Nguyen Duy Trinh, the Foreign Minister, and Tran Quoc Hoan, Minister of the Interior, all of whom were to die shortly afterwards, plus Nguyen Van Linh who later resurfaced as Party General Secretary.

had a disparaging attitude towards General Giap and sought to downplay the role and respect he enjoyed. From 1975 onwards I attended many meetings addressed by Le Duan. He made his stance clearest when he spoke to heads of section and upwards at the editorial office of *Nhan Dan* in March 1983. Inconsiderately he said, 'During the war against the Americans, the Minister of Defence was like a frightened rabbit. Therefore we could not leave him in command. We had to take over the situation and pursue the struggle. In fact we had to find somebody else to take over as Defence Minister.'

I have also heard Le Duan criticise General Giap at many other meetings in Hanoi and Saigon. I considered it a dirty game unworthy of a leader holding a position of high responsibility. However the antagonism between these two men goes back well beyond 1975, at least to 1962 in the controversial lead–up to the 9th Plenum when General Giap was suspected of being a 'revisionist'. Some cadres known for their impartiality have even asserted that Le Duan's envy of General Giap stems from 1945 when the future Party General Secretary thought that his long years of imprisonment for the cause were being ignored by a bourgeois upstart in Hanoi. There are many stories of clashes between them from that time on.

A general who used to attend the same high school as me in Hue before the Revolution told me that as an officer on the General Staff he often attended Politburo meetings during the war to jot down a record of any discussions of military matters. He said that at one session towards the end of 1972 following the major offensive that year, Le Duan deliberately provoked General Giap by claiming that he had not clearly defined the objectives of the offensive. Immediately Giap, with fists tightly clenched on the table, retorted 'Am I in supreme command of the army or not?' The fact is that when the offensive was being planned a year earlier, the Politburo records show that Le Duan wanted the main objective to be the towns of Pleiku and Kontum in the Central Highlands, whereas General Giap argued that it should be the coastal area of Quang Tri and Thua Thien just sough of the Demilitarised Zone because that area was more accessible for our army from the North than the Central Highlands, which were in any case a far less important target. As it turned out the offensive in the Central Highlands encountered many difficulties, although that in the coastal region was slowed down as well, which I myself can vouch for.

The events surroundings the Gulf of Tonkin incident in August 1964 also gave rise to a clash between the Party General Secretary and the Supreme Commander at a Politburo session when Ho Chi Minh said that we had to be well prepared to cope with the situation and not be taken by surprise. But he added that we should not strike first. We should leave it to the enemy and then retaliate. At that time, American warships including the USS *Maddox* were patrolling around an area about 35 kilometres or roughly 20 nautical miles offshore. Since they had not yet violated our sovereign territorial waters, Giap ordered the Navy not to attack but to be on the alert. But Le Duan, on being informed of the situation, immediately instructed the Chief of General Staff, General Van Tien Dung, to attack. On receiving this order from the Party General Secretary, General Dung complied straight away by passing it on to the Commander of the Navy, Admiral Giap Van Cuong, and our ships opened fire. After the battle it was announced that two of our patrol boats had been sunk and another damaged, while one enemy warship had likewise suffered damage. After that incident, Le Duan often criticised General Giap and tried to diminish his prestige by claiming that he was afraid to attack.

After the death of Ho Chi Minh, Le Duan together with Le Duc Tho tried even harder to get rid of Giap. They were unable to do so for so long because of his influence in the army coupled with his simple and exemplary life. No other General could match these standards. What is more, his ouster during the war would have caused a catastrophic upheaval in the armed forces. He had to be eased out gently.

Despite the many dirty tricks he was subjected to, General Giap continued to show that he bore no feelings of revenge and was not unhappy. However he became far more cautious and reserved in order to avoid providing other people with an opportunity to slander him. On various trips I made abroad with him, including one to East Berlin and Budapest in 1977, he always insisted that I include in my reports on his activities that he had conveyed friendly greetings from Party General Secretary Le Duan, Chairman of the Council of State Truong Chinh, and Chairman of the Council of Ministers Pham Van Dong and others to the leaders of whichever country he was visiting. It was a way of protecting himself to avoid a 'knock-out'.

Unlike Le Duan, General Giap genuinely liked talking to journalists and photographers who covered his trips, and one day he said to me 'One of our big mistakes in organisational work is our failure to distinguish between carrying out one's duty and gaining rewards.'. He explained that in feudal times the system was quite good because it was based on proper rules and regulations. In those days, he said, there was a real distinction between duties, titles, ranks, privileges and salaries. Carrying out one's duty was the most important thing. Title, rank and salary were just secondary. But he went on 'Now we do not make any distinction. There are those who use their position to gain rewards irrespective of merit. This creates chaos and danger.'

As a former professor of history and law student, General Giap talked fluently about the legal system under Hong Duc, the Tran and Le dynasties, as well as the organisation of the civil service in France, Britain and Germany in the old days.

It could be said that General Giap suffered a hard fate. After he was dropped from the Politburo in 1982, he remained a member of the Central Committee and the deputy premier responsible for scientific matters. Yet while all the other deputy premiers were members of the National Assembly, the Party Organisational Committee 'forgot' to nominate General Giap as a candidate at the next elections. Nevertheless, he continued to carry out various formal duties, for instance as a member of memorial committees or Chairman of the Family Planning Commission. That prompted one Western journalist to comment that 'these days General Giap's battlefield lies in the beds of young couples.' People on the street also coined a verse about this extraordinary situation when

> *Politicians become poets,*
> *Poets become economists,*
> *And the Field Marshal fits IUDs.*

Besides the reference to General Giap, this lampoon also took note of the fact that several members of the Politburo and most notably Le Duc Tho often expressed their views in verse, while the official Party poet To Huu tried to take over the running of the economy in the early 1980s and made a complete mess of it with a sudden change of currency. It would have been far better for him and his reputation if he had stuck to poetry.

Clearly To Huu wanted to become a major Party leader, as did his wife Mme Thanh. On the strength of her husband's crony connections, she had risen from running a small song and dance troupe in the Viet Bac region during the Resistance, to become in 1977 Deputy Director of the Party's Training and Propaganda Committee with ministerial rank, heading delegations travelling far and wide between the capitals of our fraternal allies from East Berlin to Ulaan Bator. In fact many people in the Party regarded her as a great lady but unfortunately, like her husband, she had little knowledge of politics or current affairs. Nonetheless, there was widespread belief that To Huu was being groomed by Le Duc Tho to take over as Party General Secretary from Le Duan who died in June 1986. But at that point, the Soviet Union under the leadership of Mikhail Gorbachev had just adopted the policies of *perestroika* and *glasnost*, so we had to change too.

7

RENOVATION

One of the consequences of our conflict with China and our move into Cambodia was that we became almost totally dependent on the Soviet Union. Many Vietnamese admired the Soviet people, who were regarded as the model of the 'new socialist man', dedicated workers with a high level of production. And publicly the Soviet experts who came to Vietnam in a spirit of international co-operation were held in high regard.

However, in April 1986 when I passed through Moscow on my way to and from East Germany, I happened to meet a Vietnamese delegation from our joint oil venture with the Soviet Union. Some of its members were former colonels with specialist knowledge whom I had known for a long time, and through them I came to learn a lot more about the Viet-Xo petroleum enterprise set up to explore and exploit our offshore oil. They said that joint oil exploration with the Soviet Union started off with many smiles because it was going to contribute billions of roubles for the provision of much modern and costly equipment which would be of genuine help to Vietnam. But after a few years, we became a little more clever and realised that we could do things for ourselves. On examination the receipts for the equipment they purchased for us from India, Hong Kong and Singapore showed far higher prices than the real ones. And while some of the Soviet experts sent to Vietnam were good, there were also quite a number who were only out to protect their own interests. We had to create a special village for them at Vung Tau (just as at Hoa Binh where they helped construct the hydro-electric plant). This accommodation ate up most of the money we had been advanced in aid. What is more, we were careless

136

enough to charge them 'friendship prices' for rent, vital supplies and transport. My friends painfully pointed out that the more fraternal our allies, the more they bullied us and took us for a ride because we were so dumb and innocent. In the end it was the people who had to bear the burden.

The rise to power of Gorbachev in the Soviet Union and the death of Le Duan in Vietnam provided the opportunity for a change in our relationship.

Immediately Truong Chinh took it upon himself to become Party General Secretary again, almost thirty years after he had been dismissed from the same position. He had a very clear sense of responsibility. He accepted the trend in the Soviet Union towards *perestroika* and *glasnost* and outlined a similar plan for economic renovation in Vietnam. The policy is known as *Doi Moi*, which literally means 'New Change'.

Since Truong Chinh was regarded as the first person to advocate this policy, his prestige increased considerably. So when the 6th Party Congress convened in December 1986, many of the delegations, particularly that from the army, proposed that Truong Chinh should retain his position as Party General Secretary while Pham Van Dong should become Head of State, with General Vo Nguyen Giap as Prime Minister.

General Giap still enjoyed great respect in the Party. Many delegates to the Congress stated that his broad knowledge, together with his great prestige at home and abroad, was a national asset which should be put to good use. Many military men had given considerable thought to the problems of socialism and the Party leadership, as was apparent from the extraordinary and unexpected events which took place at the Army Party Conference in September that year.

The purpose of this meeting was to discuss policy and appoint delegates to attend the forthcoming Party Congress. The debate took place in an atmosphere brimming with enthusiasm for the need to bring about change and implement the policy of *Doi Moi*. There was much plain speaking and many delegates directly criticised a number of leading generals for failing to set a good example. They were said to be rotten from top to bottom; they had become corrupted with war booty and connived at their wives and children violating Party policy at the same time as they were being fawned upon in public.

One of the main targets of attack at this conference was the Defence Minister, General Van Tien Dung. He was widely regarded as ignorant in military matters as well as being vain. Not only did he pride himself on being the hero of the liberation of Saigon, but also paraded around in a vast array of uniforms – he originated from a family of tailors. His wife was even more notorious. Given a free rein by her husband, she had acquired the reputation of being a magpie gathering property and household valuables in the South, only to commandeer military aircraft to transport her loot wherever she wanted to dispose of it. As for General Chu Huy Man, the head of the General Political Department of the Army, he caused a scandal by having the first-ever private swimming pool constructed at his home in Hanoi. At the same time these generals were accused of irresponsibility towards the hard life endured by ordinary soldiers under their command and thus damaging the essence of all we had struggled for.

This in fact was the showdown which had long been looming between those officers on the one hand who were well trained and were promoted to senior positions by General Giap because of their ability, and those mediocrities on the other hand who had risen to power thanks to their class origins. As a result, when the vote was taken to select seventy-two delegates from the army to attend the Party Congress, although there was an official list of candidates, three leading generals found themselves excluded. They were Van Tien Dung and Chu Huy Man, both of whom were actually members of the Politburo, and General Man's immediate deputy.

The exclusion of these three generals from the Party Congress was sensational news and for the next month the whole of Hanoi was in uproar. Many people were very happy that democracy had established the right of the lower ranks to act decisively and discipline their superiors. This seemed to be real democracy and not just the formality mouthed by the leadership about 'collective democracy'. In other words, genuine progress was being made.

However, it did not last long. The *Bao Ve* as well as members of the Army and Party security bodies soon launched an investigation into this manifestation of 'excessive democracy' to try to find the mastermind who had instigated what they saw as a plot to usurp power. The 'mini-revolt' had in fact stemmed from the delegates at the Army Party Conference representing several departments within the Ministry of Defence and its various training schools, in particular the Higher Military Staff College at Cho Buoi in the Hanoi suburbs, which was attended by numerous talented and experienced generals and colonels. As a result, officers working at the Ministry were no longer trusted and those from the regions were summoned back to the capital. The entire security apparatus was then mobilised to ensure that there was no further 'laxity' and that the course of events at the Army Party conference was not repeated at the full Party Congress. We all shook our heads and became very depressed again.

Nonetheless, during the first few days of the Congress, many delegates representing the southern provinces as well as Hanoi lobbied strongly for a top leadership comprising Truong Chinh, Pham Van Dong and Vo Nguyen Giap. Then suddenly, when the Congress met to decide on which personalities to appoint, the Party Organisational Committee produced a completely different scenario. Nguyen Van Linh was to become Party General Secretary with Vo Chi Cong as Head of State and Pham Hung as Prime Minister.

To ensure that this line-up was accepted without any hitch, Le Duc Tho, who had headed the Party Organisational Committee for the previous thirty years, wrote a short but persuasive letter to Truong Chinh and Pham Van Dong. In reality, it put considerable pressure on them. What Le Duc Tho stated in this letter was that many delegates at the Congress felt that these two comrades as well as himself were very old and weak. Therefore they should no longer remain members of the Politburo, but instead become senior advisers to the Central Committee. Le Duc Tho's letter continued: 'I consider this to be a reasonable idea. If all three of us continue to occupy our positions, we might be suspected of wishing to hang on to power. I very much hope you comrades will agree with this proposal.'

And that is what happened, to the regret of many Party members who regard the 6th Congress as that dominated by Brother Six, in other words Le Duc Tho. According to various people in the office of the Central Committee, it was Nguyen Khanh, the head of that office, who actually had to act as the messenger and deliver Le Duc Tho's letter to the homes of Truong Chinh and Pham Van Dong.

In addition, the Party organisational and security committees had been mobilised to prevent General Giap from being appointed as Prime Minister by informing all the delegates attending the Congress that there were various problems relating to his personal history. As evidence, translated copies were circulated of a request for a scholarship to go and study in France written by Giap to the Governor-General of Indo-China back in the early 1930s. The letter was couched in a form which was natural in those days with phrases such as 'I beg, Sir, to send you my respectful greetings' and 'I remain, Sir, your obedient servant'.

Some people suffering from the disease of having a 'firm viewpoint' – in other words those who were stubborn in their enmity towards General Giap although they could find nothing to criticise in his conduct and in his honesty and intelligence – now had a pretext to attack him. Here was a Communist who had addressed the colonialists as 'Sir' and referred to himself as an 'obedient servant', so he was beyond forgiveness. This trick gave rise to ridicule among those of us who had at least a little culture and education. But it caused some delegates from the provinces who knew nothing of formal procedure in the old days to have doubts.

I still have a photo of General Vo Nguyen Giap taken the day after the 6th Party Congress finished. He looks happy enough but I have reason to believe that deep down he felt very differently, not only because of the outcome of the Congress. During the previous six months, he had been immensely saddened by the death of two of his closest friends in the army.

One of them was General Hoang Van Thai, the Deputy Minister of Defence. He had died suddenly at home in June 1986 after a week of direct involvement in a series of tense meetings at the Ministry about preparations for the forthcoming Army and Party Congresses. General Thai's friendship with Giap dated back as far as December 1944 when he was a member of an army propaganda unit. When they reached Hanoi the following year, he was General Giap's choice as Chief of Staff, a position he continued to occupy throughout the war against the French including the battle of Dien Bien Phu. Then, in 1957, General Thai had to cede his position to General Van Tien Dung, but in reality as First Deputy Chief of Staff he remained the soul of the army staff as one generation of officers succeeded another over a period of thirty years. Nor could it be said that he lacked combat experience. General Thai spent three years in the South at R Base in Tay Ninh province and became deputy commander of the Liberation Armed Forces when guerrilla warfare developed into full-scale war.

The office of the General Staff is close to that of the Minister of Defence, so General Giap consulted his old friend on military matters almost daily. General Thai was also the person in whom the Supreme Commander could confide all his concerns. The two men were also linked through family ties. Vo Dien Bien, the eldest son of General Giap who was born in 1954 soon after our victory, married Hoang Thi Kim Phuong, the daughter of General Thai. Both of them are military officers. Dien Bien is a major in the anti-aircraft brigade while Kim Phuong is an officer in the medical corps. General Thai's wife Loan was also a colonel in the army, although she has now retired. She used to work on policy studies in the office of the General Staff and was well known as one of the four women who joined the army before the August Revolution and came down to Hanoi from the Viet Bac region with the Quang Trung brigade in August 1945 together with her future husband and General Giap.

Exactly six months after the death of General Hoang Van Thai, General Giap had cause to weep over yet another sudden death, that of General Le Trong Tan, an officer of great talent and virtue. He was highly respected throughout the army as a general who was always in the forefront of the battle wherever it was hottest. He was commander of an artillery division at Dien Bien Phu. He commanded our forces in Laos in the Sam Neua campaign. From 1966 to 1969 he was at R Base in the South and during the 1975 offensive commanded our forces when they advanced down the coast from Da Nang through Cam Ranh Bay to Bien Hoa and finally Saigon. He also led our army into Phnom Penh in 1979.

General Tan was an officer who studied the details of every campaign and applied this experience to his own command strategy. He had no other passions. He did not drink, not even beer. As such he was much respected by General Giap, who once said that in any battle where General Tan was in command, his mind could be at least fifty per cent at ease. The Politburo apparently had a similarly high opinion of General Tan. On

December 5, 1986, ten days before the Party Congress was due to convene, it decided to dismiss General Van Tien Dung from his position as Defence Minister and appoint in his stead General Le Trong Tan who was then Chief of the General Staff. But a few hours later when he was having lunch at home, General Tan suddenly collapsed and died. He had previously been in good health and his widow and children are still uncertain about the cause of his death.

As a result of this unexpected occurrence, General Van Tien Dung, who had been excluded from the Party Congress, enjoyed a 'stroke of good fortune'. Since he headed the list of failed candidates to the Party Congress, he was now able to attend thanks to the empty seat left by the tragic death of General Tan. Moreover, although General Dung lost his position in the Politburo, he was re-elected to the Party Central Committee at the Congress, much to the amazement of many military officers. Hence he was able to continue to participate in the work of drafting military and Party policy right up to the 7th Party Congress in 1991 when he was finally dropped from the Central Committee.

Still, not everything continued to go General Dung's way. He was eventually replaced as Defence Minister in early 1987 by General Le Duc Anh who thus shot to prominence. A native of Hue who studied engineering at the time of the French, he is a tall man. But unfortunately as a child he suffered from smallpox which left him with his face pock-marked and without the use of one eye. During the resistance against the French, he was an official at battalion level in charge of local militia with no military rank. However, by 1962 he had become deputy head of operations on the General Staff before going South as commander of Military Region 9 in the coastal area bordering Cambodia which he headed from 1967 onwards. It was regarded as the most peaceful region in the South because no American forces were based there, and the Saigon army did not deploy its crack units so far afield. Consequently Le Duc Anh proved so successful in expanding the liberated zones under his control after the Paris Agreements that at the end of 1974 he was promoted to the rank of general. And in May 1975, he was chosen to head the victory parade held in front of the Independence Palace in Saigon. Several years later, together with General Le Trong Tan, he led the offensive against Cambodia and remained there as commander of the Vietnamese 'volunteers' until 1985.

At that time he would invite me to a meal whenever I visited Phnom Penh to discuss the situation at home and abroad. He also twice asked me to talk about current affairs to the officers on his staff. General Anh was a placid man with a keen sense of discipline, but his knowledge of politics, economics and above all international affairs was limited. He had led a simple life on the battlefield and his elevation to the Politburo was unexpected, like that of General Doan Khue, another of the regional officers who was recalled to Hanoi in the wake of the Army Party Conference to help carry out a transformation of the Defence Ministry and the General Staff.

Originally a provincial *apparatchik* in the Vinh Linh area of Central Vietnam, Doan Khue was promoted in 1963 to become deputy political commissar of Military Region 5 covering part of the Central Highlands where he was known as Trinh, and where after 1975 he was appointed overall military commander with the rank of major-general. He was born in one of the many coastal villages of Quang Tri where I happened to stop on one occasion. As a result I discovered by chance that Doan Khue's father had been the district chief and the richest man in the village, owning a lot of copper ornaments hidden in the family house or buried under the high sand-dunes nearby. Nevertheless Doan Khue joined the Revolution early and after only two years of high school during the French period was arrested and imprisoned, which led his father to disown him for fear of becoming involved. All the high-ranking generals in Hanoi knew Doan Khue as a political officer who had little military experience and had never commanded any unit or attended staff college. He simply had a reputation as a diehard who had progressed formalistically through the political apparatus. Yet in early 1987 he was appointed Chief of General Staff.

There was a third officer who likewise rose high at the same time. This was Nguyen Quyet who had been political commissar of Military Region 3 with its headquarters near Haiphong. A man of small stature who looks like a student, he took part in the August Revolution in Hanoi and later spent a short time in the battlefield in the South, but basically he is yet another political *apparatchik*.

The rapid promotion to high political positions of these officers who had spent most of their life 'in the backwoods' exemplified a trend. Known as the 'Gang of Three', they were clearly being used to neutralise and force into retirement the better educated officers whom General Giap had previously depended upon in the Army General Staff.

Hence there were no problems in early 1987 when, following the end of the 6th Party Congress, its resolutions were circulated for endorsement by another Army Party Conference. But there was another sudden death. General Phan Binh, the head of military intelligence for the General Staff, was said to have put a pistol to his head and committed suicide. I knew him quite well. He was a slender little man from Quang Nam who had held this position since 1964, when he replaced Colonel Nguyen Minh Nghia on the latter's being detained as a 'revisionist'. Within the General Staff, many people regarded General Binh as being very close to the family of the Defence Minister Van Tien Dung, with personal knowledge of many stories about corruption and the division of war booty among senior military officers. For that reason, he remained a high-ranking Party official. So when he died in Ho Chi Minh City, his home was thoroughly searched. A week later his son, a junior army colonel who had many personal documents and letters belonging to his father, was killed in a traffic accident on the city streets. This was yet another incident which has never been satisfactorily explained.

Nevertheless, one of the main slogans to emerge from the 6th Party Congress was 'Speak the truth, the whole truth and nothing but the truth.' This still survives in theory on paper, but the people do not believe it. They are very critical and for that reason do not read newspapers. They joke bitterly about the only credible news being the weather forecasts because they are sometimes bad. Then there are obituaries: they too acknowledge that sickness can occur.

However, when *Doi Moi* was first adopted as official policy, our newspaper *Nhan Dan* was regarded as its main instrument and the forerunner of the process of democratisation. All this sounded fine. But in reality it was very difficult to carry out this task. Apart from anything else, we were required to publish the articles signed 'N.V.L.', the initials of the new Party General Secretary, Nguyen Van Linh. I had long had frequent contact with Linh because he occupied various important positions in Ho Chi Minh City after its liberation. In fact, although a northerner he had spent most of his career in the South where he was quite popular. During the resistance against the French, he was nicknamed '*Les Cent Bougies*', meaning the hundred candles, since he had negotiated a sort of co-existence with religious sects like the Cao Dai and Hoa Hao. He also lived simply and was regarded as good-natured as well as truthful.

However, Nguyen Van Linh was a 'professional' revolutionary, having learned his politics in an imperialist prison. Hence his weak point was that his level of education was inadequate for the positions he later came to occupy. He lacked imagination and was very gullible, frequently being swayed by his assistants. During the early 1980s, for instance, when he was head of the national trade union movement, he showed himself to be indecisive and hesitant, in other words lacking in the qualities necessary in a leader. He was dropped from the Politburo in 1982, and only bounced back four years later thanks to the machinations of Le Duc Tho. Then when he was promoted to Party General Secretary, he became an ardent advocate of the policy of *Doi Moi*.

I too was very enthusiastic when a two-day meeting of writers and intellectuals was held in 1987 with the Party General Secretary attending. Nguyen Van Linh spoke for only ten minutes at the beginning and forty minutes at the end. For the rest of the ten hours, he sat and listened. He also came down from the platform to shake hands with the historian Dr Nguyen Khac Vien and went on to encourage the woman writer Duong Thu Huong to expound her ideas. In fact, Linh advised everybody present not to 'bend the nibs of their pens' and distort their writing, but rather to have a sense of purpose in living and writing.

As a result, an atmosphere of freedom started to emerge. Talents which had lain hidden at the bottom of many hearts were liberated. The harsh and painful truth found a new way to worm itself into articles and stories which were allowed to be published. For instance Nguyen Ngoc, the editor of *Van Nghe*, the main cultural journal printed in Hanoi, was encouraged by Tran Do who headed the Party Committee responsible for the arts to publish various fictional stories by young writers which created a stir. One was about the plight of a soldier ordered to confiscate the property of a poor family unable to pay its taxes, who muttered to himself 'What is the Party making me do?' Then *Nong Nghiep*, the agricultural newspaper, followed suit with moving short stories about the injustice of life in the countryside with the village cadres and Cong An oppressing the people. Another frequent theme was the suffering caused by the pursuit of class warfare through the use of personal family history. All this supposedly fictional writing aroused a great deal of attention among readers throughout the country, as did the novels and short stories of the authors Duong Thu Huong and Nguyen Huy Thiep. Those of their works which appeared between 1986 and 1989 clearly show the relationship between politics and culture.

But Nguyen Van Linh soon changed. Never again did he appear so relaxed as he was at the meeting of writers in 1987. Later he just talked and no longer listened to anybody else. It was as if his thoughts were powered by a battery which did not recharge itself and just went dry. His power of concentration became progressively duller and he lost his charisma. At the same time his speeches became longer and longer, so exposing his lack of intelligence, and it became difficult to listen to him.

In my opinion there are two factors needed to make a successful official: intelligence and sympathy. Many leaders of the Party and the state have continually shown that their knowledge does not measure up to their level of responsibility. They only have a modicum of education whereas there are hundreds of people in Vietnam who have doctorates as well as hundreds of thousands with degrees, let alone all those who have completed secondary education. People with little knowledge are very subjective. They do not know how dimwitted they are. Therefore a weakness of members of the Politburo is that they do very little listening. They cannot stand it. Whenever they encounter a problem, they talk a lot and issue numerous orders and instructions.

That was also the problem with Nguyen Van Linh's articles signed 'N.V.L.' which he claimed stood for '*noi va lam*', in other words 'speak and act'. At first these articles published in *Nhan Dan* were well received, exposing as they did various specific examples of official corruption. But gradually Linh's lack of experience began to show through. For instance the Foreign Minister Nguyen Co Thach felt it necessary to protest when an 'N.V.L.' article criticised several Vietnamese embassies in South East Asia for using Western and Japanese cars instead of Soviet vehicles which were the standard official transport in Hanoi. Thach pointed out that in cities like Bangkok and Jakarta there were no spare parts or repair facilities for Soviet cars and anyway the tax on them was higher. Indeed after several such nonsenses in the 'N.V.L.' articles, they became know as '*noi va lua*' meaning 'speak and cheat'. And that finally led to their disappearance.

Still, despite the fate of these articles the policy of *Doi Moi* led to a new way of thinking, particularly at *Nhan Dan*. We debated whether our paper was the organ of the Party or the forum of the people as its name suggests. If the latter were true, how nice, how beautiful it would be! I cannot remember how many times the staff of *Nhan Dan* discussed what role they should play. The paper had to decide on which side it stood. Did it dare to speak out on behalf of the people? Or should it make clear that it was the mouthpiece of the Party and the state which it had a duty to protect, especially when they were criticised by the people and the readers?

Sometimes there was total deadlock in these discussions because the Party leadership committed so many mistakes, and corruption spread like an epidemic within the State bodies and organisations responsible for the economy. Taking advantage of the move towards free market policies and the encouragement of foreign investment, the *Nomenklatura* used the opportunity to benefit themselves first and foremost. There was for example the case of Han, the eldest son of Le Duan. An anti-aircraft officer by training, he was promoted to deputy head of Military Region 7 surrounding Saigon after 1975 and officially allocated a three-storey house with a large garden in the city. But as property prices rose, under *Doi Moi*, he paid 16 taels of gold for a certificate of ownership and promptly sold the house for 120 taels to a foreign company. Many people in Hanoi were also aware that after the 'old man' died, the second Mme Le Duan was openly selling for foreign currency the many gifts her husband had received on his travels abroad as Party General Secretary. Seeing these and many other abuses of power, the people became uneasy as well as full of anger and hatred towards the corrupt and inefficient officials who allowed such a situation to develop.

In such circumstances some of the old hands on *Nhan Dan* commented sarcastically 'The paper is the organ of the Party, so why should it be called *The People?*' Others said mischievously that we should introduce a private newspaper to represent the Party and if anybody asked us why, we should say that the Party had hijacked our real name so now we were creating a new newspaper the people could call their own. We even proposed negotiations to set up these newspapers under their own true names.

The problem is that there are no official gazettes for the government or the state in Vietnam. As a result, members of the Politburo insist that *Nhan Dan* should carry out their orders. There have been times when the Party General Secretary, the head of the State Council or the Chairman of the National Assembly and very often the Prime Minister have all insisted that we carry reports and pictures of their activities. In addition the many commissions of the Party Central Committee, of which there are over a dozen, as well as government ministers consider that *Nhan Dan* has a duty to publish reports about their work. Thus the paper has become a platform for the organs of the Party and the state, in other words a heavy and depressing sort of official gazette reporting meetings, receptions, resolutions etc., as if to torment its readers. For instance each time the name of a prominent Party member is mentioned, we have to list all his official positions such as member of the Politburo, Minister of this, member of the commission for that, and so on. In fact the editorial board a *Nhan Dan* was severely reprimanded by Nguyen Thanh Binh when, in a reference to him as Party Secretary of Hanoi, one of his many other official functions was accidentally omitted.

On the other hand, *Nhan Dan* had made some much more serious mistakes, for which in its lofty and condescending way it has never felt the need to apologise. For example in 1980, to commemorate the 600th anniversary of the birth of Nguyen Trai our great national writer, the paper devoted its front page to a major article about him illustrated with a picture. But it was not a picture of Nguyen Trai but the photo of another famous man from the end of the nineteenth century wearing the costume of the Nguyen dynasty. In other words, these two figures were five centuries apart but nobody bothered to apologise to the readers. It was a disgrace.

I regard the Vietnamese press as antediluvian and much too stick-in-the-mud. Many of our journalists have ability as well as good and heartfelt intentions, but these are suppressed and annihilated by a stifling bureaucracy. As a result I lost hope, since one of my duties was to teach journalism to students from the Party propaganda school plus those in Laos and Cambodia. Still, I did try to point out the antiquated nature of the Vietnamese press and that of the socialist world in general.

The first cardinal sin is that the press usually belittles the intelligence of its readers although it claims to be of the people and for the people. There is a whole range of bureaucratic journalists who specialise in hectoring and intimidating their readers. In the spirit of class warfare, they learnt mechanistically about the power of the press to make propaganda, although it is really distorting the truth and altogether wrong. Sometimes, too, it leads to ludicrous situations.

I remember one occasion when the deputy editor of the army newspaper severely criticised a front-page layout with a picture of Ho Chi Minh in the top left corner and a photo of one of our anti-aircraft guns bottom right. Unfortunately the gun was pointing across the page in the direction of Ho. As a result several people were disciplined although it had previously never even occurred to any of us that there might be minds devious enough among either our colleagues or the general public to make a connection between the two pictures. Nevertheless, we learned after that to be far more wary. Because our newsprint was so thin, we even worried about which photo was published on the reverse side of what article in order to avoid the wrong inferences being made.

Obituaries were another problem. On which page should they appear? Everything depended on the pecking order within the Party. Sometimes it was difficult to judge. People who had previously been prominent often fell into official disrepute without anyone being aware of the fact, let alone the reason why. One case in point was that of General Chu Van Tan, who commanded the first guerrilla unit set up by the Viet Minh close to the border with China in 1942-3. A member of the Tho' ethnic minority, he continued to be regarded as a symbol who was helpful in rallying the support of the non-Vietnamese peoples including the Lao. But he was never completely trusted. Despite having been a Politburo member and awarded numerous gold medals in the course of his career, it became apparent when he died in a Hanoi hospital in the 1980s that General Chu Van Tan had fallen from favour. His burial took place not in the heroes' cemetery but in a common grave, whence the Cong An removed and destroyed a picture of the general dressed in his uniform with all his medals on the grounds that he had been a reactionary!

Despite the policy of *Doi Moi*, old Party habits died hard. That became particularly clear in 1988 when the Prime Minister Pham Hung died. He was yet another leader who owed his prominence in the Party to imprisonment under the French. As a teenage activist he was arrested by the colonial authorities in 1931 and given a death sentence, later commuted to life imprisonment. Many people expected or hoped that Pham Hung would be succeeded by Vo Van Kiet, who was popular in the south where he had pioneered the concept of *Doi Moi* before it was adopted as official policy. Instead it was Do Muoi who became Prime Minister because he had the right revolutionary credentials.

I have known Do Muoi for a long time, in fact ever since he was political commissar in the area north of the Red River before the battle of Dien Bien Phu. I saw a lot of him again in the South after 1975, when he led the campaign for the socialist transformation of trade and industry particularly in Saigon and Cholon. This was a major ideological task which had far-reaching social effects and left a disastrous legacy of widespread corruption. However, Do Muoi himself is not regarded as corrupt. He still lives very simply. His trouble is that he talks and talks, constantly banging his fist on the table as if he were punching an enemy. He talks until he is hoarse and that still does not stop him. He speaks on every subject, every field of politics, social science and technology, every country, although having been so busy in the struggle throughout his life he has never had time to learn a single foreign language.

As a man of energy, Do Muoi has a reputation of being a cadre who pushes people to achieve results. He was in direct charge of the construction of the Ho Chi Minh mausoleum in Hanoi as well as the 'two giant projects' of this century, as conceived by Le Duan. These were the Thang Long bridge across the Red River and the Hoa Binh hydro-electricity plant. Both of them symbolised the appallingly phlegmatic Vietnamese attitude towards modern technology. Before this could be corrected, these projects were well underway, so wasting much time and money as well as causing incalculable losses. And such Stalinist-style projects continue. The latest is the construction of an electric power line from Hoa Binh near Hanoi via the Central Highlands to Can Tho in the southern Mekong Delta without a proper feasibility study being conducted beforehand. Politics of the most childish kind hold sway, and technologists are expected to fall into line.

Even the death of the old men in the Party has made little difference, except that it has saved a lot of paper. Their lengthy speeches and ideological treatises, which were really compiled by their secretaries, no longer have to be printed and reprinted in millions of wasteful copies. Still nobody dares to criticise Le Duan openly, although work on his official biography has been suspended because it is no longer of any interest. The same fate befell Truong Chinh's memoirs which he was still recounting two days before he died in October 1988, when he suffered a fatal head injury falling on a flight of stone steps. Instead it was the collapse of Communism in Eastern Europe which turned out to be the real test for the Vietnamese Communist Party. It was a test which it failed to pass.

In August 1989, when candidates from the Solidarity trade union movement proved victorious in the Polish elections held on a democratic basis, Tran Trong Tan, the head of the Party's ideological and cultural committee, hastily wrote an editorial affirming that a counter-revolutionary coup had taken place. It also called on the Polish people to close ranks and overthrow the reactionaries. He then issued a directive for Vietnamese organisations to hold meetings to support the Poles in striking back against Solidarity.

This editorial was sent to *Nhan Dan* with a demand that it be printed immediately because it had high-level approval. By that time Ha Dang had become editor-in-chief. He was a Party official who always carried out orders without any hesitation, so we had to comply although it went against the grain. Previously the staff of *Nhan Dan* had been determined to maintain an independent spirit as well as a responsible attitude towards every article published.

The outcome of this editorial was that Vietnam became a laughing-stock all over the world. What is more, the Polish embassy in Hanoi lodged a protest on the very evening of its publication. Nonetheless the editor of *Nhan Dan* and the author of the editorial, Tran Trong Tan, pretended that nothing had happened.* In fact it had become routine that mistakes with leftist tendencies could be forgiven since they were regarded simply as an excess of true revolutionary spirit. However, Nguyen Van Linh did not even realise that a mistake had been made. Rather, he compounded it.

Many people both at home and abroad placed great hope in Linh in 1986 and 1987 when they saw him as a sort of Vietnamese Gorbachev. So they were all the more disappointed in 1989 when he reacted to developments in Poland by insisting on making the National Day speech on September 2 instead of the Prime Minister as was customary. The Party General Secretary used the occasion to criticise the outcome of the Polish elections. The way he analysed the situation showed a lack of depth and objectivity. How could he blame the imperialists, the CIA and even the Vatican as the real criminals responsible for the breakdown of Communism without realising the part played by the anger of the people? He himself should be blamed for going on to express the belief that Vietnam too had become a target for destruction by the imperialists, the CIA and other reactionary forces.

I have discussed this matter with many French and American journalists, not one of whom gives any credence to this theory. They all maintain that governments in the West and even the CIA all want to see a stable Vietnam progressing on the road towards development. What purpose would it serve to create chaos? How would that benefit the United States? The Americans have not supported the Khmer Rouge, nor have they helped Vietnamese anti-Communist organisations based in the United States like that led by Hoang Co Minh. On the contrary, leading members of this organisation based in California have been investigated by the US revenue authorities for tax evasion and fraud.

Another mistake made by Nguyen Van Linh was that he went on to affirm mechanistically, like an automaton, that the Vietnamese Communist Party alone leads the country because that is its historic mission; that was always so in the past, remains

---

* Tran Trong Tan is a hypocrite who loves to lecture everybody while hiding his past. He and his brother collaborated with the Japanese fascists in Quang Tri during the Second World War, a fact recently revealed by a high-ranking judge from the same area.

so at present and will be so in the future. This rigid way of speaking is difficult to listen to and leaves no room for retreat. To mount the platform and speak thus for the whole world to hear when both friends and enemies shake their heads in amazement is appalling. It all goes to show that Linh lacked the ability to think for himself and simply followed the advice of his assistants. He turned out to be no more than an *apparatchik* who, when the system is threatened, instinctively moved to defend it. He reads few foreign books and newspapers while paying scant attention to the news. He has little intuition and has rarely been abroad. When he travelled, it was in a very formal way – as the Vietnamese saying goes, 'like riding a horse to go and look at the flowers'.

Yet after delivering the National Day speech, the Party General Secretary was even more outspoken in an off-the-record briefing he gave to the staff at *Nhan Dan*. He branded the Soviet leader Mikhail Gorbachev as an opportunist while lavishing praise on his hardline opponent Yegor Ligachev, whose works we had to publish in Vietnamese.

Then Linh insisted on going to East Berlin personally to attend the fortieth anniversary celebrations of the German Democratic Republic in October 1989. He knew that Gorbachev would be present and Linh wanted to use the occasion to tell him as well as the East German leader Erich Honecker that they had been lax in allowing the situation in Poland to slide so far out of control. In other words, Linh wanted to deliver a lecture to fellow Communist leaders about being more vigilant in protecting the system.

In the event, he was only accorded a brief meeting with Gorbachev and Honecker to exchange courtesies. According to one story which became current in both Moscow and Hanoi, Gorbachev politely doffed his hat and said with a grin 'May I greet the biggest opportunist on earth!' Only Linh and his interpreter could have been aware of what Gorbachev said, but such things have a way of travelling. The Soviet embassy in Hanoi was only 500 metres from Ba Dinh Hall where at Party plenums, particularly after the Tien An Men Square massacre, Gorbachev was often criticised as an opportunist, an agent of the CIA and the tool of American imperialism.

During the celebrations in East Germany, Linh also had to sit out in the open watching a three-hour military parade in bitterly cold weather. The next day, he fell ill with some sort of facial paralysis and returned to Vietnam literally speechless. His wife was very worried and so too was the head of the Women's Association in Saigon, who went off to consult a fortune-teller. He advised that the geomancy of Linh's family home was at fault. Accordingly the main gate facing north was blocked up and the Party financial committee paid for the opening up of a new gate facing east (towards America, as the local wags said). Linh then recovered but he was perforce still silent a few weeks later when the Berlin Wall was torn down and Germany reunited. All this came as a great shock to the ideologues of the Vietnamese Communist Party.

Then, as one Communist regime after another collapsed in Eastern Europe, feelings of panic began to engulf the Vietnamese leadership. The open-door economic policy was still maintained but politics again became a closed book. Controls were re-imposed and writers had to suffer their fate. As for those who had previously appealed to these writers 'not to bend their nibs' but rather to let their creative energy flow, they now did an about-turn. They lectured us with words of intimidation about following the rules of conduct. As a result creativity was stifled and silenced, to be replaced by insipid mediocrity. In other words, all the beautiful flowers which had bloomed on the cactus when the policy of *Doi Moi* was first launched promptly withered, although a new dawn could bring them back to life again.

Nevertheless the leadership had already begun to impose tighter censorship at the beginning of 1989 with calls for more control. For example Kim Hanh, the editor of the outspoken youth magazine *Tuoi Tre* who was eventually dismissed from her position in 1991 for publishing the story about Ho Chi Minh's marriage, was firmly disciplined in 1989. Having attended the International Youth Festival in Pyongyang, she had written an article questioning the degree of freedom in North Korea, a problem of which the whole world is aware. Other sectors of society were affected by this crackdown as well.

In the South some of the officers who had played a prominent role in the Liberation Army set up a body known as the Club of the Revolutionaries. One of its founding members was my old friend General Tran Van Tra. He was still smarting from the banning of his book on the 1975 offensive which had led to his departure from the Party Central Committee and disappearance from public life. Many other officers who had long and distinguished records of service in the South also resented the way they had been pushed aside at the end of the war when people from the North seemed to arrogate the right to run the whole country. Such views appeared in a journal which the Club of Revolutionaries started to publish. It even contained criticism of the way General Vo Nguyen Giap had been removed from power without any explanation being given to the people.

Naturally the appearance of a journal expressing such views caused a considerable stir and it had to be published semi-clandestinely. However, the problem for the Party leadership was that many of its contributors were well-known and popular figures in the South thanks to their revolutionary past. They were also old friends of Nguyen Van Linh who had spent most of his career there. The same was true of Vo Chi Cong who had become Head of State. In fact his son was married to General Tran Van Tra's daughter. Hence two of the most important men in the country had reason enough to 'persuade' General Tra that he should desist from sullying the reputation of the Party by disassociating himself from other members of the Club of Revolutionaries like Nguyen Ho and Ta Ba Tong who were placed under detention without any formal charges being brought against them. As in so many previous cases, the whole matter has been hushed up and their fate is unknown.*

During this crackdown in 1989, I had several articles pigeonholed because the editor always wanted to 'take another look at them'. I had written about the disease of arrogance following our victory in 1975. Then another article I wrote on multi-party politics and pluralism was heavily censored and then suppressed.

However, when the 5th Congress of Journalists convened in Hanoi on October 16, 1989, I had recently recovered from a serious illness, so I just penned a very short article entitled 'Our

---

* In fact, because of the pressure imposed on him, Nguyen Ho, a veteran revolutionary who joined the party in 1936, tendered his resignation from it in early 1990 and withdrew to the countryside, where he was summarily arrested later that year and placed under strict surveillance. He describes these events in a bitter 50-page denunciation of the Party which he circulated clandestinely in late 1993. As a result, he was re-arrested and imprisoned (at the age of seventy-eight) on March 10, 1994.

Village Forum'. It referred to the 6,000 or more writers and journalists throughout the country who were represented by the 300 people who actually attended the Congress. But all of them, whether present or absent, placed a lot of hope in the Congress, as did millions of readers who realised that after more than two years of *Doi Moi* the press had changed a lot. Hence the Congress was expected to be a tense affair. In the event, however, all real discussion was avoided because some people had deliberately absented themselves. One was Tran Do, the head of the Party's Cultural Commission, who knew he was under a cloud for encouraging literary freedom. Another was Nguyen Ngoc, the controversial editor of the cultural magazine *Van Nghe* who had just been sacked from this position as well as from the executive board of the Writers' Association. Nevertheless his successor was not an extreme hardliner as had been expected.

Immediately afterwards at the end of 1989, a new Press Law was promulgated. Its contents were best summed up by a correspondent for the *Nation*, an English-language newspaper published in Bangkok. Having attended the press conference held at the International Club in Hanoi where the Minister of Information spoke at length about the law, he filed a succinct report which read: 'The Vietnamese Press Law which was issued today contains two significant points. They are that the state maintains strict control over the press and prohibits private publications. That's it.' But eyes and ears that have been opened cannot be so easily shut again.

Before 1975, people in the North who listened to foreign radio stations like the BBC and Voice of America always had to keep the volume down and be wary of their neighbours, otherwise there could be problems, particularly with the Cong An. Listening to 'the enemy' was forbidden. In recent years the situation has eased and they can even listen to traditional Vietnamese opera which was previously restricted.

Freedom took another step forward in 1986 with the right in many Party branches to question why the leadership treated skilled graduates like children who were not allowed to read the 'reference documents' produced by the Vietnam News Agency. Thus, people were challenging the system which used to exist in all Communist countries whereby frank reports from the non-Communist world were translated and circulated secretly to a restricted number of high-ranking Party cadres, like in China where it is known as 'Reference News'. Many people went on to say: 'We may be only officials whose salaries are less than those of our superiors, but we are not sure that their knowledge is better than ours. To say that we oppose the ranking of the hierarchy within the Party is to admit that such a pecking order exists, whereas everybody should be equal, even non Party members.'

While there are over 40 million adults in Vietnam, only 2 million are Party members and many of them are losing faith and seeking to quit. At the same time few young people have any interest in joining since they know that the Party only accepts people who know how to kow-tow, clap their hands and approve the resolutions handed down from above by a small group of leaders. There is a story about a man who actually applies to join a Party cell and is strongly recommended by his colleagues because they want to keep the ranks of the non-Party members clean!

Within the Party itself, much attention was focused during the closing months of 1989 on Tran Xuan Bach. He was born in Ha Nam Ninh, the same province as Le Duc Tho and Nguyen Co Thach, the Foreign Minister. Early in his life, Bach was active in the youth movement in the town of Nam Dinh and became deputy secretary of the provincial Party committee. He was then promoted to the State Committee responsible for religious affairs because he was extremely well informed about the area of Phat Diem, which was the centre of the Roman Catholic religion in North Vietnam. Later he became secretary to the Party Central Committee and in 1980 was chosen to go to Cambodia to become the Party representative of the Vietnamese 'volunteers' there. That was a very important task when the question arose of creating a special relationship between the three countries of Indo-China.

Tran Xuan Bach owed this position to Le Duc Tho who was responsible not only for Party organisation but for Cambodia as well. As a result Bach became a member of the Party Secretariat at the 5th Party Congress in 1982 and of the Politburo at the 6th Congress in 1986. Aged sixty, he was its youngest member. He was then given responsibility for relations with Laos and Cambodia as well as other foreign Communist parties including those movements which had not yet achieved power. In addition his duties covered the Overseas Vietnamese organisations.

However, very few people were aware that from 1987 onwards Bach was assigned another task by the Politburo. That was to monitor the situation both at home and abroad by reading the foreign press and drawing up reports on it for the top leadership. In order to carry out this work, he assembled a team of six people who could read and translate from English, French, Russian and Chinese in order to summarise what was being said. He also made good use of the Institute of Social Sciences and the Vietnam News Agency. In fact, his office became the centre of the latest information.

For example, I went there to borrow a copy of the book *Brother Enemy* by Nayan Chanda as soon as it was published. I had known Nayan for many years. He is an Indian journalist educated in France who worked for the *Far Eastern Economic Review*. His book presented a truthful and lively account of the turbulence within the Asian Communist world during the 1970s through much revealing new information.

Thanks to the advisory group which helped him from 1987 onwards to assess and analyse the foreign media, Tran Xuan Bach began to change his views and draw up his own policy scenario. Even before the Democracy Movement erupted in China and culminated in the Tien An Men Square massacre of June 1989, he had presented an analysis of the situation to ideological and foreign affairs cadres. He stated that the re-establishment of relations between the Soviet Union and China would be a significant landmark creating a multi-polar world with the United States but at the same time creating a crisis for Communism. Therefore relations between Vietnam and China would have to be improved, although attention had to be paid to China's tendency towards hegemonism and its desire to dominate the islands of the South China Sea.

Tran Xuan Bach then turned to the crisis in the Communist world and attributed its economic problems to the shortage of consumer goods as well as low production. He also said there was a social crisis because of a lack of confidence in Communism and the leading role of the Party. There were, he said, three types of people in society – politicians, scientists and businessmen – but in Vietnam there was a lack of businessmen, so social attitudes had to be corrected. Politicians should be treated with respect, scientists should not be discriminated against, and there should be no prejudice against businessmen.

As a solution to Vietnam's problems, Bach advocated various far-reaching measures right down to the lowest political and social levels. Pointing to the way that the dong had depreciated in value by 3,000 per cent since 1986, while the money in circulation had increased to an equally astronomical extent, he suggested that the two crucial elements Vietnam had ignored were market forces and wide-ranging democracy. Even so, in developing the economy he ruled out the black market, just as he rejected the idea of a political opposition in the process of moving towards democracy.

At the end of 1989, Tran Xuan Bach explained these ideas to the 7th Plenum of the Party Central Committee with the simile that progress must take place on two legs. If the economy is to progress rapidly to increase productivity according to market forces, then the political leg must also move forward towards democracy and the acceptance of pluralism. These ideas were considered dangerous and extremist, and were therefore rejected. Still, in early 1990 Tran Xuan Bach continued to travel around explaining his views and getting articles about them published in the press. That prompted the Party Committee for Ideology and Culture to criticise the mass media for spreading the views of individuals opposed to the Party. In fact, at one of the weekly Party meetings of the mass media an official in charge of ideology upbraided Tran Xuan Bach for making mistakes such as putting Pol Pot, Stalin and Mao Tse-tung in the same basket.

When he was disciplined at the 8th Party Plenum held in March 1990, the idea was originally just to remove Bach from the Politburo and Party Secretariat while keeping him as a member of the Central Committee. But as the discussions proceeded, some delegates from the central and highland provinces as well as the army criticised him as undisciplined and unworthy of being a Party member at a time when unity and consensus were needed. Thus when a vote was taken, a majority of over 50 per cent voted in favour of his expulsion from the Central Committee.

Tran Xuan Bach accepted this disciplinary measure on the understanding that his case would be re-assessed at the forthcoming 7th Party Congress to be held the following year, but this idea did not materialise since he was not a delegate at the Congress and nobody bothered to recall his name. Nonetheless in the meantime Nguyen Co Thach, the Foreign Minister, appointed Bach as a researcher in his office in order to make use of his knowledge. There was also sympathy involved. Both men had originally been considered to be protégés of Le Duc Tho. Thach too was an educated man compared with the rest of the Politburo. He had graduated from high school and although starting his revolutionary career in the army, had participated in most of Vietnam's international diplomatic ventures from the Geneva Conference in 1954 onwards. In fact through his ability to read the American press and develop propaganda to exploit the anti-war movement in the United States during the 1960s, Nguyen Co Thach could be said to have underpinned Le Duc Tho's success in outmanoeuvring Henry Kissinger in the Paris Agreements concluded in January 1973.

Nor did Thach's interests stop there. Whenever I met him in subsequent years either in Hanoi or during his travels abroad on official duty, he wanted to talk, to discuss matters freely without the constraints of Party policy. He also liked to listen to my ideas about what I had learned on my foreign travels. Basically Thach was in favour of improving relations with our former enemies such as the Americans, the Japanese and the French in order to look to the future rather than being always drawn back into the past, as he put it. He also appreciated that General Vo Nguyen Giap might be able to play a significant role in achieving a reconciliation with France and the United States. Nor was Thach opposed to an improvement in relations with China. He merely said that if we put too much emphasis on our relationship with the Chinese, it could be disastrous for us.

This ability to understand the outside world made Tran Xuan Bach and Nguyen Co Thach natural allies, but it was not allowed to last for long. At the 9th Party Plenum held in August 1990, Thach too came under attack as a rightist because he had long been a strong proponent of a total military withdrawal from Cambodia while guaranteeing that it would soon lead to a lifting of the US trade and aid embargo. When he proved unable to produce this result, Thach tried to save his own skin by sacrificing Tran Xuan Bach, who had to retire completely and retreat to his wife's village near Gia Lam where he now lives forgotten by everybody.

Yet it is worth remembering that Bach did not advocate a multi-party system as such. He was always careful to protect himself and explain that what he favoured was a diversification of ideas in the field of economics and cultural styles as well as respect for different religions. He also accepted the need for discussing differing ideologies and political views. But he stopped short of a multi-party system.

Bach's case is also significant because he was carrying out the sort of research in which the leadership of the Vietnamese Communist Party is very weak. When facing the realities of the world as presented through the mass media, the views of the people change because of the nature of progress. The fifteen minutes of news relayed by the Soviet Union through the Lotus satellite system became a very important window on the world. It enabled viewers in Vietnam to watch vivid pictures of such events as the breaching of the Berlin Wall, President Ceausescu being shot dead in Romania, the acclamation of Vaclav Havel as President in Czechoslovakia and the multi-party elections in Mongolia.

However, control over the choice of what was shown on television soon tightened again in an attempt to avoid awkward truths, and in July 1990 the Party ideological and cultural committee issued an order banning the press, radio and television from referring to Stalin. I thought this wrong and stupid. Why, when the Soviet Union was producing articles, documents and films about Stalin's crimes, should we in Vietnam try to hush them up? It was unnatural – as if we were afraid of the truth because we had so often eulogised him in the past.

This same order also forbade all mention of pluralism, and anybody who violated it would be held responsible before the Party and the state. Again it was obvious that talking of anything that might lead to a multi-party system was anathema to the leadership. However it is impossible to revert to the old ways and hush everything up, leaving the people in total ignorance as before. Knowledge about the world is a deeply felt need. The people know that if they can acquire such knowledge there is hope for the future.

During the crucial meetings of the Party Central Committee to discuss developments in Eastern Europe and the fate of Tran Xuan Bach, one of his harshest critics was Politburo member Dao Duy Tung, who is known in inner Party circles as 'the

Toad' because he jumped up and down with so much glee on attaining this position in 1986. Previously he was editor of *Tap Chi Cong San*, the Party's monthly journal, for whom I used to write quite a lot of articles until his views became increasingly rigid and dogmatic. Indeed, on his return to Hanoi in late 1989 after attending the Romanian Party Congress, he came straight to *Nhan Dan* to tell us how stable and successful the Ceausescu regime was, just a couple of weeks before it was overthrown. Still at the crucial Party plenums held in late 1989 and early 1990, Dao Duy Tung enjoyed the full support of Nguyen Duc Binh, the head of the Nguyen Ai Quoc Party School, and Nong Duc Manh, the provincial Party Secretary of the Bac Thai region in the North, both of whom have subsequently been appointed members of the Politburo. Then there was Nguyen Ha Phan, the provincial Party Secretary in Hau Giang, a powerful figure in the South who was also opposed to Tran Xuan Bach.

In March 1990, when the resolution of the 8th Plenum expelling Bach from the Central Committee and attributing the collapse of Communism in Eastern Europe to imperialist and reactionary plots was published in *Nhan Dan*, everybody accepted it in silence. But when we met individually, most of us acknowledged that it was not easy because obviously the people of Eastern Europe had risen up and rejected bureaucracy and totalitarianism. Then all Party members, once they had studied the plenum's decisions, had to undergo sessions of criticism and self-criticism. There were two of them. Decision 8A concerned relations between the Party and the people. Decision 8B was about the situation in Eastern Europe. All the criticisms and self-criticisms had to be written by hand, signed and submitted to the Party branch organiser so that they could be attached to one's own personal file.

At the editorial office of *Nhan Dan* when such criticism and self-criticism sessions were held in June 1990, I felt I was clearly one of the major targets of the Party organisers although I held quite an important position. I was editor of the paper's Sunday Magazine as well as being responsible for arts and culture. What was more, I still continued to be involved in editorial work relating to international current affairs with particular reference to national defence and security matters. I have never tried to avoid my duty and have always been determined to maintain a correct attitude as well as my self-confidence. After the editor of *Nhan Dan* conducted his self-criticism, it was my turn.

On this occasion I repeated my view that the collapse of Communism in Eastern Europe was mainly due to internal factors although there could have been external influence as well. That however was a judgement based on the principles of dialectical materialism, whereas the problem really arose from a lack of democracy, an excess of bureaucracy and irresponsible attitudes. I went on to say that the concept of diversifying ideas is both correct and necessary. It is the basis of the policy of *Doi Moi*, therefore the Party was going too far in disciplining Tran Xuan Bach by expelling him from all the positions he held.

This meeting was attended by about thirty officials from *Nhan Dan* ranging from sub-editors to heads of department. One of them who was in charge of readers' letters asked me whether I should review my ideas to conform with those of the Party. He then stated that in his neighbourhood some forty to fifty people had crammed into a small room to listen to a tape-recording of a speech I had made, and one of them had commented that it was high time everybody spoke out in this way without bothering to waste time listening to propagandists.

But during this criticism session at *Nhan Dan*, another colleague challenged me by saying that an article I had written about the situation in Eastern Europe was at variance with the Party line. I replied that it was true I had spoken about the brutality of man towards man coupled with bureaucracy, corruption and totalitarianism. That always alienates true Communists. No one can accept these characteristics, and therefore it is essential that every Communist Party should review its attitude.

Following this meeting quite a lot of young cadres who had been present came to talk to me. They said that while they sympathised with my statement, they were worried about what would happen to me since I had expressed my views so strongly. On the other hand, they said that I was fortunate in that I enjoyed a certain status within the Party whereas if they had spoken out as I did they would be gambling with their jobs and their future. In fact for several years I had been quite daring in expressing my views openly at meetings and was amused to watch the reaction. Some people were very surprised but others nodded their heads in agreement with obvious pleasure.

At the Nguyen Ai Quoc Party School in April 1990, for instance, I expressed the view that the Party had long usurped the power of the government and it was high time that such duties were handed back to duly elected bodies. Otherwise the Party could be said to be violating the constitution which has long been the fundamental law of the state. I then pointed out that the constitution states clearly that in Vietnam government rests in the hands of the people through the representatives whom they have elected to the National Assembly. The people have not elected the members of the Politburo or Central Commitee; yet these two bodies make decisions about policy and planning both in the short and longer term concerning agriculture, industry and handicrafts etc. All of this is wrong in principle since it overlaps the authority of the National Assembly and the local Peoples' Committees.

In May 1990 the Ministry of the Interior also invited me to come and talk about domestic and international affairs to various medium- and high-ranking cadres of the Cong An in Hanoi. I chose to speak about how our armed forces, including the Cong An, far exceeded in numbers those of other countries comparable in size with Vietnam. I also expressed the view that Vietnam had lost a lot of international goodwill when Le Duc Tho refused to accept the Nobel Peace Prize back in 1973. After the meeting I asked some of the officials present whether they found my views too strong. They replied that they had enjoyed my briefing because I was straightforward and had interesting and useful ideas to put forward.

Likewise I was invited to go and talk to people in Ha Nam Ninh province. That was an experience I will not easily forget. The deputy head of the province took me and several young journalists to visit the coastal region of Xuan Thuy where various sandbanks have been developing into islands in recent years because the sea is withdrawing. Then we went to Bach Long where sixty years ago my father had been district chief and supervised the construction of dykes to stop the sea swallowing up thousands of hectares of land. These dykes still exist as a memorial to those who built them as well as all those who have owed their living to them ever since. I still remember my father telling us children how the dykes were built when we were studying in Hue.

Later, I learned that the General Department of the Security

Forces had sent an official to Ha Nam Ninh to investigate what I had been doing there in speaking to people at the port enterprise at Ninh Binh as well as the mechanical engineering works. Those responsible replied calmly that they had invited me to come and speak because they knew I had addressed the Nguyen Ai Quoc Party School and cadres at the Interior Ministry in my capacity as deputy editor of *Nhan Dan*, so they too wanted to hear what I had to say and found it very useful. I had talked about my observations of life in America, Japan and the neighbouring countries of South East Asia.

In this same context, a friend informed me that in August 1990, when he went on a trip to Vinh, Nha Trang and Ho Chi Minh City, he found tapes of one of my speeches at Ninh Binh on sale there for 3,000 dong each. I have also heard that these tapes have reached the markets of places as far apart as Rach Gia in the extreme south and Lai Chau on the Chinese border although, as I jokingly remarked, I have never received any copyright fees.

Some short articles I wrote about life abroad likewise attracted favourable comment from readers of *Nhan Dan*. These articles talked about the spirit of discipline and public health prevailing in some cities in the world in contrast to Hanoi where the streets are used for all purposes from relieving oneself to playing football, with people eating and sleeping in between. I also wrote about the standards of public service in foreign countries as well as the fact that people there who are only thirty years old can attain important positions as university professors or government ministers.

The trouble with Vietnam is that it has been isolated for so long from the outside world and has continued with its own way of living and working which is old-fashioned, even primitive. It has therefore missed out on a lot of experience gained by other countries. I know that young people in particular are thirsty for new information that is truthful and direct, and are fed up with articles and speeches full of empty morality and jargon which goes in one ear and out of the other. For instance they have so often heard the phrase 'We have committed mistakes and shortcomings' without any explanation of whom the word 'we' is intended to signify and whether these mistakes will ever be punished.

Even Vietnamese embassies abroad know little of the outside world. According to a very old formula, they divide Overseas Vietnamese into good and bad, in other words the patriots and the reactionaries. Hence in January 1990, when over 700 Vietnamese living abroad – many of whom had previously been regarded as patriots – signed what they called a 'heartfelt' petition, they were all labelled as reactionaries. The petition had 'dared' to refer to events in Romania and request the separation of the Party from the state. As a result the signatories of the petition were refused permission to visit Vietnam which, as I told the Deputy Interior Minister Tam Long in July 1990, was a senseless and foolish decision.

For instance several foreign affairs and economic administration institutes invited Professor Nguyen Manh Hung, who teaches economics in Canada, to come and give some lectures in Hanoi. But when he arrived at Hanoi's Noi Bai airport, he was refused entry by the Cong An in a way that was rude and lacking in any courtesy. It was also politically counter-productive because while it manifestly did nothing to contribute to national security, it evoked a sharp reaction both from the organisations which had invited Professor Hung in the first place and from many Overseas Vietnamese.

Then there was the case of Nguyen Thanh Long, an engineer trained in France who invented a method, which has been widely applied in Europe, of using old tyres to reinforce the construction of roads and dykes. He was invited by the Ministry of Education to make a working visit to Vietnam with several French engineers. Although he carries a Vietnamese passport and also wished to see his elderly mother who was ill, he was not allowed to return home. The reason was because he had allowed his address in France to be used as a contact point for signatures to the petition, so eliminating the need for a post office box. As a result, the authorities regarded him as a dangerous person who had possibly initiated and even masterminded the whole affair. However, those Overseas Vietnamese who are familiar with this case point out that the strangest aspect is that passport-holding nationals of most countries do not have to apply for a visa to return home.

On various occasions, Vietnamese intellectuals abroad who remain loyal to the country and are involved in research projects have invited me to their homes on my own with just a notebook and admitted how discouraged they are. They feel that they have to request stateless travel documents in spite of being no less patriotic than those of us who live within the country.

One cannot really blame all the diplomats and officials involved. Vietnamese embassies – and during the course of my travels, I have visited many of them in various parts of the world including Eastern Europe and South East Asia – are a reflection in miniature of the situation back home. There is a lack of any sense of urgency, and salaries are low so that the staff often engage in trafficking in order to survive. There is considerable advantage to be gained from this practice and some diplomats even make a fortune. I know that on one occasion when the diplomatic bag from an embassy in Eastern Europe was opened in transit through Moscow, it was found to include 800 pairs of jeans and 2,000 digital watches belonging to a high-ranking diplomat who was actually the Party branch secretary within the embassy concerned. There have even been cases of container-loads of goods sent home under diplomatic cover.

Perhaps one of the most notorious incidents occurred in 1985 on what turned out to be Le Duan's last visit to Moscow. Its purpose was stated to be official consultations, but it amounted to a holiday coupled with medical care. He was accompanied by twelve officials and sixteen assistants who arrived at Moscow airport for the return flight to Hanoi with three lorries carrying 6 tons of accompanying luggage rather than the concessionary rate of 60 kilos per person allowed to prominent passengers. Since the era of reforms had already begun to take root in the Soviet Union, airport officials decided to teach the Vietnamese a lesson. They refused to let the plane carrying the Party General Secretary take off with so much baggage, saying it constituted a safety hazard. The Vietnamese ambassador implored and entreated, but in vain. The Russians knew full well that Le Duan's delegation had engaged in a shopping spree in the Soviet Union buying up water pumps, sewing machines, pressure cookers, irons, medicines, Western cigarettes etc. to take back home duty-free to sell on the open market. In the end Le Duan's flight took off late and the goods had to be shipped afterwards by sea via Vladivostok or Odessa.

There must have been many more such consignments which reached their destination successfully and undetected under cover of a red passport. Everything has its price. But there are still some diplomats who are conscious of what is right and wrong even when living in a prosperous country where they cannot afford to take a friend out for a meal for the essential purpose of improving relations.

All this made me realise in 1990 that it was necessary to adopt a strong and determined attitude in order to help the country through such a major crisis, which I regarded as more serious than any it had previously experienced. I also wanted to do something to remedy the plight of the press and those who worked for it. The patience of my friends and indeed of the whole people had been stretched to the limit.

Back in 1986 when Truong Chinh became Party General Secretary again, I sent him a petition through his personal secretary Ha Nghiep. This petition consisting of five pages of typescript of which I still have a copy, suggested that the policy of *Doi Moi* should be pursued strongly and with determination in both the economic and political spheres while we mended relations with all our former enemies such as Japan, France, China and the United States. I proposed that we should seize the initiative to send delegations to those countries as well as convening a special conference to discuss major changes in our economic and political system. In this petition I also suggested reducing the armed forces from 1.6 million to 600,000 within three years in line with the rest of the world. But Truong Chinh just glanced at this petition and said that my ideas were powerful and would have to be considered by the Central Committee. The rest was silence.

I now understand more clearly than before how the system had been distorted, and how democracy had become a formality with the leadership exploiting truth and patriotism in the name of the masses united in support of the Party. Therefore I had to find a different, more roundabout way to convey my message; – a way that was hit-and-miss as well as fraught with danger.

8

DEPARTURE

I know that the Party considered long and hard whether to let me accept the invitation I had received from the French Communist Party newspaper *L'Humanité* to visit Paris in September 1990. After all, I had voiced a lot of criticism of the situation in Vietnam during the previous few months. But then I too had to think about the implications of my departure.

I had taken many major steps in my life like leaving home in my youth to join the Resistance and the Communist Party. I had also embarked on several hazardous trips down the Ho Chi Minh Trail as well as being in the forefront of our troops entering Saigon and later Phnom Penh. Going to France seemed to me no less of an adventure, perhaps the last in my life. But in all my earlier expeditions and behind all my anxieties there was a belief in our cause, based on hope. It may have been shallow and unstable, but it was there.

It is true that in certain ways it was like returning to my past because I was French-educated, but there were so many unanswered questions. What was France really like? What would the attitude of the French authorities be towards someone like myself who had fought against them? And what about the Vietnamese living in France? How would they react? And how would I be able to survive there? I was also worried about my health following a minor heart attack in June 1989. What would happen if I had another one? There were many nights when I tossed about sleeplessly with such worries.

There was also the fact that I had a stable occupation. From February 1989, in other words for nearly two years, I had been directly responsible for the Sunday Magazine of *Nhan Dan*. I

169

had conceived the idea and directed the project to construct a team of twelve people who believed and trusted in one another to create a new sort of magazine. We wanted to forge something different which was useful without appearing arrogant or loud-mouthed. We tried to raise the level of information with short articles of ten to thirty lines, compared with those in *Nhan Dan* which could be up to 200 lines long. We also tried to provide differing ideas as a discussion forum for our readers. Then we introduced colour photos, a trend followed by other papers. As a result we started off by printing 60,000 copies in February 1989 at 350 dong a copy and had increased our sales to 140,000 by the end of the year, so making a considerable profit. Thus the magazine provided marketable and *Nhan Dan* no longer needed to be subsidised as before with Party funds provided by the Ministry of Finance. We even had money to set up a welfare fund for the staff and to invest in new technology. Then we branched out into producing special issues for Women's Day, Children's Day, National Day etc. which enabled us to grant a bonus to all 300 members of staff, for whom life consequently became easier. Thus the staff of the Sunday Magazine, myself included, gained a lot of praise.

Even so, although I enjoyed this new form of journalism, there were still obstacles. In theory I was the editor of the Sunday Magazine as well as continuing to write for the daily newspaper. Nonetheless, despite the fact that for the past four years I had been a Grade 8 official equivalent to a deputy minister, my articles still had to go through all the various stages of vetting, and some of them were censored and in the end banned from publication.

In this situation I felt a deep sadness for the country and the people who were in such a state of poverty and despair from which there seemed no way out. I wanted to play a part in rescuing Vietnam from its misery and isolation. Yet if I went abroad I might have to face many difficulties in getting my ideas accepted. Would I be wasting my time and bringing misfortune on myself and my family? However, I could not just sit back and do nothing while I thought about my own fate. That would have been irresponsible towards my dear compatriots. I decided I had to act.

My children had grown up and were successful. My daughter was a doctor at the Central Eye Hospital, and her husband worked as an official at the State Commission for Cooperation and Investment. My son had left for Hong Kong as a boat person sailing from Haiphong at the beginning of 1989. He was a mechanical engineer who after graduating from Hanoi Polytechnic became fed up with the way people of talent were treated and wanted to improve his educational qualifications. Since facilities in Vietnam are so bad, he decided to find a way of going abroad.

Within the family my wife did not encourage him, but she also did not try to stop him when he suddenly decided to depart despite all the dangers involved. My son and his girlfriend, who had just graduated in English from the Foreign Languages Institute of Hanoi University, went to the District Committee to get the papers to register their marriage the day before they left. Then many months later we received a letter saying that the two of them had spent twenty-eight days at sea before reaching Hong Kong. There they were subsequently held in Whitehead Detention Centre for a year and a half before gaining their freedom in July 1990 to await acceptance for resettlement in Canada on the guarantee of one of my sisters who lives in La Puente, California. I was both worried about my son and proud of him because he has an independent mind, determination and personality.

A week before I myself departed, I managed to visit the village of Lien Bat in the Ung Hoa district of Ha Dong province where my parents were buried. Despite having been a communist since the age of nineteen, I still believe it is right and proper to respect our traditions and honour the ancestors. Then I said good-bye to my family as well as my close friends in a mixed frame of mind. I was happy to have the opportunity to go and do something useful. On the other hand, I was worried about taking a leap into the unknown. I was sad too about going so far away on my own.

In particular, I had to brush away my tears when embracing my granddaughters Hoai Anh and Quynh Anh who were nearly four and eight years old. They regarded their grandfather as a friend and often asked him to take them shopping to buy pictures and books or go to the park to eat ice cream. Above all they liked to go to the hall of mirrors where all three of us would stand and laugh at the way out shapes became distorted. The two girls also felt they could talk to their grandfather about 'important' and secret stories concerning friends or school and their teachers which they could not tell their parents.

I left for France at the end of September 1990 alone. All I had with me was an air ticket to Moscow, a diplomatic passport a – privilege extended to all Vietnamese journalists travelling abroad, although it has to be surrendered automatically at the airport on return – and a small case containing little more than a couple of shirts and pairs of trousers.

As usual because Vietnam was such a small, poor country 'walking with other people's legs', I had to stop off in Moscow to collect my onward ticket to Paris from the office of *Pravda*, which was paying for it. I also used the occasion to visit the organisation responsible for state planning, but its offices were quite deserted because the staff had to stand in long queues to buy bread and even matches! At Moscow Radio, too, many people were expressing concern about the introduction of food rationing as well as rising prices.

By contrast, when I arrived in France, I discovered a very different society, although if I praise it I know some people at home will criticise me. But while I too have not forgotten that it was the French who killed my mother and many of my friends, I have come to appreciate a lot about France including the freedom of choice and the rule of law. Therefore after attending the celebrations at *L'Humanité* and then the conference organised by the Leclerc Foundation, I asked the Vietnamese Ambassador in Paris, Pham Binh, to forward to Hanoi a request from me to stay on in France for health care. The French too agreed to let me remain, although I did not request political asylum.

At the same time, I contacted the BBC in London. It was something I had decided to do even before leaving Vietnam. It is a radio station which has a good signal, it speaks clearly and is rarely 'jammed'. The times of its transmissions in the morning, evening and night are very convenient for listeners and I know many people who tune in, ranging from peasants and ordinary families to officials and Party members. They all prefer the BBC. I also know that several members of the leadership including Pham Van Dong, Vo Nguyen Giap and Nguyen Van Linh all listen to the BBC although during the war it carried news and comments which on occasion were biased against the North. But in recent years it has become very objective, providing extremely up-to-date and comprehensive news in many forms with attractive voices. The BBC Vietnamese Section has a mixture of Northern and Southern accents, both male and female, all of which are highly expressive. Clearly it attracts millions more listeners than Hanoi Radio.

One of the people who works for the BBC Vietnamese Section is Do Van whom I met when he visited Hanoi in 1988 and again in 1990. On those occasions I found he spoke straight to the point and asked questions which went to the heart of the matter. He also showed deep concern for the crisis in which Vietnam is currently involved. So I asked him if he could come over to Paris. It was after talking to him and other Overseas Vietnamese in France that I decided to draw up a twelve point Petition from a Citizen under my pen-name Thanh Tin calling for major changes in the country.

Among other things in this petition, I singled out the role of three bodies responsible for the present situation in the country. They are the people in charge of indoctrination, Party organisation and the Cong An. I have many friends in all these bodies and many of them are well-intentioned. But these three bodies have committed innumerable mistakes.

The Nguyen Ai Quoc Party School, which is responsible for indoctrination, is very backward in keeping up to date with developments not only inside the country but also in the world at large. Its opinions are conservative, using dogma lagging thirty or forty years behind the times. I know for instance that Nguyen Duc Binh, the head of the School, led a delegation to Moscow in 1987 to discuss Party policy and met with considerable criticism there. His views were regarded as dogmatic and outmoded, particularly the claim that capitalism was facing a crisis of confidence throughout the world and would inevitably wither away, so proving the pre-eminence of socialism. Yet he was one of the fiercest critics of Tran Xuan Bach and has subsequently become a member of the Politburo.

The same is true of Le Phuc Tho, the head of the Party Organisational Committee. Nonetheless the influence of this body diminished somewhat following Le Duc Tho's death from cancer in October 1990. For instance it could not protect the career of his younger brother Mai Chi Tho, who in early 1987 was appointed Minister of the Interior and hence head of the Cong

An, although he had never been an officer in this body. Even when Mai Chi Tho had himself promoted to the rank of full general after his brother's death, he was still replaced as Minister of the Interior by Bui Thien Ngo, a professional Cong An officer.

Under him, the Cong An continues to commit serious mistakes and these have been increasing. There are hundreds of cases in which people have been branded as anti-Party, anti-leadership, anti- socialist, revisionists and reactionaries or alternatively as having acted as 'the paid agents of colonialism' or 'imperialist spies'. These cases have still not been corrected or brought to justice. I have mentioned some names but the list is not complete. For example, in May 1990 Father Chan Tin as well as the former Catholic priest, Nguyen Ngoc Lan, both of whom had previously campaigned on behalf of those people detained either by the Saigon regime or later by our authorities, suddenly found themselves subjected to three years of house arrest. Although there were never any formal proceedings against them, they were regarded as 'hostile elements' because during the observance of the Christian period of Lent that year, Father Chan Tin had preached several sermons calling on the leadership in Hanoi to 'repent for its sins'.

Apart from such well-known political dissidents, there are literally thousands of ordinary people who have been victimised and detained in a whole network of prisons, sometimes for decades. There they exist in insanitary conditions and have been ill-treated, oppressed and dishonoured. At the same time their families and friends have suffered discrimination. Some of them have even died unjustly in ignominy and shame. Meanwhile their families have continued endlessly to demand an explanation, but without ever getting a response.

On the other hand, not a single representative in the National Assembly has ever raised the question of who is responsible for all this suffering. I just hope that the day will come when the people realise that our various security branches, including the Cong An and the *Bao Ve*, hold myriads of files on individuals. Perhaps then public opinion both at home and abroad will appreciate what Vietnam has had to endure for so many years.

In my petition I described a regime which has no sense of personal responsibility before the law. Instead we give prominence to the high degree of unity among our collective leadership to the point where individuals no longer matter. But that is where the fault lies. Collectivity is a shield behind which individuals can happily conceal and dodge their own personal responsibility.

In November 1990 I sent a copy of my petition to Pham Binh, the ambassador in Paris, to be forwarded to the leadership in Hanoi through official diplomatic channels. But I knew that the likelihood of my proposals being officially accepted was very slim. So I also handed the text to the international press as well as the BBC, which agreed to broadcast it followed by a series of interviews in the course of which Do Van posed to me many searching questions not just about the present situation in Vietnam but also about past history.

On December 3, the Reuter correspondent in Hanoi reported: 'Listeners to the BBC in Vietnam and particularly in Hanoi and Saigon are paying a great deal of attention to Bui Tin's interviews because he has been saying what a lot of people including those in official positions think but have never dared state in public.'

Then, ten days later, a French journalist who had just returned from Vietnam phoned to congratulate me. He said that it was just as if an atomic bomb had dropped on Ho Chi Minh City. Everybody there was talking about my interviews, and every Saturday and Sunday evening when they were broadcast, the streets were deserted as people stayed home to listen to the BBC.

I was very moved but still cautious. I told him he must be exaggerating, but he insisted he was not. Then I started to get letters from friends all over Vietnam. They related how on hearing my petition, intellectuals, professors, students and artists had held heated discussions and there was a general tendency to speak the truth more boldly without fear or hesitation as previously. And the more boldly people spoke out, the bolder they became. I considered that an important sign. I never regarded my ideas as the sole solution – they were merely intended as a stimulus to make people think about the situation in Vietnam and develop their own views about how to resolve its many problems.

At the beginning of January 1991 the text of another petition reached Paris and was published there. It took the form of a personal letter written to Nguyen Huu Tho, the head of the Fatherland Front, by Dr Nguyen Khac Vien. He was a well-known figure who had studied medicine in France and continued to maintain contact with the Overseas Vietnamese community there through his articles about the need for patriotism. He also wrote several books on the history of Vietnam and acted for many years as editor of *Vietnam Courier*, the newspaper produced in Hanoi in several languages for distribution to friends abroad. Now retired but still writing books about child care, Dr Vien was already disillusioned about the situation in Vietnam in 1982 when he wrote a letter to Truong Chinh, then Chairman of the National Assembly, calling among other things for this body to be granted more real power. This letter was never published in Vietnam, nor was Dr Vien's subsequent letter to Nguyen Huu Tho.

A similar fate awaited other letters and petitions which emerged in the early months of 1991. One came from the pen of Hoang Minh Chinh who was first detained as a 'revisionist' back in 1964. On his release a couple of years later, he was unrepentant and wrote a treatise entitled 'Dogmatism in Vietnam' which earned him another long spell in prison. Still he has never desisted from expressing his opinion that Asian communism in the form of Maoism is little different from feudalism. This theme recurred in his 1991 petition where he outlined the history of the Vietnamese Party and claimed that it been infected with the disease of infantilism from the very outset and so needed to be completely overhauled. What is more, Hoang Minh Chinh was not afraid to circulate this statement under his own name, giving the address where he now lives in Hanoi under constant surveillance by the security forces.

Then there was the petition entitled 'An Urgent Programme for Overcoming the Current Crisis and Creating Proper Conditions for Developing the Country'. This was written by the well-known mathematician Phan Dinh Dieu, deputy head of the Scientific Studies Institute of Vietnam. He even advocated the introduction of a multi-party system.

In the South too, Lu Phuong, the noted writer who was formerly Deputy Minister of Culture in the Provisional Revolutionary Government of South Vietnam, wrote an article entitled 'Vietnamese Socialism, its Legacy and *Doi Moi*'. Very daringly and lucidly, it put forward the view that the Communist Party should hand over full power to the state and the people, as well as placing itself within the law on an equal footing with all other political and social organisations. Thus it would re-affirm its ability and qualities. Soon afterwards the elderly journalist Vu Hanh also sent an article, 'Brazen-faced towards the People', to Radio Moscow. On March 31, 1991, this article appeared in *Moscow News*, the weekly published in twelve languages (though not Vietnamese). It was accompanied by the comment 'The leaders of the Vietnamese regime are worried because they feel themselves isolated. They have been accustomed to depend on the support and "spirit of solidarity" among the so-called socialist countries, but in reality these were dictatorships which have just collapsed. The Vietnamese leaders now feel abandoned in confronting the people to whom they will have to answer for all the hardship and backwardness the country has had to endure for the past couple of decades.'

As a result of such comments the circulation of *Moscow News* and other Soviet newspapers was banned in Vietnam. The local press, radio and television also remained silent about all these articles and petitions. However one has to be mindful of the technology of modern communications in the world these days. It is not like in the old days when news from Hue had to be conveyed by messengers on foot or horseback to Hanoi or later by rail or car. Nor is the situation as it was during the time of the Resistance in the jungle when newspapers and letters took weeks to arrive and such news of the outside world as we received was scrappy and out-of-date. These days people throughout the country have access to radio, television, photocopiers and even fax machines so it is difficult to keep them in the dark about what is going on.

What is more, the official press drew attention to my petition by criticising it and me. Then in an interview given to the Bangkok newspaper *The Nation*, Mai Chi Tho the Minister of the Interior denounced me as a 'reactionary' and made disparaging remarks about my class origins. But it took four months before I was finally expelled from the Party and dismissed from *Nhan Dan* in March 1991.

I did not respond to the abuse heaped on me by the Party. I even retained my self-control when I was accused of having been brought up by imperialist elements. It is not that I am proud or obstinate, but then neither am I dejected by all this, or even surprised. The Party always reacts in the same way, as if its main slogan is 'Protect the Party and Protect the Regime'. Yet the crucial fact is that not even Party members, let alone the people, have much faith in its slogans which lack justice and enlightenment.

One of the main lessons I have learnt in almost fifty years of political activism is always to be oneself and not to lose one's identity. It is essential to think for oneself and not blindly imitate other people. This may be difficult, but to be lazy, frightened or over-cautious is to gamble away one's own self.

However, my attitude came as a shock to my wife. She is a native of Vinh and we married in 1956 when I was stationed there. In 1990 she retired from her work as a schoolteacher. Previously she was often worried when I went away on long trips and left her to look after our two children, but when she heard my interviews on the BBC and learned that I had decided to remain temporarily in France, she was astonished. Yet at the end of one of her letters she said that on occasions as she rode her bicycle through the streets of Hanoi, other unknown cyclists had approached her with words of encouragement for what I was doing and to express sympathy for all the family was suffering as a result. I remember the way the families of the writers involved in the *Nhan Van, Giai Pham* affair were also subject to discrimination as well as abuse and scorn for many years.

My family became the object of surveillance and my son-in-law, who had been nominated by the head of his institute to study at Harvard, was refused permission to go. Then somebody in Paris noted that I had received a letter from a person called Quynh Anh. A week later the National Security Agency in Hanoi started an investigation to find out who Quynh Anh was, what she did and whether she was part of the Bui Tin group. Obviously the existence of her letter had been reported to the embassy in Paris. So I wrote to the ambassador Pham Binh that if any of his security officials wanted to know anything about me, they had simply to ask and I would tell them because I was acting completely on my own initiative without any links with anybody and without any group or gang backing me up. As for Quynh Anh, I told the ambassador she was my eight-year-old grand-daughter who attended the Trung Vuong School in Hanoi.

In fact I knew from a friend in the embassy that the day after I issued my petition, the Party Secretariat sent a telegram to the ambassador in Paris seeking information about me and who I was working with. In other words, was I subject to the influence of Vietnamese or of foreigners? I soon learnt that Pham Binh had replied that as far as he was aware, I was acting on my own and had planned to do so even before leaving Vietnam. He added that he had met me on various occasions spread over many years and knew me to be a person who had long had his own ideas.

That was a very straightforward attitude on the part of Pham Binh. Naturally he did not approve of what I was doing but he still let his staff contact me personally or by phone to inquire after my health and at the same time to find out what I was up to. And I continued to meet and talk to members of the embassy staff in the normal way. Some of them criticised me but several of the younger ones were more sympathetic. They even broke the rules and went to considerable lengths to visit and help me. To stop them getting into trouble, I expressed my gratitude and asked them to cease providing such help. Even now that I have been in France for quite a long time, there are people at the embassy who are concerned about me and worry about whether I am sad about not returning home.

However at the end of 1990 there was an amusing incident. During the last week of the year, a group of over twenty Vietnamese journalists from various countries in Western Europe gathered in Paris to discuss the situation back home as well as professional matters. They invited me as a fellow journalist to join them for dinner on December 29 at the semi–official Vietnamese government restaurant in the Rue Monge. By coincidence it happened to be my birthday so there was a lot of conviviality and congratulations but that was all. Nevertheless an important official at the embassy cabled a report back to Hanoi. Then the Party Secretariat issued a letter to all cells stating that Bui Tin had assembled a group of reactionaries from Western Europe in Paris to plot a coup. It was alleged I had made a speech at this meeting and those present had shouted counter-revolutionary slogans!

On hearing this, I wrote a letter to Duong Thong, the head of the Counter-Espionage Department in Hanoi, with whom I have long been acquainted. I said clearly 'You should be aware of the way your subordinates work. They use inferences, imagination and fabrications. You have assessed and victimised so many people, treating them unfairly without ever realising your mistakes or learning from experience. Everything I do here is done publicly, openly and with my cards on the table. There is nothing shady or underhand that has to be hidden.'

Also at the end of 1990, I asked an Overseas Vietnamese couple from Lille who were returning to Hanoi for a visit to take with them two small dolls for my granddaughters. That prompted an official from the embassy in Paris to run around asking who it was who was going to convey these gifts because it was essential for the authorities to know. Thereupon I telephoned the embassy and provided the names of the people concerned. I added that the gifts were intended as a token of affection and did not signify that my granddaughters supported or approved of what I was doing. The embassy could so easily have caused problems for my grandchildren through its usual methods of trying to punish and take revenge on innocent people. So I was later very touched to receive a photo of the two little girls embracing the dolls I had sent them.

Then in March 1991 the official organisation of Vietnamese in Lyon invited me to come and give a talk. Immediately an official at the embassy tried to sabotage the idea by telephoning several elderly workers in Lyons to announce that I had asked for political asylum in France (there was an erroneous news story on French radio about this which I had corrected) and that therefore I was a reactionary who should not be invited to speak. Yet my invitation still stood. Members of the organisation in Lyons pointed out that contrary to what the embassy said, I had not requested political asylum and that Dr Nguyen Khac Vien, who for many years had been responsible for their organisation, had described me as a person of conviction, while even the leadership in Hanoi had to pay serious attention to my petition. Finally even the old-timers who were subject to pressure from the embassy had to agree.

This sort of thoughtless and foolish action by the Vietnamese embassy in Paris diminishes its credibility, which in any case does not rate very highly. There are nearly a quarter of a million Vietnamese living in France. Ten years ago 6,000 of them had close links with the Vietnamese embassy, but today that figure has shrunk to 200. Some officials at the embassy are known to resort to tricks. They threaten Overseas Vietnamese who want to return to visit their families that they will have to wait a long time to get a visa unless they toe the embassy line. In addition some embassy officials are known to collude with businessmen who want to visit Vietnam in order to make a quick profit by exploiting inflation and the unstable exchange rate, regardless of the suffering of the working people.

Even people who get a visa are not always welcome in Vietnam. In March 1991, the half-French, half-Vietnamese film maker Bernard Gesbert was detained in Hanoi for several weeks before being deported. Then an Overseas Vietnamese from the United States, Dr Bui Duy Tam, was similarly treated. In both cases the Cong An were suspicious of the local contacts they had made. This campaign culminated in April when the writer Duong Thu Huong, who had been expelled from the Party the previous year, was arrested in Hanoi on the grounds that she had violated national security and revealed state secrets. She was accused of trying to send secret documents out of the country. But these were none other than the letter which Dr Nguyen Khac Vien had written to Nguyen Huu Tho and Hoang Minh Chinh's petition, copies of which were already being widely circulated abroad.

Some of the paranoia of the security forces in early 1991 stemmed from the preparations for the 7th Party Congress to be held in June. The unexpected events at the previous congress in 1986 continued to worry the leadership, so numerous circulars were issued in an attempt to ensure that the run-up to this Congress proceeded smoothly. Absolutely no one with democratic or pluralist views was to be allowed to participate in the preparatory conferences. One person excluded on these grounds was Dang Quoc Bao, the younger brother of Truong Chinh who had joined the Revolution in 1945 and risen high to become a Party Central Committee member as well as head of the Ho Chi Minh Youth Union. But having travelled widely in Eastern Europe after 1986, he had become disillusioned with the lack of democracy and what he saw as the distortion of Marxist policy in Vietnam.

Also during the closing months of 1990, more than 1,000 high-ranking officers from generals to colonels were retired to ensure that they would not be able to attend the Party conferences of their units. Among these officers were obviously many 'incurable' individuals who were familiar with the internal affairs of the army, liked to speak frankly and wanted to see the armed forces bring themselves up-to-date in organisation, weaponry and ideas. They were the people who would have demanded an end to irresponsible corruption, injustice, bureaucracy and militarism. They wanted measures leading to broader democracy and individual justice. For such people to be retired or sent on sick leave was to create a dangerous time-bomb where the implementation of the Party's policy of *Doi Moi* was concerned. All the solemn promises of four years earlier were reshaped to emphasise mass effort and discipline.

Even so, before the 7th Party Congress there were rumours that General Vo Nguyen Giap would return to the Politburo and become head of the State Council, in other words Head of State, because that was the wish of the people. In my view, this was like a sweet drink laced with poison. General Giap was almost eighty years old and his health was deteriorating. Still he remained an intellectual with broad knowledge and a sense of honesty which is rare these days and all the more precious because it is so rare. What is more, he is respected both at home and abroad. However at the Party Congress he was dropped from the Central Committee and has subsequently lost all his other positions.

Indeed the 7th Party Congress showed no signs of true democracy. It was merely formalistic, which does not correspond with the wishes of the people. Just as at previous Party Congresses, nobody raised any problems at all. The resolutions had been prepared in advance. The only thing those attending had to do was express their approval like children at school obeying their teachers.

Nguyen Van Linh was replaced as Party General Secretary by Do Muoi. But these days a man in such a position should have a solid base of knowledge and an understanding of society as well as of the world at large rather than being just an enthusiastic *apparatchik*. Many intellectuals in Hanoi say that lack of knowledge combined with eagerness equals destructions. Clearly Do Muoi had never lacked enthusiasm in his campaigns to reform industry and construct major projects. But the question of health is no less important with him than it was Nguyen Van Linh. When Linh became Party General Secretary, he was seventy-one, but Do Muoi took over the position at the age of seventy-four. And during the 7th Party Congress he gave the impression of the eternal campaigner who would run and run without any concessions to the next generation, even though his health was poor.

At the same time, the Congress also rubber-stamped the demotion from the Politburo and departure from office of the long-standing Foreign Minister, Nguyen Co Thach. Not only was he regarded as a 'rightist' who had long advocated moves towards normalising relations with the United States while continuing to be unenthusiastic about any rapprochement with China, but he was also vulnerable to the charge of nepotism. More than thirty members of his extended family were believed to occupy privileged diplomatic positions abroad, while his wife, originally trained as a medical assistant, had been co-opted into the Foreign Ministry as head of the department responsible for liaison with the United Nations, which likewise brought perks and prestige in its wake.

Nevertheless many Western diplomats with whom I have discussed the matter were sorry to see Thach go. They regarded him as a man who had been able to build up much personal understanding for Vietnam's foreign policy both in the West and in South East Asia. But over the choice of his successor, numerous people shrugged their shoulders in dismay.

Rather than selecting one of the internationally experienced deputy Foreign Ministers like Le Mai or Tran Quan Co, the Party organisational committee promoted Nguyen Manh Cam, a mediocre official of limited intellect. Having started his career as a student interpreter of Russian, he had risen through the bureaucratic process to become ambassador in Moscow, albeit not without controversy. He too was known to have taken advantage of his position to traffic in goods smuggled back to Vietnam under diplomatic cover. And he has no other compensating qualifications to help him cope with the increasingly complex world of the 1990s. I know that a lot of people in Hanoi were aware of this but dared not express their views openly about the poor image this has given to our foreign policy. Nguyen Manh Cam was appointed simply to appease China, and he is not even a Politburo member which would give weight to his authority as Foreign Minister. Instead the new people who joined the Politburo after the 7th Party Congress were those who had been most critical of Tran Xuan Bach a year earlier. Most prominent of all was Dao Duy Tung, who began to act as if he was the Deputy Party General Secretary preparing to take over from Do Muoi.

Still, after the Party Congress was concluded the press as usual proclaimed it a brilliant success. But these days how many Party members believe its claims that within the next five years Vietnam will have emerged from its crisis? And who believes that within ten years national *per capita* income will have increased by 100 per cent? Even within a month after the end of the Party Congress, the price of a tael of gold had risen from 380,000 to 460,000 dong while the value of the US dollar had jumped from 8,600 to over 10,000 dong. The earnings of workers and officials, which were low enough already, were reduced even further and people turned in their mind the question 'Which way is life going?' But they are not blind. The people as a whole can see that Party cadres who used to travel around in Soviet-made cars now have Toyotas, Mazdas or even Mercedes while respected intellectuals continue to pedal long distances to work on their bicycles.

One such person was our prominent Marxist philosopher Tran Duc Thao. A graduate of the prestigious Ecole Normale Supérieure in Paris in the 1940s, he acquired fame in France by publishing a book entitled *Phenomenology and Dialectical Materialism* based on a series of conversations he had with Jean-Paul Sartre. The book never appeared in Vietnamese because although Professor Thao returned to join the Viet Minh in 1952, he later became associated with the *Nhan Van, Giai Pham* group (as they are called in private, though not publicly) and was banished to a rural commune some 40 miles from Hanoi. But in recent years he often cycled into the capital to keep in touch with the wider world, until 1991 when the Party granted his request to visit France again. Once there, he declined to return home, and before his death in April 1993 started writing a new book claiming that the present Party leadership in Vietnam knows nothing about Marxism. All it knows is how to mouth Marxist slogans; it is an intellectual disgrace which is ignorant of science, technology and so much else compared with many other people in our country.

In my opinion, what we have now is a 'New Class' as described by Milovan Djilas, the dissident Yugoslav Communist leader who parted company with Tito in the early 1950s. Likewise in Vietnam, the 'New Class' Communists although they were originally stained with the same blood and sweat as their compatriots during the war, have thrown themselves into activities which are illegal, immoral and often inhuman. By running after their own advantage they and their families have become 'Red Capitalists'.

However, they did at least learn one lesson from the collapse of Communism in Eastern Europe. Because they were afraid of the possible public reaction, many of the special holiday resorts and villas reserved for the leadership, including the Party's West Lake complex in Hanoi and the former royal residence in Dalat, were opened to the public or those people who could pay in foreign currency, in other words mainly tourists from abroad. But the companies running these ventures are essentially offshoots of the Party Finance and Administration Committee.

However, one very important factor these days is to acknowledge the property rights of the peasants and their rights of inheritance. But the programme of the 7th Congress was still equivocal on this subject by stressing that land remains the property of all the people, with peasant families only having the right to use it. As a result, the peasants are still not completely at ease and remain wary of investing money to improve the land because they still do not regard it as their property. The same ambiguities persist in the field of industry and trade.

Indeed the 7th Party Congress did not provide any answers to many serious questions. It was as if the pulse of the country was felt but no prescription was provided. During the past sixteen years, with four Party Congresses being held, the same has always been true. Each time people thought a solution could be found but we have been slow to identify the source of the disease, and when we did, its nature changed and became more serious. In fact when the country is in danger, there are a host of ideas and petitions, but like the traditional head of a Vietnamese family, the leadership closes its eyes and covers its ears. Its ability to listen, which is in any case very poor, returns to zero.

The conservatism of the 7th Party Congress was summed up in the statement 'Stability must be maintained at all costs. Progress towards democracy must be carefully thought out, not carried out hastily. While democracy plays a leading role, it goes hand in hand with collectivism closely linked with discipline.' This statement is very dangerous. It condemns the country to a state of political backwardness, so obstructing the policy of *Doi Moi* in the economic field. It runs contrary to the aspirations of the people. And it contradicts the principle that the working people are the masters, since it violates their rights.

The basis for the construction of socialism as stated by the 7th Party Congress is that it was the path chosen by Ho Chi Minh so it can never be abandoned. In fact there are dozens of references to Ho Chi Minh's choice of socialism in the documents approved by the Congress which to my mind are not scientific. He died over twenty years ago and it was he who, together with the Party, planned the rapid and total transformation of agriculture which in these days is recognised as a mistake. Even so this can never be mentioned because it was Ho Chi Minh's idea. He also envisaged the high-speed industrialisation of Vietnam, with heavy industry to the forefront, which has proved to be another mistake. What is more, Ho Chi Minh did not live to witness the serious crisis arising from the current collapse of Communism. Nor could he have foreseen the profound effect this would have on international relations, so changing the face of the world. In my opinion all programmes and viewpoints, no matter how clever, should simply be seen as a matter for discussion. Only those who have enough responsibility and are capable of understanding the current situation should take decisions affecting the present generation.

For instance, two months after the end of the Vietnamese Party Congress came the coup in the Soviet Union on August 19, 1991 when the conservatives seized power. In Hanoi Thai Ninh, the deputy head of the Party Committee for Ideology and Culture, was beside himself with joy and quickly informed the Party propaganda network and the press that it was staunch Communists who had taken action in Moscow. He went on to say that the overthrow of Gorbachev was to be welcomed because it could save socialism and Marxism-Leninism in the Soviet Union which would have a lot of advantages for Vietnam! In the same spirit Mme Ho The Lan, the spokesperson for the Ministry of Foreign Affairs, happily stated at a press conference on the afternoon of August 20, that the coup in the Soviet Union was a major new development that was beneficial for Vietnam. She expressed the hope that the Soviet Union would now return to its former happy self.

At the same time, a high-ranking official from the Party's cultural and ideological committee, replying to a question from Reuters news agency, went further and talked about the crimes of Gorbachev, saying that he was a 'radical opportunist'. But he had to eat his own words within seventy hours when Vietnam's 'staunch comrades' in Moscow were overwhelmed, having shown their true colours as criminals and reactionaries who were caught in the act and now had to face up to the law.

After these events Thai Ninh, the deputy head of the Party's committee on ideology and culture who had just been elevated to the Central Committee at the 7th Congress, continued to praise the 'staunch Soviet comrades' and so missed the boat again. And he was in charge of the media! Those journalists who had at least some independent power of thought shook their heads in despair about this symbolic 'wooden tongue'. It continued to go on shamelessly talking about the two blocs and the four contradictions which would lead to the death of capitalism. In fact many of the top leaders in Hanoi continue to believe that the collapse of Communism in the Soviet Union and Eastern Europe is only a temporary phenomenon, a storm which will soon pass and allow the skies to become clear again.

Hanoi is now one of the few cities in the world where one can still see a statue of Lenin. It stands in the park on Dien Bien Phu Avenue, and the plaque on the pedestal states that it was erected by the army in 1987 to mark the seventieth anniversary of the October Revolution. The statue portrays Lenin grasping his overcoat with one hand and pointing straight ahead with the other. According to the sarcastic wits of Hanoi, when Lenin arrived in Vietnam he was worried about pickpockets and is shouting 'Stop thief!' There is also a popular verse which mockingly asks why he, a Russian, has come to Vietnam. Is it to impose socialism for ever? Then on the eve of Vietnam's National Day on September 2, 1991, somebody climbed up the statue and placed one of our traditional peasant hats on Lenin's head. At dawn the next day it was removed by the Cong An. The Vietnamese people still have a love of political satire which is lacking in their proletarian leaders.

Even before the total collapse of the Soviet Union, one French journalist, commenting on the outcome of the Vietnamese Party Congress, wrote: 'This was a show staged for the Chinese leader Deng Xiaoping. The Vietnamese, having fallen to one side in the Sino-Soviet dispute, tried to find a good friend and rushed into the arms of their major enemy thinking they would find comfort. Because they share a common ideology and a similar system, the Vietnamese now think they can rebuild the comradeship they once shared with China in order to find a way out of their current predicament.'

However, it was not that simple. True, Nguyen Co Thach had been dropped from the Politburo partly because of his anti-Chinese stance. So too had Mai Chi Tho, the younger brother of Le Duc Tho and Minister of the Interior, who was earlier held responsible for the expulsion of the Chinese from Cholon in 1978. But when General Le Duc Anh, one of the architects of our military takeover of Cambodia, who had just been promoted to the number two slot in the Politburo, travelled to Peking to make his peace, he had a rude awakening. Not only did the Chinese leadership seem prepared to support the other four permanent members of the UN Security Council in bringing about a peaceful negotiated settlement to the Cambodian problem irrespective of any Vietnamese concerns, but they also hedged on a Vietnamese request for aid. One of the major sources of disagreement between Peking and Hanoi back in the 1970s was Vietnam's lack of gratitude for all the loans previously received from China.

Bereft of any further Soviet – let alone Russian – aid, the leadership in Hanoi then had to try another tack. With little hope of an early lifting of the US trade and aid embargo, despite increased efforts to resolve the MIA issue, other Western countries were regarded as possibly more forthcoming, but here too there was a price to pay. Vietnam has been coming under growing criticism for its human rights record. More than 1,000 well-known Western writers and other personalities signed a petition for the release of the author Duong Thu Huong. Just before the visit to Hanoi in October 1991 of the French Foreign Minister, who had indicated that he intended to raise this issue, she was suddenly allowed to return home after eight months in detention without even being formally charged or placed on trial.

At the same time several other well-known writers were released, including the poet Nguyen Chi Thien. He had been in prison for most of the preceding thirty years, although during a brief spell of freedom in the late 1970s he managed to pass his poems *Flowers from Hell* to the British Embassy in Hanoi for publication in the outside world. In fact he is better known abroad, where Amnesty International has campaigned actively on his behalf, than he is in Vietnam because his name has never been mentioned in the press. And now he is not being allowed to go abroad for medical care, of which he is in desperate need, because he would provide devastating evidence of the cruelty of our prison system. I would like to ask Pham Van Dong, who prides himself on being a cultured man and a poet, whether during all the years he was Prime Minister he was aware of the case of Nguyen Chi Thien and the inhumanity he suffered.

And it still continues. While some of the people implicated in the *Nhan Van, Giai Pham* affair over thirty-five years ago have been rehabilitated, albeit not publicly, other intellectuals have been detained. They include Dr Nguyen Dan Que, a European-educated endocrinologist who has been sentenced to twenty years imprisonment for circulating a petition in 1990 calling for more democracy. More recently an American-trained educationalist, Professor Doan Viet Hoat has suffered a similar fate. The list goes on and on, with many Buddhist priests now being detained for demanding more religious freedom.

This lack of respect for human rights makes natural allies of the leaders in Hanoi and Peking. Thus in November 1991 a large delegation headed by Do Muoi swallowed its pride and went to China to kowtow and officially normalise relations. In my opinion, this is a rapprochement between Parties and governments which share the same paranoia about the wave of democracy and pluralism sweeping through most countries in the world. It is a rapprochement between political diehards who have rushed into one another's arms for self-preservation and to squeeze out the aspirations of the people. But nobody has dared speak out about this development or the true consequences for Vietnam of the settlement in Cambodia.

Personally I think the person who should be challenged on the issue of Cambodia is General Le Duc Anh. For ten years he was responsible for the situation there, first as commander on the ground of our forces in the country and later as Minister of Defence. In this light, his subsequent elevation in September 1992 to Head of State by unanimous vote in the National Assembly seems extraordinary except for his high ranking in the Party. It must have prompted at least a hundred generals who were for years far senior to him to shake their heads in wonder. Of course it is normal for talented officers to be promoted rapidly over the heads of their superiors in rank and age, but General Anh is known to have little experience off the battlefield, and the current state of our armed forces also raises many questions.

I am often asked whether these days Vietnam still has a lot of competent generals. It is difficult to reply. When Le Duc Anh moved up to become Head of State, the other two members of the 'gang of three' which took over the leadership of the army in early 1987 were likewise promoted. General Doan Khue became Defence Minister with Nguyen Quyet as his immediate deputy. And now we have the 'gang of four' because the new Chief of the General Staff is Major-General Dao Dinh Luyen who was quickly raised to a rank commensurate with this position. His appointment is highly unusual because he is an Air Force officer with no experience of military tactics or the deployment of troops, unlike everybody else who has ever served on the General Staff.* Certainly General Luyen was one of the first of our combatants to learn to fly, and as a result he was sent to both China and the Soviet Union for advanced training as a pilot and commanded the Air Force throughout the war against the Americans. He is also diligent, careful and well regarded by his junior officers. But although a tall man of dark complexion who originates from Thai Binh in the North, he is considered among his friends to have the mannerisms of a woman. He blushes in female company and is clearly afraid of his superiors. Perhaps he was chosen to become Chief of Staff because of his high sense of discipline. He always carries out orders immediately without question like a well-oiled machine. If, sometime in the future, the armed forces have to be used to suppress a democratic

---

* Another person who shot to prominence at the same time is General Le Kha Phieu. He replaced Nguyen Quyet as head of the Army General Political Department although hardly anybody had ever heard of him before 1986. Coming from a 'pure peasant' background, he was simply a lieutenant-colonel in 1974 serving as a divisional political commissar out in the field. But then he was brought into the Defence Ministry and rapidly promoted to the point where in 1991 he became a member of the Party Secretariat. He is regarded as one of the younger generation being just over fifty. On the other hand, I can list numerous generals who are far more competent and intelligent than all those who currently head our armed forces.

movement, General Luyen will be the ideal person to have in command. As General Doan Khue wrote in a recent article, 'The army must be ready to protect the regime. It must be ready to inflict direct punishment on the agents of imperialism who are plotting 'peaceful evolution' and all other reactionaries.'

In this context, I know that extracts from books by Zbigniev Brzezinski and Richard Nixon, where they talk about the end of Communism through peaceful evolution, have been translated into Vietnamese and circulated to members of the Party Central Committee with the warning that this policy is aimed directly at Vietnam. But these are books written quite a few years ago by men no longer in positions of power. The Party does not seem to realise that the world has moved on since then and continues to change.

Instead in late 1992 the Party Central Committee redefined our foreign policy in a secret resolution which categorises Vietnam's relations with various countries according to a list of priorities. In the first category are China, Cuba and North Korea together with Cambodia and Laos, since they are all considered to be Marxist-Leninist states. Second come the countries of Eastern Europe and the former Soviet Union because our leadership believes they have the capability to revert to Communism. India too is included in this category as a former close ally of the socialist bloc. Third come Vietnam's neighbours in ASEAN who have to be won over to co-operate. Next are friends in the Third World such as Egypt, Iran, Iraq and Algeria. Also falling within this category are the countries of Western Europe as well as Australia and Japan which are currently expanding their relations with us. Fifth and last there is the United States which is still regarded as Vietnam's long-term enemy.

Because the Vietnamese Communist Party learned its Marxism-Leninism by taking a shortcut through the works of Stalin and Mao Tse-tung, its ideology is strongly imbued with the traits of those two discredited leaders. These include feudalism, a peasant mentality, clannishness, authoritarianism, conservatism and immobilism, all of which are completely at odds with the spirit of democracy in the modern world, no matter where.

Some people have the illusion that things are different in Asia because the spirit of feudalism still prevails and peasants are politically inactive. This is not true. Asians and Vietnamese are changing.

They are desperate for democracy, freedom and development. Nothing can restrain them any longer and it is only a matter of time before the situation erupts. The political stability which appears to exist in Vietnam at the moment is a fake.

For many years, the *Nomenklatura* has engaged in a frenzy of dispossessing and splitting society into the 'haves and have-nots' so that they themselves can become rich quickly. These people apparently feel that time is short. Abusing their positions of power, they tie up illegal contracts with foreign companies. They do not even mind being imprisoned for bribery and corruption, because, they believe, their accomplices will have stored up enough gold and valuables for them to live comfortably on on their release. Every day they become more like the Mafia, Red Capitalists who have emerged from the jungle in a way never before witnessed in our country's history. Thanks to those in power, Vietnam is losing its traditional values and being overwhelmed by robbery, gambling, prostitution, drug addiction and the spread of AIDS, while the health and education systems continue to decline.

Nowadays the aspiration of the vast majority of the Vietnamese people, both at home and abroad, is to see an early end to the politically conservative, despotic and authoritarian regime in Hanoi so that we can have a truly democratic government of the people, by the people, for the people. There are many who also hope that the Communist Party will take part in the democratisation process, leading to a new era in which Vietnam can catch up with the modern world. But some of our top leaders are recalcitrant. They are fearful of taking the necessary steps. Instead they calumniate such ideas as part of an imperialist and reactionary plot to overthrow the regime through 'peaceful evolution'. These allegations have been elaborated in documents drawn up by the leadership and circulated internally to all Party branches. They are being used to justify further repression and the arbitrary arrest of any dissenters. In this so-called period of *Doi Moi*, the security forces have not changed. But the 1990s are not the same as the 1950s and 1960s when nobody dared to protest against the repression of the *Nhan Van, Giai Pham* group and those accused of 'revisionism'. And after the lifting of the US trade embargo, the Party leadership is well aware that foreign contacts will increase and with them the concept of legality. It knows too that there will be a growing demand for democracy. In this situation, as the leadership finds itself more and more isolated and on the defensive against the people, it could become increasingly repressive. This will be a great test for democracy in Vietnam. Those who have already been arrested know that they enjoy widespread support, so that they continue bravely to defy their oppressors. The battle for democracy against tyranny is heating up. Ironically the leadership clamours at the same time in articles written for the press that people are becoming richer, the country stronger and society more civilised. I believe that real stability and prosperity will only come to Vietnam through democracy, coupled with good planning to achieve national development.

POSTFACE

The sight of the snowdrops breaking through the ice has remained with me throughout this journey back through my life and my thoughts. I know that many of my friends have led similar lives and sometimes ones which have been even more exciting and rich in experience. They may however be surprised at some of the things I have said. Many young people too will find my words unusual and at times difficult to understand. But what I have written is the truth, the real truth.

Everybody's experience of life is a profound lesson and one which is very useful. In the old days, wise men educated themselves through much study. They still do even now. Besides, every nation grows up by experiencing glory and shame, victory and defeat, and learning through its own experience and the experience of others. If it is incapable of doing so, then it becomes subjective and complacent, sufficient unto itself and isolated from the rest of the world like an orphan who cannot relate to society or its prevailing discipline.

In writing this book, I have tried for the sake of my readers to make a distinction between the puerile, the erroneous and the sincere.

CHRONOLOGY

1879. First French Governor-General of Indo-China appointed.

1912. Nguyen Tat Thanh (later known as Ho Chi Minh) leaves Vietnam for France.

1921. Nguyen Ai Quoc (later known as Ho Chi Minh) addresses 1st Congress of French Communist Party in Tours.

1925. Bao Dai becomes Emperor of Annam.

1927. Vuong (later known as Ho Chi Minh) sets up a training school for Vietnamese revolutionaries in Canton.

1930. Indo-China Communist Party (ICP) established at a meeting in Hong Kong.

1935. 1st Congress of ICP held in Macau.

June 1940. France capitulates to Germany, and French administration in Indo-China decides to support the Vichy regime while the Japanese start to apply pressure.

May 1941. Nguyen Ai Quoc appears in Cao Bang on the Sino-Vietnamese border at 8th Plenum of the Indo-Chinese Communist Party (ICP), which appoints Truong Chinh as Party General Secretary and sets up the Viet Minh to fight Japanese imperialism and French colonialism.

July 1941. Japanese forces move into the whole of Indo-China.

Dec. 1941. War in the Pacific breaks out.

Nov. 1944. General de Gaulle enters Paris as the head of a Free French government.

Mar. 9, 1945. Japanese forces oust the French administration in Indo-China and encourage Emperor Bao Dai to establish an independent Vietnamese government.

Apr. 17, 1945. Tran Trong Kim becomes Prime Minister of Vietnam.

July 1945. US, Soviet and British heads of government meeting in Potsdam decide Indo-China should be divided at 16th parallel for the purpose of disarming the Japanese.

Aug. 15, 1945. Emperor of Japan orders his troops to surrender.

Aug. 18, 1945. Meeting held at Hanoi Opera House to support Tran Trong Kim is taken over by Viet Minh at the start of August Revolution.

Aug. 23, 1945. Provisional government established in Hanoi under the Presidency of Ho Chi Minh.

Aug. 25, 1945. Emperor Bao Dai abdicates at request of Viet Minh.

Sep. 2, 1945. Proclamation of independence of Democratic Republic of

195

Vietnam (DRV) by Ho Chi Minh in Ba Dinh Square, Hanoi.
Sep. 3, 1945. Chinese forces arrive in Hanoi to disarm Japanese north of 16th parallel.
Sep. 11, 1945. British forces arrive in Saigon to disarm Japanese.
Sep. 23, 1945. Full-scale fighting breaks out in Saigon.
Oct. 1945. French forces start to arrive in southern Vietnam under the command of General Leclerc.
Nov. 11, 1945. Ho Chi Minh formally dissolves ICP.
Jan. 6, 1946. National Assembly elections held.
Feb. 28, 1946. China signs agreement with France to withdraw troops from Indo-China north of 16th parallel.
Mar. 6, 1946. Ho Chi Minh signs agreement with France providing for recognition of Vietnamese independence within the French Union and the stationing of French troops in northern Indo-China.
June–Sep. 1946. Ho Chi Minh attends Fontainebleau Conference in France.
Sep. 14, 1946. Ho Chi Minh signs '*modus vivendi*' agreement with France before returning to Hanoi.
Nov. 20, 1946. Serious fighting in port of Haiphong as French forces arrive.
Dec. 19, 1946. Viet Minh attack on Yen Phu power station in Hanoi marks outbreak of full-scale war and Ho Chi Minh departs to Viet Bac.
Jan. 8, 1948. France agrees with Emperor Bao Dai to establishment of the State of Vietnam with Associated status.
June 2, 1948. State of Vietnam established within the French Union.
Jan. 18, 1950. Chinese People's Republic recognises DRV during visit of Ho Chi Minh to Peking.
Jan. 30, 1950. Soviet Union recognises DRV.
Feb. 7, 1950. US and Britain recognise Associated State of Vietnam under Bao Dai.
Jan. 1952. 2nd Party Congress held in Viet Bac region when it re-emerges as Lao Dong or Workers Party.
Mar. 13–May 7, 1954. Battle of Dien Bien Phu.
May 8, 1954. International Conference opens in Geneva to discuss peace in Indo-China.
June 4, 1954. France grants full independence to State of Vietnam under Bao Dai who appoints Ngo Dinh Diem as Prime Minister.
July 21, 1954. Geneva Agreements provide for partitioning of Vietnam at 17th parallel, the withdrawal of French forces and the '*regroupement*' of the population within a year.
Oct. 15, 1954. Ho Chi Mihn and DRV government return to Hanoi.
Oct. 1955. Referendum in South Vietnam approves creation of Republic of Vietnam (RVN). Ngo Dinh Diem becomes President replacing Bao Dai as Head of State.

1956. Ngo Dinh Diem ignores provision of Geneva Agreements on nationwide elections.

Sep. 1956. Truong Chinh dismissed as Party General Secretary.

Oct. 1956. Vo Nguyen Giap acknowledges mistakes of land reform.

Nov. 1956. *Nhan Van* and *Giai Pham* journals closed down.

Oct. 1957. Le Duan becomes acting Party General Secretary.

Jan. 1959. 15th Party Plenum decides to start infiltration of the South.

1959. US increases aid to RVN and starts guerrilla warfare.

Sep. 1, 1959. Nguyen Chi Thanh promoted to general, second in rank to Vo Nguyen Giap.

Sep. 1960. 3rd Party Congress confirms Le Duan as Party General Secretary.

Nov. 1960. 81 Party Conference in Moscow attended by Ho Chi Minh, Le Duan and Nguyen Chi Thanh.

Dec. 1960. National Liberation Front of South Vietnam established.

Dec. 1961. Chinese military delegation headed by Marshal Yeh Chien-ying visits Hanoi and Vinh.

Nov. 2, 1963. Ngo Dinh Diem and his brother assassinated during military coup in Saigon.

Nov. 22, 1963. President Kennedy assassinated in Dallas.

Dec. 1963. 9th Party Plenum decides to step up war in the South.

Aug. 1964. Gulf of Tonkin incident marks start of US bombing of DRV.

Apr. 11, 1965. First US ground troops arrive in South Vietnam.

June 1965. General Nguyen Van Thieu becomes RVN Head of State.

June 1967. Nguyen Chi Thanh dies in Hanoi after a conference to plan Tet Offensive.

Jan. 31, 1968. Start of Tet Offensive.

May 1968. Negotiations begin in Paris between US and Vietnamese.

Sep. 2, 1969. Ho Chi Minh dies.

Feb. 1970. First secret talks in Paris between Le Duc Tho and Henry Kissinger.

Feb. 1972. President Nixon visits Peking.

Apr. 1972. Viet Cong launches Spring Offensive in south Vietnam.

Aug.-Nov. 1972. Intensive negotiations in Paris between Le Duc Tho and Henry Kissinger.

Dec. 1972. US Christmas bombing offensive against Hanoi and Haiphong.

Jan. 27, 1973. Signing of Paris Agreements providing for exchange of prisoners of war and withdrawal of US forces from Vietnam within 60 days. Joint Liaison Committee set up in Saigon.

Aug. 9, 1974. President Nixon resigns.

Nov. 1974. Meetings in Hanoi to plan new offensive in the South.

Mar. 10, 1975. Viet Cong attack on Ban Me Thuot marks beginning of Ho Chi Minh campaign.

Mar. 29, 1975. Communist capture of Da Nang.

Apr. 17, 1975. Khmer Rouge assume power in Phnom Penh.

Apr. 21, 1975. President Nguyen Van Thieu resigns.

Apr. 28, 1975. General Duong Van Minh becomes President of RVN.

Apr. 30, 1975. Communist forces enter Saigon and Duong Van Minh orders surrender of RVN army.

May 15, 1975. Victory parade in Saigon.

June 1975. Re-education for RVN officers and officials begins.

July 1976. Reunification of Vietnam as a Socialist Republic (SRV).

Dec. 1976. 4th Congress of renamed Communist Party of Vietnam (CPV).

Apr. 30, 1977. First major Khmer Rouge attack on Vietnam.

Dec. 31, 1977. Cambodia breaks off diplomatic relations with Vietnam.

Apr. 1978. Campaign for nationalisation of private property and socialist transformation of agriculture launched in the South. Boat people exodus begins.

May. 1978. China ends aid to SRV.

Sep. 1978. Talks on normalisation of relations between US and SRV collapse.

Nov. 1978. Soviet Union and SRV sign treaty of friendship in Moscow.

Dec. 25, 1978. Vietnam launches invasion of Cambodia.

Jan. 7, 1979. Vietnamese forces capture Phnom Penh and install Heng Samrin regime.

Feb. 1979. Chinese forces invade northern Vietnam.

Dec. 1980. Van Tien Dung replaces Vo Nguyen Giap as Defence Minister in major cabinet reshuffle.

Feb. 1982. 5th Party Congress. Vo Nguyen Giap dropped from Politburo together with other leading members.

June 1986. Le Duan dies and Truong Chinh becomes Party Secretary General again.

Dec. 1986. 6th Party Congress. Truong Chinh, Le Duc Tho and Pham Van Dong retire from Politburo and Nguyen Van Linh becomes Party General Secretary with Pham Hung as Prime Minister.

Apr. 1988. Pham Hung dies and Do Muoi takes over as Prime Minister.

Oct. 1988. Truong Chinh dies.

Aug. 1989. SRV condemns result of Polish elections.

Oct. 1989. Nguyen Van Linh visits East Germany.

Nov. 1989. Berlin Wall falls.

Mar. 1990. 8th Party Plenum expels Tran Xuan Bach from Politburo.

June 1991. 7th Party Congress. Nguyen Van Linh retires as Party General Secretary and is replaced by Do Muoi. Vo Van Kiet becomes Prime Minister.

July 1991. General Le Duc Anh makes secret visit to Peking.

Aug. 1991. Coup in Moscow leads to dissolution of Soviet Communist Party.

Nov. 1991. Vietnam normalises relations with China.

Sep. 1992. General Le Duc Anh becomes Head of State.

INDEX